More Praise for *L&D Order Taker No More!*

"Jess has a deep understanding of the state of L&D and a compelling vision for where we need to go. Her no-nonsense strategy is grounded in real stories. Follow the advice on these pages and take your department to the partnership level."
—**Rance Greene,** Founder, School of Story Design

"This book couldn't be more timely. The L&D role is evolving rapidly, and Jess captures one of the most crucial transitions we're facing with authenticity and clarity. Every L&D professional should see this as a guide to the future—one where simply taking orders is no longer enough, and becoming a true business partner is essential for our role's survival."
—**Lavinia Mehedintu,** Co-Founder and Learning Architect, Offbeat

"Jess Almlie constantly challenges L&D professionals to focus on producing real business results. This book provides a clear road map for learning leaders who feel stuck in an 'order taker' role."
—**Christopher Adams, PhD,** Principal Consultant, Performance Change Strategies

"*L&D Order Taker No More!* is an empowering guide for L&D professionals who want to elevate their role from service providers to strategic business partners. Jess offers practical insights and tools that complement the work of building a strong, capable L&D team poised to drive business impact. This book is a must-read for those ready to shift perspectives and deliver real value to their organizations."
—**Robyn A. Defelice, PhD,** Learning Intrapreneur and Strategist, RADLearning

"Like an MBA program tailored specifically for L&D professionals, this book delivers practical frameworks that help you prioritize initiatives and manage limited resources. It's the only book I've encountered offering a playbook for both becoming a strategic business partner and also building strong relationships with other strategic partners in your organization—exactly what learning leaders need to maximize their impact."
—**Alaina Szlachta, PhD,** Measurement Architect, By Design Development Solutions

"This book is a practical guide for L&D professionals striving to do more, help more, and provide greater value to the people they support. It will empower you to break free from legacy practices, change the way people think about L&D, and become an integral partner within your business."
—**JD Dillon,** CLO, Axonify; Founder, LearnGeek

L&D Order Taker No More!

Become a Strategic Business Partner

JESS ALMLIE

PRESS

ALEXANDRIA, VA

© 2025 ASTD DBA the Association for Talent Development (ATD)
All rights reserved.

28 27 26 25   1 2 3 4 5

No part of this publication may be reproduced, distributed, or transmitted in any form or by any means, including photocopying, recording, information storage and retrieval systems, or other electronic or mechanical methods, without the prior written permission of the publisher, except in the case of brief quotations embodied in critical reviews and certain other noncommercial uses permitted by copyright law. For permission requests, please go to copyright.com, or contact Copyright Clearance Center (CCC), 222 Rosewood Drive, Danvers, MA 01923 (telephone: 978.750.8400; fax: 978.646.8600).

ATD Press is an internationally renowned source of insightful and practical information on talent development, training, and professional development.

ATD Press
1640 King Street
Alexandria, VA 22314 USA

Ordering information: Books published by ATD Press can be purchased by visiting ATD's website at td.org/books or by calling 800.628.2783 or 703.683.8100.

Library of Congress Control Number: 2025931158

ISBN-10: 1-96023-126-X
ISBN-13: 978-1-960231-26-0
e-ISBN: 978-1-96023-127-7

ATD Press Editorial Staff
Director: Sarah Halgas
Manager: Melissa Jones
Content Manager, Managing the Learning Function: Bianca Woods
Developmental Editor: Shelley Sperry
Production Editor: Katy Wiley Stewts
Text Designer: Shirley E.M. Raybuck
Cover Designer: Rose Richey

Contents

Preface vii

Introduction: Order Takers No More! xi

Part 1. Stuck
    Chapter 1. How We Got Here 3
    Chapter 2. Why We Stay Stuck 15
    Chapter 3. What a Strategic Business Partner Looks Like 35

Part 2. Foundations
    Chapter 4. Understand the Business First 65
    Chapter 5. Build Your Internal and External L&D Playbooks 89
    Chapter 6. Determine Your Key Stakeholders 129

Part 3. Daily Practice
    Chapter 7. Partner With Your Key Stakeholders 159
    Chapter 8. Create Your Learning Strategy 189
    Chapter 9. Master the Strategic Yes and No 215
    Chapter 10. Measure to Make Decisions 249
    Chapter 11. Develop a Team of SBPs 273
    Chapter 12. Find the Opportunity in Every Order 291

Conclusion: Become a Strategic Business Partner 305

Acknowledgments 307

References 309

Index 311

About the Author 317

About ATD 319

Preface

During college, I worked part time at a little restaurant in northern Minnesota. Maybe you've heard of it? It was called McDonald's. Other than the layer of grease that covered my face after each shift, I enjoyed everything about that job. I knew what was expected of me, which meant I knew how to be successful. It wasn't difficult. I just had to remain positive while taking and delivering food orders. Easy peasy.

After several months of making French fries, boxing up Happy Meals, and crushing it at the drive-thru window, my success was rewarded with a promotion to the position of crew trainer. This made me enjoy my job even more. As I helped new employees learn and excel in their jobs, I began to wonder if training others might be a career path for me.

One day, after I'd been working at the franchise for about a year, the regional manager stopped in our store as he was making his rounds. He caught up with me near the ice machine and told me he was impressed with my ability to take and execute orders. "Jess," he said, "I just know you're going to be a McDonald's *lifer.*"

I didn't know what to say. I paused for a moment to process his words. He was a sincere guy, and I knew he meant what he'd said as a compliment—a way of recognizing my hard work and positive attitude. I smiled and thanked him while my brain churned. I appreciated all I had learned in the fast-food world, where taking orders, delivering what the customers asked for, and training others to do the same was literally my whole job description.

Did I want to do that for the rest of my life?

After I finished college, I left McDonald's. Equipped with my love of training others, I started to work in entry-level learning and development roles at other companies. I facilitated new employee orientations, coordinated training courses, and rose through the ranks to manage learning programs and L&D teams. The work I did was consistently engaging and interactive, and I was proud of it. Plus, I rarely went home with grease on my face.

My love of helping others grow and excel drew me to the L&D profession, but it was my desire to maximize my impact that made me stay. I quickly realized that if I could lead groups of people to improve their skills, the potential to make a difference multiplied. Even better, if I could figure out how to do it effectively and efficiently (without wasting time, money, or resources), my work could become transformative for the organizations and teams I was a part of. This became the type of challenge I lived for each day.

While working to maximize growth and impact, I forgot about that conversation with the McDonald's regional manager and my reflections on taking orders—until one day, many years later. I was leading a team of L&D rock stars, but we were getting complaints about the way we delivered on the orders from our stakeholders—it wasn't good enough. That's when I started wondering if I had become a lifer after all. Was I still just taking and delivering orders? And why were my customers not as happy as the ones who got burgers and fries?

At McDonald's, our customers' problem was simple: hunger. When we took a food order and delivered it well, we solved that problem. In most other businesses, the problems are more complex. Training alone can't solve every problem, so simply taking and delivering on training orders often isn't the right answer.

Several years ago, I set out on a quest to find the right answer. Once I found it, I knew I had to share it with more L&D leaders, who—like me—need to find their way out of an older, order-taking mindset to become powerful partners in their organizations. That's how I ended up writing this book and sharing it with all of you.

My quest was driven by my desire to discover the keys to maximizing L&D's effectiveness in any organization. I'm excited to share what I learned through the many questions, research, failures, and successes I found along the way. I'm even more excited for you to join me in this journey. My hope is that this book both affirms your current situation, no matter what that is, and empowers you with practical ideas to move forward—ideas that will equip your own quest to step away from taking orders and start increasing the impact of L&D in your organization. Let's do this!

Introduction
Order Takers No More!

Several years ago, I was vice president of learning at Discovery Benefits, a midsize financial services company, working with a team of rock star L&D pros who created engaging experiences and loved their jobs. We received high praise from learners for our outputs. But, as I watched never-ending requests for new learning experiences come across my desk, I knew something was wrong. Stakeholders began to express dissatisfaction with our training programs. Again and again, a problem that leaders had hoped to solve with a great learning experience remained unsolved after that experience was complete. We were all frustrated. The stakeholders blamed our L&D team for "failed" learning experiences. But, from our perspective, we had delivered precisely what they had requested—and done our jobs well.

Does any of this seem familiar? If you picked up this book, I'll bet you're engaged in a similar struggle. You probably feel frustrated and stuck, just like I did.

I hated that feeling of being stuck. I knew I had to find a way out, but there was no map or handbook to guide me.

Within the L&D community, we often find ourselves in conversations about how the system of taking and delivering orders is failing us and our stakeholders. Part of the problem can be traced to the evolution of L&D as a field, legacy thinking about the components of effective learning, and organizational roadblocks. Other aspects relate to that feeling of just being trapped in an outdated mindset. We know that we have more to contribute but don't know how to make the transition from order takers to more productive roles as strategic partners in our organizations.

In the years since facing my own stuck moment, I've discovered that our solution to that challenge is to transform the way we see ourselves, improve the ways we interact with stakeholders and our companies, and break out of the order-taker mold. Instead of expert order takers, we must become strategic business partners (SBPs).

I came to this realization after I dove headfirst into an investigation of internal consulting practices, performance improvement, project and stakeholder management, and impact measurement. I assumed that no one at my organization—neither the L&D team nor the stakeholders—understood the real, underlying problems, but I knew we needed to unpack them. I started asking more critical questions at the onset of each request for a learning solution that made its way to my team.

To our stakeholders' surprise, I started to push back on requests, refusing to commit to taking an order without a thorough analysis and confidence that my L&D team could solve the problem. For a while, we all struggled to pinpoint the right approach. It wasn't easy. But then I had one of those "lightbulb moments."

A New Mindset

After months of research, I suddenly recognized that to accomplish a full transformation, I needed a new mindset that *put business concerns first*. I put myself in my stakeholders' shoes, studied performance data and goals, and even shadowed some of my organization's leaders. Instead of asking questions about learning objectives, I now asked questions about the business challenges shown in monthly reports. In response, my organization's stakeholders stopped asking for training courses and started asking my L&D team to solve business and talent challenges.

What does that sound like? Well, instead of saying, "We need an e-learning course on effective communication next month," a company leader would say, "We're having a problem with communication among team members in this department. Can you help us?"

As my L&D team left order-taker mode behind, I watched stakeholders start seeing us as part of their strategic solutions team, contributing opinions and expertise to a variety of conversations about talent and large-scale organizational initiatives. We were now partnering with stakeholders to solve challenges related to talent development that would have a significant impact on the overall success of the company.

My final lightbulb moment came when I recognized that the transformation of our approach had not only been good for the L&D department—which was my original goal—but it also produced much better results for the organization and for each individual on my team, including me. Organizations that embrace a partnership with L&D get better solutions to the challenges they face including finding and retaining talent, driving stronger alignment between business objectives and L&D programs, and seeing an improved return on investment for those programs. On an individual level, as L&D pros, we can take pride in gaining more influence and visibility throughout our organizations, new skills, and (from my own experience at least) a greater sense of purpose and satisfaction.

Why Change Now?

Today's learning landscape is primed for us to shift the narrative from L&D leaders as order takers to L&D leaders as SBPs. During periods of economic challenge, every dollar an organization spends is scrutinized, and functions that don't solve problems will be seen as expendable. Employee engagement and smile sheets alone won't cut it.

At the same time, companies are fighting a difficult and costly battle to find and retain talent, especially people who can learn and evolve when technology and business trends change. L&D groups must upskill and reskill the workforce to meet these needs.

This mismatch is, in some ways, our own fault. We tend to perpetuate legacy thinking. We have trained our stakeholders to think that doing business with us means putting in a request, answering questions about learning objectives, helping us gather information to meet those objectives by working with subject matter experts, participating in reviews of the material, and then accepting the result. We complain that we aren't involved in strategic conversations, but we have never acted in a way that gives our stakeholders confidence that we could participate in and add value to such conversations. Acting like order takers only perpetuates *more* of that behavior.

It's time for us to change the narrative. It's time to use our expertise, skills, and strengths to work as SBPs and to serve our organizations strategically. As an L&D leader, you can lead the way, creating the right conditions for this shift in mindset and practices. The purpose of this book is to share my experiences and knowledge, as well as the experiences of others in similar roles, to help you and your organization make that shift.

What's on the Menu

In this book, I'll share my own successes and failures and the tools I've developed along the way. In addition, I've gathered insights from in-depth interviews with dozens of L&D leaders who shared their challenges and successes in small (less than 2,000 employees), midsize (2,000 to 10,000 employees), and large (more than 10,000 employees) companies across multiple industries. Many of these leaders are also trying to change the order-taker narrative and are facing similar roadblocks, which partially explains why our profession as a whole is still stuck. I've drawn on these interviews throughout the book, keeping the contributors and their organizations anonymous to protect their privacy.

This book is organized into three sections that are designed to help you more easily navigate the process of becoming an SBP.

Part 1, Stuck, considers the origins and shape of our profession's challenges, or why we're "stuck," and then outlines a new mindset to overcome those challenges, transforming L&D into an SBP in every organization we work with and for. Chapter 1 focuses on the history that got us in our current predicament. Chapter 2 examines external and internal roadblocks that keep L&D pros in an order-taking mindset. For many of us, practices that start logically will eventually become acts of self-sabotage, stopping us from fulfilling our potential in the profession. Chapter 3 suggests how we can spot someone who has succeeded in the SBP role, demonstrating how they approach their work differently, inspired by a specific set of beliefs the rest of us can learn.

At the end of part 1, you will find a tool for assessing your own strengths and knowledge and experience gaps when it comes to working as an SBP. I urge you to complete the assessment before moving on to part 2 to help gauge your opportunity areas throughout the remainder of the book.

Part 2, Foundations, is a handbook—complete with definitions, strategies, tools, stories, and best practices—for building the foundation you need to become an SBP. The foundation starts in chapter 4 with understanding business basics. Chapter 5 will help you build a new playbook for your L&D career that supports internal and external goals, including how to run the L&D function like the rest of the business and how to train the business to work with you. Chapter 6 is devoted to defining and understanding your key stakeholders—anyone in your organization who has a vested interest in learning and development. They are essential to your work and have the power to influence L&D projects in various ways. Do they see you as an order taker or an SBP? How can you tell?

In part 3, Daily Practice, you will learn the practices that will help you move with confidence beyond the role of order taker. In chapter 7, you'll learn techniques for partnering effectively with stakeholders, and in chapter 8, you'll learn how to create a successful learning strategy. Chapter 9 covers the art of saying yes—and no—strategically, something most of us struggle to master. Chapter 10 explains how to create and follow a measurement plan to inform your business decisions. Chapter 11 provides clear, effective best practices for developing your own team of supportive SBPs.

Finally, in chapter 12, I'll address the L&D elephant in the room. What if all you've learned about becoming a partner rather than an order taker seems great in theory, but simply can't be implemented in your organization? What can you do? When you are still constrained by the role of order taker, is it possible to take small steps toward becoming an SBP? Don't worry. I've been there, the answer is *yes,* and I've got your back.

I wrote this book as a practical how-to guide for L&D leaders who are in the trenches every day. It's the handbook I wanted but couldn't find when I embarked on my own journey to change my team from a group of order takers to partners with our organization's stakeholders. I've included tools and templates throughout, including self-assessments, checklists, questionnaires, and models. I also hope I've made each chapter more engaging by including some fascinating stories and data from my colleagues in the field.

I truly believe that we can better use our expertise and make a bigger impact on our organizations by embracing the SBP role. We can help solve business problems and engage and inspire more people in the process. We can improve our organizations' performance, achieve critical goals, and move our profession forward. My own experience proves that it *can* be done. Let's get started!

PART 1
Stuck

CHAPTER 1
How We Got Here

Every superhero has an origin story. Often, it's about an ordinary person suddenly gifted with superpowers who struggles to harness them for good. This story provides the framework for the hero's eventual rise to save the world. As L&D professionals, we can think of our skills in learning design and training as our superpowers. We may not harness them to save the world (that's a bit dramatic), but we can harness them to improve our organizations. We can use them to maximize our impact, move away from working primarily as order takers, and become strategic partners instead. But, just like any good superhero, we need to know something about our origin story first.

In this chapter, we'll briefly review the origins of L&D, a few key points about how humans learn, and how those are related to what we do today as L&D professionals. We'll consider how our stakeholders' learning experiences influence how they understand—or don't understand—what we do as L&D leaders to help us become more effective strategic business partners (SBPs).

From Social Learning to Modern L&D Training

Formal classroom learning is a relatively recent addition to the many ways people learn and develop new skills. Yet many of the stakeholders in our organizations retain rigid, outdated ideas about how learning occurs and what L&D teams should and should not do. To understand where those ideas come from, let's quickly review a little history.

Social Learning

For most of human history, people learned by watching and imitating others, trying new methods, adjusting for failures, and repeating that process. Since before the Stone Age, children watched and mimicked their parents, gathering knowledge and learning new skills through trial and error. The same was true of ancient and medieval apprentices who learned their trades simply by working alongside expert craftspeople. Today, we call this process of learning in collaboration with others *social learning*.

The study of complex, abstract subjects such as philosophy and ethics also occurred first through social learning. The ancient Greek philosopher Socrates originated a form of social learning aptly named *Socratic dialogue*. As the term suggests, this practice involves people discussing a topic and questioning their fellow learners to reach a better understanding of the truth (Garner and Ferguson 2023).

Most of us in L&D still use our own versions of social learning and Socratic dialogue, both informally and in formal settings led by trainers and facilitators. The techniques and skills associated with social learning are some of our most valuable superpowers.

Formal Learning

Most social learning traditionally takes place in informal settings—at home, in social gatherings, and among colleagues in the workplace. As L&D leaders, we often lean less on informal, social learning techniques in formal settings. These are places like schools or training classrooms where we follow a set plan or curriculum, guided by a teacher or trainer. Historically, this type of formal learning occurred in universities that were only available to elites. The most dramatic change to formal learning opportunities came in the 18th and 19th centuries, when many countries made elementary education compulsory and began using classroom-style models to train large numbers of workers during the Industrial Revolution.

In the United States, modern, taxpayer-supported public schools started to emerge in the 1830s and 1840s under the leadership of education reformer Horace Mann. Learning in these schools was modeled after the formal lectures and assessments of universities. A well-trained teacher at the front of the classroom shared knowledge, assigned homework, and tested students through quizzes and exams. Gradually, other approaches, including the use of simulations and small-group activities, became popular.

Eventually, as the L&D profession developed and expanded in the mid-20th century, social learning, formal classroom learning, simulations, and small-group activities all served as foundational elements.

Evolution of Employee Training

Training for employees initially followed the models of elementary and university learning, which were easy to scale for large groups of people. In the late 19th century, when millions of people shifted their work from farms to factories, businesses needed to upskill new employees quickly and effectively (Garner and Ferguson 2023). In response, companies scaled their training programs from one-to-one to one-to-many using the classroom model. Like schoolteachers and college professors, trainers in factories stood in front of new workers and lectured them about their jobs.

In the 1940s, when US manufacturing expanded dramatically to meet the demands of World War II, businesses adopted a new hybrid technique called "job instruction training" (JIT), now known as "on-the-job training" (AllenComm 2016). Similar to the old social learning model, on-the-job training (OJT) required a supervisor or co-worker to explain a job to a new employee, demonstrate the job, ask the learner to demonstrate the job, and then follow up later with inspections and evaluations of the new worker. This was a more formal, structured approach to the one-to-one training of apprentices.

The Corporate University

Employee education inspired by university models remained popular in employee training programs throughout the 20th century. Companies established corporate universities with lecture-based classroom programs for training and upskilling employees. As early as 1913, Ford Motor Company established the Ford English School, which offered English language classes for immigrant workers before and after factory shifts (The Henry Ford n.d.). The value of these classes for the company was clear: When employees all spoke the same language and could easily communicate with one another, safety and efficiency improved on the factory floor.

Corporate universities became more common by the 1960s. For example, in 1961, McDonald's Hamburger University started teaching franchise owners about restaurant operations (Varghese 2015). In 1981, Motorola University began teaching its workers about problem solving, running effective meetings, and goal setting (Wiggenhorn 1990). Just like training in factory settings, these programs required workers to leave the daily routine of their jobs and enter a new learning environment to acquire the skills they needed. For L&D functions, this meant designing and delivering formalized curricula much like their university professor counterparts.

Team Building and Personality Assessments

In the 1980s and 1990s, team building exercises bubbled up in the L&D profession as new, highly valued approaches to ensure employee success (Robinson 2022). Teams left the confines of work sites to engage in physical activities, such as rafting or adventurous ropes courses. The challenge for L&D was to facilitate a reflective process in which participants understood the parallels to workplace life. Ideally, these takeaways would improve relationships and the company culture, leading to more effective organizations.

New personality-based team building techniques also took off in the 1980s and 1990s. L&D teams used assessments like the Myers-Briggs Type Indicator instrument to focus on relationships between employees as well as between employees and the managers with whom they were working on a regular basis. Although they didn't all take place in a classroom, completing these assessments did require time away from the everyday tasks that needed to be done, reiterating the concept that real learning happens in formal, preplanned, structured environments. The topics may have shifted from tasks to relationships, but L&D leaders again found themselves designing and leading a formal curriculum in some type of classroom.

Computer-Based Training

When computer-based training (CBT) appeared in the 1980s, employees left traditional classrooms with chalkboards and flip charts to sit in front of computers to learn key concepts (AllenComm 2016). This shifted L&D professionals' focus somewhat, from teaching classes to designing computer-based training. But trainers quickly discovered that e-learning via computer wasn't enough to accomplish stakeholders' goals, and at that point, hybrid or blended learning models became more popular.

By the early 2000s, many L&D teams and organization leaders determined that a combination of classroom learning, CBT, and OJT worked best to achieve their desired learning outcomes.

Modern L&D's Multiple Modalities

As you look at the timeline of learning modalities in Figure 1-1, notice that once a certain modality appears, teaching and learning communities never really abandon it—although they've certainly all evolved over years, decades, and even centuries. For example, we can imagine a clear line of continuity between the one-to-one training of an apprentice working under a master stone mason in 1550 and the structured, OJT of an apprentice working with a master electrician in 1950. After thousands of years of adapting learning to new circumstances and needs, we now have more modalities to choose from than ever.

Figure 1-1. A Brief History of Learning Modalities

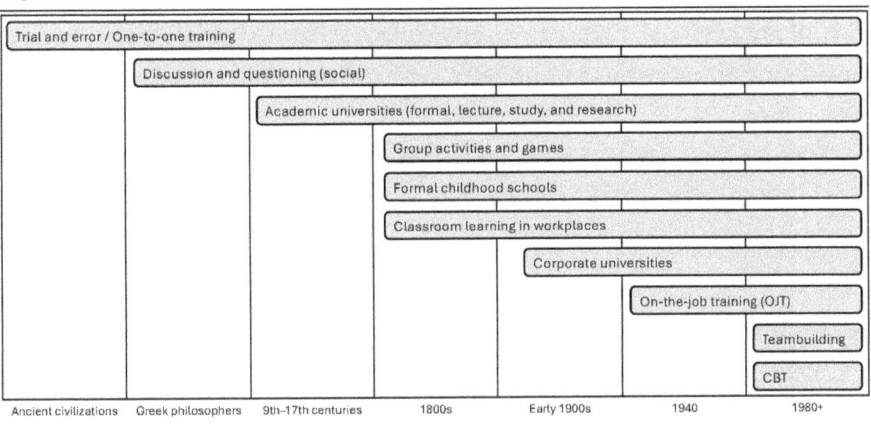

As L&D leaders, we are well-versed in a broad variety of effective modalities, including classroom training, group discussions, team building, and other group activities, as well as CBT and structured OJT. These are the superpowers we have at our fingertips. Like all good superheroes, we often combine these powers (modalities), using all our knowledge and skills as creatively as possible to meet learning outcomes.

But here's the problem: Most of us still spend the majority of our time designing formal learning experiences that are not that different from those in a 19th-century schoolhouse. These experiences usually pull people away from their daily work and out of production. Why are we so faithful to thinking that is almost 200 years old?

Our Experiences Teach Us About Learning

I suspect your memories of elementary and high school are much the same as mine: A teacher stands in front of a chalkboard or whiteboard, handing out assignments designed to ensure we practice and review the concepts bestowed in the daily lesson. We can all remember cramming for exams that were supposed to measure whether we had retained the knowledge we'd learned—and let's not forget the dreaded pop quiz! In most classes beyond music and art, the focus was on conveying theoretical knowledge, rather than the practical application of that knowledge or changing our behavior.

My children's experiences in school haven't been much different from my own, except for the addition of computers, phones, and virtual classes. Every year of grade school, high school, and college seems to include a series of lectures, written assignments, and tests, with little access to practical, hands-on experience.

My son enrolled in a trade school program during 11th and 12th grade, seeking an experience that would allow him to *learn by doing* instead of sitting in a chair and listening to a lecture every day. He got more hands-on experience than he would have in a traditional high school, but lectures, assignments, and tests still dominated his days.

Because most of us—including our stakeholders and everyone on their teams—share a common type of educational experience in our formative years, we also share many assumptions about how learning works and what it should look like. Consider Table 1-1, which compares a traditional educational experience with how we usually design and deliver workplace learning experiences.

Table 1-1. Traditional Education vs. Common Workplace Learning Experiences

A Traditional Educational Experience	A Common Workplace Learning Experience
A teacher with formal credentials stands at the front of a room full of students.	A prepared facilitator, trainer, or subject matter expert (or a computer-based e-learning program) runs the experience from start to finish.
The time is set aside for learning. It is separate from everything else going on in the students' lives.	The time is set aside for learning. It is separate from the rest of the work each person needs to complete that day.
Students are required to attend.	The learners are assigned to participate in the experience because they are new employees, the experience relates to their performance goals, or the experience explains or demonstrates a new skill or software tool they need to use on the job.
Students in the room (ideally) have approximately the same level of knowledge and, therefore, are at the same starting point.	Participants (ideally) have approximately the same level of background knowledge and experience, and the learning content is designed with that in mind.
The teacher spends time lecturing and may employ visual aids.	The trainer or facilitator shares knowledge using slides or other visual representations of key points, or the employees click through e-learning modules with voice-overs and visual representations of key points.
From time to time, the teacher may engage students in discussion, hold question-and-answer periods, or ask them to talk in small groups.	The facilitator tries to engage employees in discussion, allows for questions and answers, and may ask them to participate in small group activities.
The teacher assigns homework and administers exams designed to judge the degree to which the students are learning the presented concepts.	The facilitator may assign follow-up tasks to help employees use the new skills in their work roles. The facilitator may use assessments or evaluations designed to measure perceived learning or behavior change in a classroom or e-learning situation.
The teacher or other official issues grades that are considered a sign of students' accomplishments.	A facilitator or other official may determine whether employees have learned the required skill or knowledge. These determinations are especially important in certification courses.
Eventually, the accumulation of grades helps determine students' access to future opportunities, such as additional study or employment.	Eventually, if employees satisfactorily complete certain programs, they earn certification or access to promotions and additional experiences, which may include an increase in salary.

The resemblance is uncanny, isn't it?

One thing to note about the similarity between traditional education and workplace training is that very often, as L&D leaders, we understand the weaknesses of traditional education and try to avoid them. We know that high-quality experiences don't always require us to pull people out of production lines or make them watch an instructor read PowerPoint slides. And we know which aspects of traditional curricula are not effective for workplace learning and behavior change because we have spent so much time thinking about, studying, and debating our practices. Yet we often face pushback when we attempt to do something different and (we hope) more effective than traditional training. The people pushing back are usually our stakeholders.

Our Stakeholders' Legacy Mode of Thinking

The key stakeholders in our organizations—the people who have a vested interest in the work of our L&D function—are often in their positions because they *thrived* in the traditional education system.

To be fair, C-suite executives, managers, and other key stakeholders spend most of their time thinking about how to improve the business, produce more, solve big challenges, manage change, and get the most out of their teams. They don't have time to consider how learning happens in the brain or how well traditional learning translates to the workplace. And they have no reason to question an approach to education that worked effectively for them and the people they know. This legacy mode of thinking is a key reason that as L&D leaders, we end up feeling stuck.

From the stakeholders' point of view, the L&D team is there to create and deliver learning experiences. They assume learning needs to happen in a formal scenario like a classroom or e-learning course, based on their own past experiences. Their legacy thinking assumes L&D is the team credentialed to create and deliver those learning experiences. We know what usually happens: When stakeholders need to resolve a problem in the organization, they think the solution is a learning experience for employees, so they simply send a request to L&D to create it.

Many employees are also conditioned to see learning in more traditional terms. In interviews about their learning experiences, employees often mention the importance of *development*, which, all too often, is code for formally planned and executed learning experiences. In exit interviews, they cite a lack of developmental opportunities among the reasons they are leaving their organizations, and again, we're stuck, because the opportunities they seem to want are more formal classroom experiences led by L&D.

When we start thinking about how we got here, perpetually feeling stuck in the role of order takers, we can see that centuries of history plus current personal and organization-based experiences inform and reinforce everyone's assumptions of how learning does and should happen.

> **The Learning Cliff**
>
> My friend Stephen Mostrom coined a great term a few years ago for the sudden drop-off in structured learning most of us experience after we complete our formal education. He calls it the *learning cliff*. In his inspiring blog post, "How to Avoid the Dreaded 'Learning Cliff,'" he explains that we've spent the vast majority of our lives in a carefully controlled environment, and then the day we graduate, it's like falling off a cliff into a new world where we're expected to just "Figure it out!"
>
> We enter the workplace and must immediately shift from a *learning mindset* to a *doing mindset*. No more learning objectives and quizzes. Bring on the project management tools and performance reviews. Instead of relying on teachers and administrators to guide us, we are thrown, for the most part, into a do-it-yourself world. But our prior experience dictates that to learn, we should show up to a preplanned experience, formally structured by an educational professional. Check the box and done!
>
> So, is it any wonder that our stakeholders are looking for formal learning experiences in which employees show up and are told what they need to know or do? We don't know how to learn any differently. The learning cliff is a real part of our lives, and we still haven't figured out how to overcome it.

Our L&D Point of View Needs a Makeover

Maybe we, as L&D leaders, should be grateful for these structured, formalized learning environments. After all, they helped create our profession in the first place, and this is one arena in which we can show off our superpowers. Without formal structures, we might not be able to do the work we love. Our jobs might not exist.

But if we broaden our viewpoint a bit, we see that we haven't yet considered whether these traditional, formal methods are *effective*. For example:

- Are employees really learning and developing?
- Are we solving the talent challenges in our organizations?
- Are our efforts helping or hurting important business initiatives?

By asking these questions we can start to imagine a better way forward in which our impact as L&D leaders isn't limited to the expectations set by our own, our stakeholders', or our learners' experiences in formal education. We can see that we need to use our superpowers differently, which is the purpose of this book.

But before we can explore what a different, better future might look like, we need to examine one more piece of our puzzle as order takers: We need to know *why*, after recognizing what is trapping us, we choose to stay stuck.

> **YOUR TURN**
>
> **Dive Deeper Into Your Own Learning Experiences**
> Answer the following questions to explore your own story about the current L&D dilemma, in which employees, stakeholders, and many L&D leaders see our function as just taking orders for traditional learning experiences.
> - **Consider your own educational experiences.** Describe your memories of the learning modalities typically used when you were in elementary school. What about in high school? Did those modalities change as you moved into higher education? How?
> - **How often do you seek out new learning experiences today?**
> - **When learning on your own, where do you most often find information?** How often does your independent learning include a formal experience, such as an in-person or e-learning class?
> - **How often do you believe your organization's stakeholders are seeking out new learning experiences?** What about their team members?
> - **For your purposes, what is the most useful takeaway from this chapter?**

Summary

The great variety of learning modalities we practice as L&D professionals today—which are our superpowers—are based on the informal and formal learning practices developed over centuries and reinforced by our stakeholders' and learners' experiences in primary, secondary, and higher education. As a profession, L&D emerged in the 20th century in response to the need to scale learning for factory workers and others in a growing economy. The first L&D programs were based on a traditional model of lecture-based learning that was popular in schools and universities in the 19th century.

Today, L&D includes multiple modalities, but the majority are formalized and structured and depend on pulling people away from their work to learn.

Our formal education system creates many assumptions among our stakeholders about how learning happens. Stakeholders often base their L&D requests on these assumptions and their personal experiences, and that has led to our entrenched system of transactional training requests in which we have become order takers rather than partners.

Remember, we have to change the way key stakeholders think about learning to become the SBPs we want to be.

CHAPTER 2
Why We Stay Stuck

We understand objectively that we are stuck, hemmed in by others' perceptions of L&D leaders as *only* order takers who deliver formal training. We got here because of the way employee education evolved and the fact that most of us share common experiences of what it means to be a learner in a traditional school. Instead of freeing our superpowers, our L&D origin story ties us to old ways of thinking about learning and training.

Our current path—in which we remain order takers in transactional relationships with stakeholders who want only simple, formalized training—isn't the best route for us, our organizations, or our learners. We aren't making the big, positive impacts we want to make; we aren't solving the most pressing talent challenges.

If we know this is all true and our frustration is real, why don't we change the path we're on? Why don't we just work differently?

Before we can free our L&D superpowers to better serve our learners and our organizations, we need to understand why we've remained stuck for so long. Like most complex problems, many factors are involved. In this chapter, we'll discuss the key barriers, or what I call *blockers*, that are keeping us stuck.

Identifying Our Blockers

The blockers keeping us squarely in our place as order takers fall into two categories. The first one points the finger of blame elsewhere—at the organizations we work with and for. These *organizational blockers* vary from company to company, but we will discuss the four most prevalent. The second category, *personal blockers*, is more significant and uncomfortable to face because we are a large part of the problem. We will examine nine personal blockers, all of which are a form of unintentional self-sabotage keeping us from leaving the role of order taker behind and becoming SBPs.

For most L&D teams, a combination of organizational and personal blockers is at play. As we explore each blocker, please take note of whether it is present in your own team. The tool at the end of this chapter is designed to help you summarize your thoughts and get a clear picture of your own organizational and personal blockers. We can't address what we don't see.

Organizational Blockers

Unfortunately, organizational blockers are usually beyond our control and too big to just shove out of the way. They are embedded in systems, processes, and rules (written and unwritten). So, we need to work within them, build bridges over them, and sometimes create roads around them. We'll address how to do this in parts 2 and 3 of this book.

The most common organizational blockers, and the ones we'll consider in this chapter, are:
- Lack of maturity in organizational culture and processes
- Lack of support from leadership
- Lack of clear organizational goals and objectives
- Lack of resources

Lack of Maturity in Organizational Culture and Processes

Is the red tape in your company endless? Do you have to run every idea past 16 different leadership groups? Does the rollout of a new program take months or even years? An organization set up like this is destined to move slowly and inefficiently, whether leadership acknowledges that challenge or not.

Consider the situation of Nate, the senior manager of talent management design and leadership at a large retailer. Nate is frustrated because his team lacks autonomy. The family-owned and operated company has been around for nearly 100 years, and the current CEO wants to be involved in all decisions. For Nate, that means every idea he has needs to go up through the senior leadership team for approval, slowing his ability to create and iterate with agility. Although successful, the company hasn't matured culturally to allow for more autonomy among the business units.

This blocker stifles the ability of L&D leaders and their teams to work strategically and proactively to solve the most important talent challenges at the moment of need. Instead, they are stuck delivering solutions to old problems while they wait for processes to catch up.

Lack of Support From Leadership

Sometimes, the words and actions of key leaders in an organization do not support the L&D team's efforts to do anything other than take orders. Often, these leaders don't understand why L&D needs more autonomy and haven't taken the necessary time to learn. They can't see beyond L&D's traditional transactional function and see no benefits in making a change.

An unsupportive leader, especially one who is in a position of influence, can become a significant barrier to doing strategic work. Denise, the training and development manager at a small healthcare technology company, reported a situation in which one influential executive was outspoken about not supporting L&D in a more strategic function. This executive halted a new leadership development program without discussion just before launch, demanding a focus on performance management instead. Denise and her team lacked the political power to push back or open a dialogue, so they had to abandon a program they had worked on for months.

Remember: The organization also requires a mindset shift to see L&D leaders as SBPs. Some people will have a harder time than others making that shift.

Lack of Clear Organizational Goals and Objectives

It's difficult for L&D leaders to strategically align to an organizations' goals and objectives if they are unclear or simply don't exist. Lack of clarity is typical in smaller and fast-growing organizations, although it may exist in larger organizations as well.

At Denise's small healthcare technology company, the leadership team frequently says that the company goal is to "be the best" in the work they do, but their statements end there. The executives share no specifics about how they intend to meet this goal and seem to lack any focus areas or targeted initiatives.

It's difficult or impossible to align to a strategy described only in broad brush strokes. In Denise's words, "How do we partner with the organization when we don't even know what we're supporting?"

Lack of Resources

In many organizations, L&D teams are often last to get needed resources and among the first to lose their resources in times of economic strain. It's difficult to align strategically with the larger organization when we only have the time, money, and staff to complete the minimum daily tasks.

Julianne, the head of talent at a large global logistics company, saw multiple rounds of layoffs over a few years, including losses in L&D. In three years, Julianne's team was reduced by more than half. They were forced to "skinny their scope" and focus less on strategic initiatives and more on the maintenance of existing programs.

This is a story I hear frequently during and after economic downturns. It's also an indicator that the L&D function is operating as transactional, expendable order takers. If L&D is unable to contribute directly to organizational goals or demonstrate impact, there is no economic reason to keep a large staff of L&D team members.

We all see organizational blockers to varying degrees in our organizations. We didn't create them, but we must recognize and gradually work to change them—or change the way we respond to them—so we can be more effective partners. In parts 2 and 3, we'll discuss strategies that will help you overcome some of these barriers over the long term.

Now, we will explore the blockers we can work to change more quickly because they are rooted in our own unintentional self-sabotaging behaviors. The good news is that our personal blockers are within our power to change; the bad news is that we can be our own worst enemies.

Personal Blockers

When I was growing up, my mom was fond of the phrase, "If I had a nickel for every time _____, I'd be rich!" Usually, she filled in the blank with, "your sister is late." While I seriously doubt the nickels she gathered would have made her rich, the concept was clear.

If I had a proverbial nickel for every time I've seen an L&D leader unintentionally sabotaging their own success to the point where they remained indefinitely stuck in an order-taker role, however, I probably *would* be rich. We are all masters in the art of unintentional self-sabotage. I stress the word *unintentional* because I do believe we all have positive intentions. We aren't trying to make it harder to become strategic partners or keep ourselves stuck in order-taking mode. We believe we are doing good work and making the right choices to help our stakeholders and organizations. But the longer-term results of our actions send a different message—one that perpetuates the order-taking narrative.

Personal blockers are almost always in play for a learning team that is stuck. Fortunately, changing our own behavior is always easier than eliminating organizational blockers. This is where we have the power to make meaningful changes that ultimately lead to strategic partnership.

In my research, I discovered many acts of unintentional self-sabotage; these are the nine most common:

- Taking and delivering orders
- Striving to be helpful, easy to work with, and successful
- Assuming others have determined that learning is the best solution
- Aligning projects to legacy expectations
- Employing a flavor-of-the-month approach to content creation
- Reinforcing the wrong purpose for learning
- Letting ego run the show
- Taking too little time to understand the business
- Lacking metrics that show real-world results

Which of these applies to you and your team? If you had a nickel for every time you've engaged in one of these acts, would you be rich?

Taking and Delivering Orders

The number 1 way we perpetuate the order-taking narrative is by taking and delivering orders. Period.

Every time we automatically say yes to providing training, exactly as requested, we reinforce the message that this is how the L&D function works. We've all seen this self-sabotage play out in a sequence of events like this:

1. A stakeholder comes to us with a request for training.
2. We ask questions about the desired learning outcomes.
3. We may also ask for access to subject matter experts (SMEs) to better understand the content.
4. We begin to work on creating the training solution.

Each time we follow this predictable process without diving deeper, understanding the true need, knowing how the ask applies to larger organizational initiatives, and determining whether learning will solve the problem, we are telling the rest of the organization that we are primarily order takers, and this is how they should work with us.

This makes sense, right? What gets rewarded gets repeated.

Of course, sometimes we do need to take and deliver on an order, but when we say yes to and fulfill a request, we should do so with a strategic and nuanced approach.

Striving to Be Helpful, Easy to Work With, and Successful

Being helpful, easy to work with, and successful are all positive traits, aren't they? Yes, but without planning and balance, they can also lead to self-sabotage. The more we prioritize being easy to work with and saying yes to all projects, including those that won't move the needle strategically, the less time we have for more important projects.

Travis—the senior vice president (SVP) of talent at a midsize insurance, financial services, and HR consulting company—explains the core of the problem succinctly: "We [in L&D] are people who want to be helpful, so we want to say yes. It's much easier to say yes than it is to push back."

Travis is right. We got into our profession because we genuinely want to help others, and this is how we show our value in our organizations. We are a good-hearted bunch! If we consistently push back on requests, eventually stakeholders will just stop coming to us, right?

Pushing back gets even harder when we add power dynamics. The L&D team doesn't normally go toe-to-toe with senior leaders. The people making requests typically have some kind of power over us, directly or indirectly, and therefore, any pushback takes a certain amount of courage and confidence.

Let's also consider the issue of success. Most of us go to work wanting to do a good job, which we equate to success. We all know how to be successful as an order taker by creating and delivering exactly what was requested on time. We collect our kudos and then move to the next request. And let's face it; we like kudos more than conflict. If we push back, what are the parameters of success? Will anyone offer kudos if we say no?

Our desire to help and succeed in our jobs, our natural aversion to conflict and discomfort, and our lack of courage and confidence in pushing back on requests all create a major barrier to working more strategically. Can we sacrifice discomfort in the moment for a bigger version of success down the road? Pushing back, thinking differently, and challenging the status quo are all hard, but trying not to rock the boat is part of what keeps us stuck rowing in circles.

Assuming Others Have Determined That Learning Is the Best Solution

When a stakeholder comes to us requesting a training solution for one of their pain points, we usually assume they know this will solve the problem and that they have already vetted other options. I'll be the first to admit that stakeholders can be quite convincing. They use our language, telling us that people need training because they don't know how to do x. We believe them. Why wouldn't we? Don't they know their team better than we do?

Sometimes, yes. But, in my experience, stakeholders are usually overwhelmed, buried in the details of their work, and lack time to do a thorough analysis or involve themselves in crafting a time-consuming solution. They need changes quickly. The immediate and easiest assumption is that their problem stems from a lack of knowledge or skills among employees.

Unfortunately, our stakeholders are often too close to a problem to see the full picture. If we provide a training solution in a situation where training won't actually solve the problem, we waste everyone's time and resources, sabotage our own credibility, and reinforce the idea that all we do is take and deliver on orders.

Aligning Projects to Legacy Expectations

In many organizations, taking and delivering orders is the way L&D work has always been done. We buy into this narrative when we enter our positions and rise through the ranks, and we never question it. We don't give ourselves permission to think differently.

L&D professionals who grew up in business operations roles, as opposed to what we now call *people development* or *talent development*, are especially susceptible to aligning their work with legacy expectations. These are people who were so good at their jobs that they were asked to help train new members of their team and were eventually promoted to the title of *trainer* and perhaps transferred to the L&D department. They have no reason to question whether their methods are as effective as they could or should be and may not have thought about how to help more than just a few employees at a time.

As L&D leaders, we are responsible for helping people on our team break from traditional thinking. We must help them understand how to build learning at scale, explain why a classroom model of training might not be the best approach, and introduce them to new learning methods. The goal is for everyone to work strategically instead of reactively. Just like leadership skills don't develop solely through instinct, neither does thinking about L&D as a strategic function.

When we simply accept the legacy mindset of taking and delivering on orders, we reinforce the traditional narrative and unintentionally sabotage our ability to grow toward strategic partnership. When we fail to help others in the profession learn that they can be more than order takers, we unintentionally sabotage their ability to grow as well.

Employing a Flavor-of-the-Month Approach to Content Creation

In food industry lore, Sealtest Dairy (an ice cream parlor chain in the Eastern United States) was the first to use a "flavor of the month" as an advertising strategy back in the 1930s (Tréguer 2018). Their ads stressed that for "just a few pennies more," your family could enjoy a specially selected, limited-time dessert! It wasn't long before other restaurants saw the genius in this scarcity marketing campaign to build a recurring customer base. Nowadays, there are flavor-of-the-month-inspired subscription delivery services for everything from wine to pickles. Yum!

This marketing approach is perfect for food and drinks, but not for L&D. Unlike learning a new skill or concept, a flavor of the month isn't meant to make it into our long-term memory or change our behavior. Too many L&D teams take a flavor-of-the-month approach to creating learning content because they lack a longer-term strategy. They hop from topic to topic—one month focusing on how to navigate challenging conversations and the next discussing effective decision making with no links between the two. They also frequently lack a strategy for the continued development of each skill. This approach again reinforces the order-taking narrative because stakeholders looking at programs from the outside see no obvious development continuum for employees.

In a flavor-of-the-month approach, your L&D team is constantly creating and pushing out new content, only to have it sit on a proverbial shelf collecting dust. The organization's training library grows, but its employees' memory of each item in the library does not. If existing content is only rarely reinforced or reused, neither managers nor employees will know what's available.

A related challenge for L&D teams is dealing with trends in the marketplace. In just one walk through the expo hall at a large talent development conference, we are hit with a myriad of fun, exciting new solutions tugging at our nerdy L&D hearts. They all might be fun and exciting, but are they really what our organizations need at the moment, or are they just solutions searching for a problem? More isn't always better, even if it's new and exciting.

For example, personality-type assessments—including the Myers-Briggs Type Indicator instrument, CliftonStrengths (formerly StrengthsFinder), Insights, and DiSC—are designed to help people learn more about themselves and how to better work with others. The latest addition to the list is the Enneagram, which many colleagues, clients, and even my young adult daughter are all eager to learn more about.

For L&D leaders, the problem is not any particular program or assessment. The problem is that we often feel compelled to change strategies and adopt whatever's most popular at the moment. When we do that, we use a constantly shifting language when investigating a person's personality instead of developing a deeper understanding based on a single framework.

You need to ask yourself a few questions before adopting a flavor-of-the-month approach to any of your key tools or techniques:
- Do you need a new version?
- Was the old one not working for the people you're serving?
- Was the old version causing a problem in your organization that required a new solution?
- Is the L&D team simply bored with the current content?
- Are you just responding to the fact that the new trending tool or technique sounds more fun and exciting?

I've chosen a simple, benign example in the form of personality assessments, but my point applies to all the emerging technology solutions that cross our desks each day. Yes, we do need to keep up with current trends, but continuously shifting our approaches without considering whether we have a real problem to solve doesn't help us work strategically. In fact, it sabotages our ability to do so because our goalposts are continuously shifting. Simply put, while L&D offerings that aren't part of a larger strategy may meet a short-term need, they don't have any staying power. Short-term solutions sabotage our position as a strategic partner working to improve talent capacity over time in the business.

Reinforcing the Wrong Purpose for Learning

If you're reading this book, you've probably had to require people to attend, participate in, or complete a specific training at least once. Perhaps the directive came from someone higher up the chain of command or an outside entity like a governing or legal body. Most frequently, mandatory training happens around compliance.

I once worked with a large healthcare organization on a project linked to the implementation of a new software system that would affect the way employees in accounting, human resources, and the supply chain did their work. Each employee was required to attend several lab-style learning sessions designed for hands-on practice in the new system. The trainer gave the employees a task and demonstrated it, asking those in the room to follow along. Participants then practiced the task while the trainer walked around and assisted. Because there were some remote employees, we offered the lab sessions with a simultaneous virtual option.

The training team (who were flown to headquarters for the event) and I couldn't believe that almost no one attended the in-person practice sessions even though the training room was located just down the hall from their workspaces. Participants dialed in from a few feet away, and most were completely disengaged.

I asked the manager about this strange situation. She said, "Well, they don't really need this training. They're just attending so they get the credit in the learning management system and don't get in trouble later."

I couldn't believe my ears. "That's not the purpose of this training," I told her. "Can we get clear on what they really *need* and ask them to attend only those sessions?"

Unfortunately, the culture of disengagement in the company had been reinforced for years, and the damage was done. Employees participated in learning only when absolutely required to check a box. If they didn't take an assigned class, they were reprimanded. Any lack of attendance was entered into each employee's performance file and eventually influenced raises and bonuses for the year. The employees were devoted to fulfilling their requirements not because they wanted to learn, but because they wanted to remain in good standing, avoid trouble with leadership, and ultimately, get better raises.

We completed the project, but I can confidently say that very few employees learned anything. When the new system launched, everyone struggled to use it, which led employees and company leaders to complain and blame our contracted training team.

"What type of training was that? I don't know how to use the system any better than I did before I went," they told us.

The reality was that it didn't matter how awesome the training was in design and delivery. For years, this company had been reinforcing the wrong message: Learning is nothing but a required assignment.

Another way we often send the wrong message about learning is by using it as the only solution for poor performance. Too often, those who need improvement only see training as a negative reprimand, rather than a positive form of help.

For example, I remember once training Todd, a veteran employee who was on the verge of being fired for a lack of professionalism in his communication with colleagues and customers. His performance improvement plan required him to attend an email communication class I had created for new hires.

For Todd, the experience was like having graduated from high school and then being told he had to return to first grade to make up for something he hadn't learned. He arrived angry, muttered sarcastic comments under his breath, and made it clear to everyone that he didn't want to be there. He refused to participate in activities and poisoned the new employees' experience with his attitude. You won't be shocked that Todd didn't pass his performance improvement plan and was eventually fired anyway.

Using training as a fix for poor employee performance just doesn't work.

But what about all the required compliance training we can't change or question? In those cases, I like to ask how we can meet the requirement in a way that allows employees to truly benefit without giving in to the "all training is boring and unnecessary" narrative. The purpose of compliance training is usually to reduce or eliminate costly errors and unsafe practices. We need to find ways of helping employees do this instead of simply hitting "next" to continue a slide show or multitasking while in a Zoom training.

Letting Ego Run the Show

Most L&D programs are well-designed, and employees enjoy them. You probably have a team that works hard to create excellent products. Congratulations! Pat yourself on the back!

Now, look around. The rest of your organization, including its leaders, doesn't care about L&D. They don't come to work thinking about flashy training modules. They care about responding to demanding customers, meeting metrics, and understanding how their people can improve and be successful in their jobs.

We can't allow our egos to control what we do. This work isn't about us, and if we think it is, we'll sabotage our success. We put ourselves in the position of doing things *for* the business instead of *with* the business.

Julianne, the head of talent at a large global logistics company, talked to me about Carl, a particularly brilliant L&D team member she had worked with in the past. Carl had all the academic accolades behind his name. When he was asked to create a leadership development program for the business, he took everything he had learned about leadership development and put it into a beautifully designed program. He was proud of it and expected rave reviews. But, during the program's rollout, very few people engaged. There was no traction. Why?

Carl was so sure of his knowledge and skills that he didn't ask questions about the business. He didn't involve the organization's leaders to ask questions about their experiences or request their feedback. As a result, they didn't trust him or his expertise. Carl's ego got in the way of his success.

Please don't jump to the conclusion that Carl was just an egotistical, self-involved guy. He wasn't, and his intentions were good. He wanted to provide the business with the best leadership development program possible and had the expertise to do so. You may be in the same position.

Have you ever not involved a stakeholder because they are too busy? Have you ever trusted that you had all the necessary information without digging deeper? Have you ever assumed your organization's leaders just want you to go away and come back a few weeks later with some wonderful solution—no questions asked?

If so, don't make the same mistake Carl made of focusing *only* on your own expertise without first focusing on the business and its needs. When we create something *for* the business instead of in partnership *with* the business, we lose an opportunity to build trust, ignore critical needs, and fail to solve real problems.

Taking Too Little Time to Understand the Business

When it comes to understanding the ins and outs of our organizations, we often think we get a pass. Of course, we can all go to a family reunion and give our aunts and uncles the elevator pitch about what our business does. I'm talking about a deeper understanding of how the business operates. This includes everything from sources of revenue and major expenses to the everyday challenges and pressures faced by frontline employees.

The most obvious way this plays out is when the L&D solution doesn't meet the business need. We miss the mark by providing a learning solution that is ineffective because we don't understand employees' daily lives on the job.

I worked in an organization in which an acquiring company's talent development team was told to "level set" all the people leaders to ensure everyone understood the new expectations. On the surface, sharing expectations with those new to the company sounds like it could be a good idea, right?

Unfortunately, the way this directive was executed simply didn't work for the leaders of the newly acquired companies. The talent development team pulled every people leader off the floor into eight hours of required, live, virtual classroom training, two hours at a time over four weeks. The training happened during the busiest quarter of the year when everyone was working overtime, no one took a lunch break, and people barely had time for normal human biological functions! Furthermore, this "level set" was required for all people leaders, whether they had been on the job for 15 days or 15 years and whether they already had a stellar performance record, low staff turnover, or a file full of glowing reviews or the worst record in the organization.

The training was content heavy—the facilitator read most of the slides to those in attendance, quoted statistics, and stressed the main points through visuals and repetition, with only a few short breakout groups. The talent development team had so much content to get through that they ignored their own best practices.

In the final training session, attendees were asked to share what they had learned, but most were hard-pressed to come up with takeaways because very little new information or ideas had been presented. The participants were stressed and frustrated by the requirement, and the program's poor timing made it hard for them to fully engage.

The talent development team delivered on the order they had received, but in doing so they did a lot of damage. Their reputation was squashed in those eight required hours, which negatively colored the perception of future programs in the eyes of influential people leaders throughout the newly acquired organization. Perhaps most troubling was the fact that the talent development team had, unintentionally, implied that the daily work of the business wasn't important.

How different would this situation have been if they had first looked at the order to level set from the standpoint of the leaders doing the work? What if they had asked questions about cadence, timing, and the best modality?

Business leaders will never see our L&D teams as strategic partners if we don't understand their daily experiences. Not taking the time to understand the organization keeps us in perpetual order-taking mode.

Lacking Metrics That Show Real-World Results

We've all seen a lot of buzz about measurement in the L&D community, and we know we need to be better at it. In addition to other challenges, our lack of effective measurement sabotages our ability to work as SBPs.

Almost all business teams are held accountable to certain metrics that show the value of their contributions to greater business goals, whether they are daily operating goals, efficiency goals, safety goals, or goals related to costs and revenue. Each team reports its metrics to the larger organization, and those numbers add up to show overall business successes and challenges. In my experience, most employees know what they need to do to help their team meet its numbers.

However, the typical L&D team doesn't operate this way. Often, we aren't held accountable, by ourselves or others, to specific metrics. We may report on the number of people in classes, hours spent creating content, or number of clicks registered in on-demand courses. But we don't report on issues critical to overall business success or failure. Our team members rarely know our numbers or their role in meeting them.

Without good data, L&D leaders can't make informed business decisions about what works and what doesn't. No other part of the organization relies solely on impressions and feelings to determine whether their efforts were worth it. Why should we? Our lack of relevant data also reinforces the perception that we add less value to the organization and contributes to the fact that we aren't seen as strategic partners on a level playing field with everyone else.

Understanding how to find and present relevant metrics was a long journey for me. I first needed specific program outcomes, and later, as I gained a wider scope of responsibility, I began to look for ways to account for L&D as a whole.

In one of my first L&D leadership roles, I worked for a growing organization that was defining its best practices. Every part of the business had to regularly report its performance metrics to the senior leadership team, and L&D was no exception. Our measurement system at the time certainly wasn't robust, and I worked hard to find metrics to report. After some creative scrambling, I turned in what I thought was a lovely dashboard.

My boss took one look at it and kindly said, "Thank you. This is great. But the only story it's telling is that we are busy. Everyone's busy. Why are we busy? What is the outcome of all this work?"

I knew she was right. I read the carefully curated numbers that showed how many people had taken our classes, how many new courses we had created, how many new videos and articles we had produced, and how many people had clicked on or enrolled in online courses. Our days were full of activity—*but for what?*

In response to my boss's urging, I used the lens of business goals to look again. I started asking different questions about our team measures. How were our initiatives contributing to organizational or team success? What was different as a result of our work? Did we reduce expenses or help increase revenue in some way? Did we contribute to customer satisfaction? These questions led to a completely different type of measurement dashboard.

As L&D leaders, we sabotage ourselves when we choose to show activity and feedback instead of real, meaningful results. We aren't showing value, just that we are busy (and perhaps creating things that add to the busyness of others). In that case, why would anyone think that we have value to add?

Understanding Why You Stay Stuck

So, here we sit. Stuck in the position of order takers. We sometimes wish that we could point the finger at others, blaming our organization or leadership— and sometimes we can. But most of the time, we are our own worst enemies, creating and maintaining personal blockers. Our intentions are good, but the long-term outcomes come back to haunt us in the end and reinforce our position as order takers.

We can't change something if we don't know it exists, so identifying our blockers is the first step to overcoming or working around them. Now that we know, it's time to start doing our work differently—and to become true SBPs.

Summary

As L&D leaders, we face a variety of blockers that keep us stuck taking orders rather than becoming true strategic partners in our organizations, and our first task is to recognize those blockers. We deal with some at the organizational level, and those are difficult to change. Others are personal and arise from unintentional self-sabotage. These are easier to change.

Organizational blockers include:
- Lack of maturity in organizational culture and processes
- Lack of supportive leadership
- Lack of clear organizational goals and objectives
- Lack of resources

Personal blockers include:
- Taking and delivering on orders
- Striving to be helpful, easy to work with, and successful
- Assuming others have determined that learning is the best solution
- Aligning projects to legacy expectations
- Employing a flavor-of-the-month approach to content creation
- Reinforcing the wrong purpose for learning
- Letting ego run the show
- Taking too little time to understand the business
- Lacking metrics that show real-world results

Tool 2-1. Self-Assessment: Why Do You Stay Stuck?

To what degree is your L&D team facing the blockers we've discussed in this chapter? Use this assessment to reflect on your situation and the situation of your team. Which of these blockers are present most often for you? For your team members? Be honest.

Don't worry—if your numbers are high, you haven't failed. But, you do have a clear starting point and specific areas to focus on throughout the rest of the book.

For now, the goal is to increase your awareness of blockers so you know where to spend the most energy to remove them. It doesn't matter whether you have one area to improve or many. The most important task is defining those areas for your unique situation.

Using this simple scale—0=never, 1=rarely, 2=about half the time, 3=almost always, 4=always—circle the answer that comes closest to how often you or your team experience the blocking scenarios described.

Organizational Blockers	Rating				
Lack of maturity in organizational culture and processes	0	1	2	3	4
Lack of support from leadership	0	1	2	3	4
Lack of clear organizational goals and objectives	0	1	2	3	4
Lack of resources	0	1	2	3	4

Personal Blockers (Unintentional Self-Sabotage)	Rating				
Taking and delivering on orders	0	1	2	3	4
Striving to be helpful, easy to work with, and successful	0	1	2	3	4
Assuming others have determined that learning is the best solution	0	1	2	3	4
Aligning projects to legacy expectations	0	1	2	3	4
Employing a flavor-of-the-month approach to content creation	0	1	2	3	4
Reinforcing the wrong purpose for learning	0	1	2	3	4
Letting ego run the show	0	1	2	3	4
Taking too little time to understand the business	0	1	2	3	4
Lacking metrics to show real-world results	0	1	2	3	4

Scoring

Look at your rating for each blocker. A zero indicates that the blocker probably isn't a problem for you or your team. A four indicates the blocker is significant and should be addressed.

Your Areas of Success

Based on the assessment, identify the areas in which you and your team are doing well. In other words, which areas did you rate a zero or one (indicating that they're rarely or never present)? Make notes that will help you to refer back to specific situations later. Also, good job!

Your Most Pervasive Blockers

Based on the assessment, where is your best opportunity for improvement? In other words, which areas did you rate between two and four (indicating that they are present at least half the time)? These are your significant blockers. List them out and include examples from your work to help you as you move through the rest of the book.

CHAPTER 3
What a Strategic Business Partner Looks Like

In chapters 1 and 2, we explored some problems we face as L&D leaders and the reasons we find ourselves stuck in the role of order taker. Those are challenging topics for me because I prefer to focus on optimism and growth. In this chapter, as we strive to change the way we work and increase our positive impact, optimism and growth both come into play in charting a new path forward—a path where, instead of becoming order takers supporting our colleagues, we work on becoming SBPs.

Each element of the term *strategic business partner* is equally important. The word *strategic* highlights the fact that we focus on achieving the most significant and critical business goals and solving the most pervasive talent challenges. It also means we are making all our L&D decisions intentionally, with an eye on long-term impact. The word *business* represents the lens through which we analyze our options and understand how our organization functions. And *partner* indicates that, as L&D leaders, we have equal standing with other leaders and teams throughout our organization and work *with*, not *for* them.

Simply put, an L&D leader who is an SBP pairs deep expertise in learning with a big-picture vision and the passion and skills to move their business forward. In chapters 4–12, we will discuss the specific steps you can take to become an SBP, but in this chapter, we discuss the mindset that has to come first. We'll consider how to ensure others recognize that strategic partner mindset from the outside and how to recognize and cultivate it in ourselves.

Strategic Partnership From the Outside

For observers, it's typically easy to determine whether an L&D leader is an SBP based on a few external indicators:
- Collaborative conversations
- Positive rapport, reputation, and relationships with others
- Early involvement in key initiatives

Collaborative Conversations

Learning leaders who work as SBPs are pulled into conversations to serve as collaborators in problem solving, not silent adherents to predetermined solutions. Other organization leaders treat an SBP as an equal and trust them to understand, ask good questions, and bring L&D expertise to the table when relevant.

I knew my team had shifted from order takers to SBPs when key stakeholders throughout the organization stopped coming to me with transactional requests like, "We need a one-hour workshop on time management." Instead, they started conversations with information like, "We are having problems with our team members getting all their work done in a timely manner. What ideas do you have to help?"

Notice the dramatic difference? As SBPs, we were invited to solve problems collaboratively. The stakeholders' questions didn't assume a training solution was the best option but instead displayed curiosity and openness. Together, we had the opportunity to explore whether a learning solution would solve the problem, and if it would, we moved on to determine the best modality for each team. Improved access to resources or job aids? Leader coaching? A multiweek course or program? Or a combination of several solutions?

Our collaborative conversations always demonstrated that we were seen by our stakeholders as partners whose expertise could help solve problems.

Positive Rapport, Reputation, and Relationships

Sarah, a learning and organization development manager at a midsize retailer, told me that she can spot an SBP based on what she calls the three Rs: positive rapport, reputation, and relationships. In other words, a learning leader who is working as an SBP has:

- Positive rapport with stakeholders throughout the business
- A solid reputation for high-quality work that moves the organization forward, whether that work involves a learning solution or a recommendation to pursue another avenue
- Trusting relationships with business stakeholders that demonstrate that learning leaders are both allies and advocates.

In the presence of a positive rapport, a solid reputation, and trusted relationships with L&D as SBPs, stakeholders quickly begin to understand that learning isn't limited to a classroom or program. They see the L&D team as experts with specific skill sets.

Joe, the director of L&D at a midsize automotive manufacturer, described his transformation into an SBP using the power of positive rapport, reputation, and relationships, while his company was overhauling and updating its product development life cycle. During the project, organization leaders came to Joe, not for an immediate learning strategy, but to facilitate a cross-functional conversation that would determine and map new processes because he had established a reputation for fairness and effective leadership. With more than 15 people in the room from engineering, manufacturing, and IT, Joe led the conversation using skills he had gained during years as an L&D facilitator to establish rapport and strengthen new relationships. He ensured that everyone's voice was heard and no one person dominated the discussion.

"I knew, at that point, I was definitely considered a business partner," Joe said, "because literally, I had nothing else to do with the whole process other than to help functional leaders work together effectively to come up with a better process for developing new products—from concept to launch and manufacturing."

Not every L&D SBP will be asked to step outside L&D's traditional scope, but all will be seen as trusted experts with solid reputations for success in communication and relationship building.

Early Involvement in Key Initiatives

Imagine a world in which you are asked to collaborate on solutions to problems, are seen and trusted as an expert who delivers quality solutions, and get pulled into key conversations from their inception. How might your day-to-day work be different? The next key determinant of success as an SBP is all about when and how a partner becomes involved in strategic initiative conversations, large-scale decisions, and major organization changes.

Transactional order takers normally join business conversations near the end and are asked to produce training content based on decisions already made. In these cases, training seems like a last-minute request, as if the stakeholders were wrapping up a final meeting and someone said, "Oh shoot, we probably need training for this!" The result is that the L&D team must scramble quickly to pull off a miracle on time and within the budget.

In contrast, SBPs are always involved in business planning early, woven into the overall strategy of any large-scale initiative, decision, or organizational change. They are in meetings listening, asking thoughtful questions, and offering solutions.

Sarah, who introduced us to the three Rs, says she knew she was working as an SBP when she was invited into conversations about business changes quite early and asked her opinion about how best to prepare the workforce. She no longer got messages just 30 days before the rollout of a new initiative, saying, "Oh gosh, we need your help with training ASAP!"

I have yet to meet a learning leader who doesn't want to experience these external determinants of SBP status. But the external determinants form only one aspect of the picture. Our success as strategic partners requires that our actions also be informed and reinforced by *internal beliefs*, *assumptions*, and *ideas*. These internal drivers are essential to the mindsets of world-class athletes, well-known artists, highly respected leaders—and successful learning leaders.

Strategic Partnership From the Inside

If we consider strategic partnerships from the L&D leader's point of view, we see four determinants of success. Each begins with an internal mindset shift that later informs their actions. Strategic business partners are:
- Business focused
- Proactive, not reactive
- Continuously adding value
- Truly collaborative

Business Focused

First and foremost, learning leaders who are strategic partners focus intensely on the business and its overall goals. They understand that L&D's work is important for the business to succeed and grow, and they see their role as equal to that of any other function in ensuring that success and growth.

Unfortunately, most L&D teams relegate themselves to the status of supporting cast members. They take orders from others, doing everything they can to support other functions, rather than partnering with them to achieve shared goals.

I've heard of L&D leaders who are functioning as SBPs shift their use of language to change their team's mindset outlawing the words *support* and *help* from their vocabulary. For example, instead of asking stakeholders, "How can we help?" or talking with their team about "how we can best support the business," they make a conscious shift to discuss *partnering*. They ask, "How can we best partner with you?" and talk about "how we can partner effectively with the business." This simple change sends a strong message to stakeholders and reinforces the L&D team members' understanding of their work as equal to—not less than—the work of others.

Thinking and operating as a partner who focuses time and energy on the business also encompasses other changes in mindset, including:
- Functioning like the rest of the organization
- Thinking big picture, and then taking small steps
- Prioritizing business improvement
- Viewing organizational politics and culture as a force for good

Functioning Like the Rest of the Organization

We can't expect to work as strategic partners if we operate under different rules from our colleagues. Leaders must know what their business is trying to achieve in terms of overall goals and initiatives and must understand revenue, expenses, and the impact of both on the company. Leaders also must know how each component of the company, including their own, contributes to the whole. They should provide meaningful metrics and performance goals and exercise good leadership practices. Learning leaders working as SBPs hold themselves to the same expectations.

When I was leading teams, I wanted to ensure that our actions always matched those of the larger organization. That meant reporting how our function was contributing to revenue and expenses and how we were moving the needle on larger-scale initiatives. I also felt strongly that we should never ask our colleagues to take on a task without also doing it ourselves.

At one point, we partnered with the business in an initiative to improve performance management and reporting. We came up with an initiative in which every team member had to create SMART goals that aligned with the company's top four initiatives, as well as key leadership behaviors or values. Leaders were asked to review the goals and behaviors regularly with their team members. I believed that the L&D team should lead the way, so we outlined team goals and then defined how each member of the team would contribute in a SMART way. We did our best to discuss progress in regular one-on-ones. Leaders also set up quarterly goal progress meetings with each of their direct reports to discuss what they had accomplished, if the team member was on track, and what needed to happen next to stay on course or improve.

I'll be honest; all that reviewing and reporting was a lot of work, and my team learned that we were asking for a lot when we tasked managers with executing leadership in this way. We needed to know that. However, the results were worth the extra work. L&D team members knew exactly what was expected of them, knew how their work contributed to larger company goals, and knew where they stood at all times as a result of the initiative.

At the end of the year, when the company gave out performance ratings, the L&D team experienced no surprises. As a bonus, team members were much less likely to blame managers for a subjective performance rating or accuse managers of just not liking them. The clarity that this work created made everyone better and raised the morale of our team. I concluded that for SBPs, holding ourselves and our team members accountable for working just like the rest of the organization is simply non-negotiable.

Thinking Big Picture, and Then Taking Small Steps

Understanding and acting like others in the business also means practicing what I like to call *big-picture, small-step thinking* (Figure 3-1). This means you can see and understand the big picture and break it down into the small, incremental steps needed to get there. This is a skill that many L&D professionals possess naturally or as a result of formal and informal training because designing learning experiences often requires weeding through and simplifying a large amount of information. This skill transfers well to thinking and working strategically.

Figure 3-1. Big-Picture, Small-Step Thinking

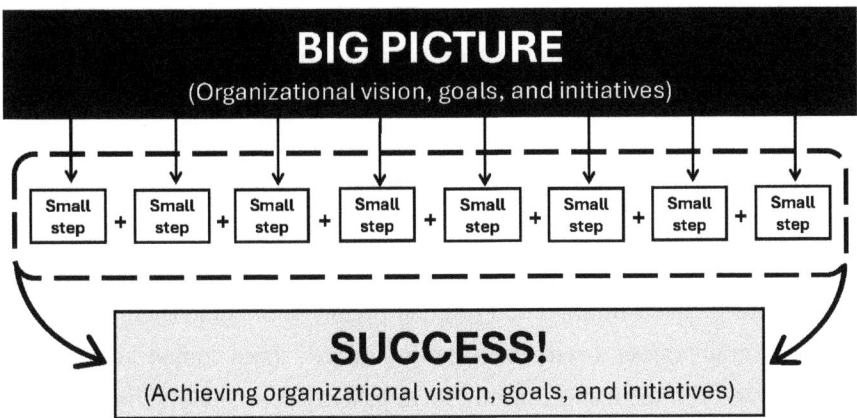

Strategic business partners take their big-picture, small-step skills and level up, applying them to a variety of work in L&D. They understand the larger goals of the organization, pair that knowledge with how the organization operates, and then break it all down to determine the smaller steps needed to contribute to goals and operations. Thinking about the big picture also allows an SBP to effectively determine L&D team priorities.

It's important to point out that this is *big-picture, small-step thinking* and not *small-step, big-picture thinking*. The order is important—big-picture thinking always comes first. You need to understand the larger business vision and goals long before defining the steps to get there, and as an SBP, you will always keep the vision and goals in mind when making decisions. If something seems confusing or unclear, you will look to the big picture first to determine your alignment before diving into the details or small steps.

For example, a sales leader asked my L&D team to create a communication "boot camp." He was eager to discuss when this would happen and what it would entail. Wearing my big-picture hat, I asked that we back up a bit. Instead of diving into the details of how the training program would be delivered, we first needed to consider the organization's goals. Was this offering part of a larger initiative? What led to this leader asking for training in the first place? The last thing we wanted to do was waste time creating and executing the small steps of a training boot camp without determining whether it tied into an overall strategy. The *how* (small steps) should always come after the *why* (big picture).

This way of thinking, in which the small steps forward are determined and guided by the big picture, combined with a thorough understanding of the business as a whole, allows learning leaders to reliably think beyond their single task or function.

Prioritizing Business Improvement

By considering overall business improvement to be their most important priority, SBPs can work under the umbrella of organization strategy instead of waiting for little droplets of unrelated tasks and requests to fall in their direction.

Early in my career, I remember getting excited about cool ideas to execute as part of an L&D team and running them past my boss (the best boss I've ever had) who responded, "That's a great idea for the learning team. I'm just wondering if it's what's best for the business overall. What do you think?"

At first, I hated that she dampened my excitement with a challenge to reconsider the big picture. But she shared that question when I needed to hear it most. She believed in using company time and resources as wisely as possible, and so did I. But sometimes, I needed a reminder.

Grounded by the question, "What's best for the business overall?" an SBP shows up without an ego. They aren't trying to prove their worth or argue for the value of their programs. They are invested in the best outcome for everyone. No heels dug in, just a desire to improve the organization, no matter who gets the credit. When a learning leader embraces this mindset, understands the business, sees the big picture, and helps to determine solutions based on what's best for overall success, they cultivate respect as a strong leader and partner.

Viewing Organizational Culture and Politics as Forces for Good

Organizational politics and culture are the unspoken rules that often dictate the success or failure of a business initiative. For our purposes, *organizational politics* refers to who wields power and influence, often based on their titles and position in the company's hierarchy. Political conflicts emerge from a scarcity of resources, preferences about whom to trust or engage with on projects, and, of course, the human ego. Organizational politics often influence decisions about where and when resources are assigned.

Organizational culture, on the other hand, includes the values, expectations, beliefs, norms, and practices that guide and inform employees' actions. Sometimes, components of culture are written down explicitly or reinforced in various ways, but just as often, we absorb our company's culture through unwritten ways of working together that emerge over time.

One example of unwritten cultural norms is how a company schedules and conducts meetings. (Expectations about proper meeting behavior usually aren't written down in formal documents.) Consider the following questions about meetings in your company:

- **Who attends meetings?** Is everyone who could possibly be involved in a project invited or just a small representative group?
- **How are meetings scheduled?** Can anyone put a meeting on someone's calendar, or do only certain people have access?
- **What is the expectation for attendance?** If you are invited to a meeting, does that mean you *need* to attend or just that you should *consider* attending?
- **When and how do meetings start?** Does the host wait for everyone to arrive or start precisely on time? Do most meetings begin with small talk or with items on the agenda?
- **How do meetings usually end?** On time, early, or late? With a recap or action items?
- **How is information gathered and reported?** Is someone assigned to take notes and send them out later, or do attendees take their own notes? Do you use an AI notetaking tool? Is it acceptable to record meetings?

When employees understand what a culturally acceptable meeting includes, they can be much more successful, but I have yet to work at an organization that puts the answers to all these questions in writing. They are simply part of the culture.

Learning leaders who work as SBPs are savvy about their organization's politics and culture. They understand that while these are powerful forces, they're not inherently positive or negative. Everything depends on how we use them.

A successful SBP tries to use organizational politics and culture for good, tapping into the norms for business improvement rather than personal gain. They know who needs to be involved in decisions, as well as all the other unwritten rules that are unique to each workplace (like how to conduct a culturally acceptable meeting).

Proactive, Not Reactive

Taking and delivering on an order is a reactive approach to learning and development. Those who have moved toward working as SBPs have transcended reactive work in favor of *proactive* work.

It would be easy to assume that all SBPs start their proactive work with an invitation to sit in and contribute to business conversations where big decisions were being made, but this is rarely the case. Working proactively tends to happen as a result of the sheer will of scrappy learning leaders who insert themselves into conversations, continuously gather information from a wide variety of sources, and then take the initiative, offering solutions before they are asked. In other words, they are proactive about working proactively!

Working proactively in L&D means:
- Inserting yourself across the organization
- Learning by overhearing
- Making recommendations without requests

Inserting Yourself Across the Organization

Elizabeth, the head of learning and leadership development at a large global manufacturing organization, invites herself to a lot of meetings because she believes that a large portion of her job is understanding the business on many levels. To understand, she needs to know how various business units do their work, what challenges they are encountering, and what initiatives they are working on. When she catches wind of a meeting where valuable information might be shared, she reaches out to the organizer and asks for an invitation.

Sometimes, they add her to the list, but other times, she gets pushback like, "Why would we invite you to this meeting?" or "We aren't doing training right now. Why would you, a learning person, want to attend our meeting?" She replies, "I just want to listen and learn more about your work so the learning team can better partner with you."

Elizabeth sometimes promises that she will sit quietly like a mouse in the corner, taking in information without contributing to the conversation. She has also offered to record meeting notes and hand them off to the organizer afterward.

"You aren't a secretary," a former boss once scolded her. "Why are you taking notes in this meeting?" Elizabeth respectfully responded, "I don't think you understand the value I get from sitting here, listening to all these conversations. I learn so much about how the business is operating, where the gaps exist, and what critical issues are popping up. All this informs where we can best spend our time, as a learning function, to help the business succeed."

Inserting ourselves into conversations like Elizabeth does is a strategic move. Colleagues across the organization will soon become familiar with our names, and ideally, they will admire and appreciate our desire to understand their work. By inserting ourselves into new spaces and discussions, we build relationships, credibility, and business knowledge one hour at a time without saying a word.

Jason, the senior manager of L&D at a midsize solar energy company likes to tell his team that if they aren't invited, they should "drag their own chair up to the table."

"I want you to envision an old-school metal chair with a cardboard back that is kind of falling apart," Jason instructs. "And then, like in any good sitcom, I want you to drag that chair across the room in such a way that it's loud, scraping the floor, and completely awkward. Now, it's quiet and all the people hear is you dragging your chair across the room to sit next to [a group of other leaders in your organization]. I want them to stop and notice that you are joining the conversation. But, don't pull that chair up to the table angry. Pull it up kindly and excitedly, thinking about how you are there to help. Invite yourself to the party."

Jason believes that a winning combination of awkwardness and positivity will help people remember us, so we will be more likely to be invited to the next party.

Strategic business partners don't wait for an invitation and they're not mad about it. They simply put on their learning hats and invite themselves to the party.

Learning by Overhearing

The learning leader who operates as an SBP considers any interaction with other aspects of the business an opportunity to learn. To the SBP, the organization is a giant puzzle, and every bit of information they pick up is a missing piece that helps reveal a clearer picture of where they can add value. They tend to find these pieces on an improvised scavenger hunt that goes from meeting to meeting or communication to communication. They might pick up one piece in the quarterly all-hands meeting, another when overhearing casual banter on a weekly call with the operations team, and another from an announcement on the main page of the company intranet. It doesn't matter where these opportunities to learn happen; the learning leader is there listening and putting the puzzle pieces together behind the scenes.

Adam, an organization development consultant for a large healthcare system is new to his role and isn't (yet) invited to many meetings where big decisions are made, but he does attend every quarterly town hall. These gatherings have become valuable windows into how the business operates, who the key players are, and what's coming next. He told me the online town halls are his best opportunities to pick up new puzzle pieces and determine the questions he needs to ask and who might be able to answer them. As the executives behind the screen share numbers and initiatives, Adam jots down questions to research later to better understand the business: Where are these numbers coming from? And who has control over changes in these numbers? When someone uses an acronym he doesn't understand, he notes that too and quickly finds out what it means.

Mechelle, the VP of student services at a small higher education institution told me how much she learns in meetings simply by closing her mouth, picking up her pen, and listening for themes. She focuses on identifying topics that keep coming up in conversations across multiple departments. If she doesn't understand why a topic is being discussed, she writes it down with a question mark to remind her to research it later. Mechelle also watches for clues about the dynamics of organizational culture. Did some people take the floor more than others? Who exhibited a negative attitude when another department spoke up or disagreed with them?

Learning leaders who work as SBPs are constantly looking for the bigger picture and proactively gathering clues, in any way they can.

Making Recommendations Without Requests

In the ultimate proactive action, SBPs offer recommendations for learning-related solutions that are aligned to business needs *before* they get a request from a stakeholder. They are so in tune with the business that they know the challenges and initiatives each area is facing, in part because they have inserted themselves across the organization and learned from every interaction.

Amber, the director of talent development at a midsize agricultural company, is a great example of someone who acts before anyone makes a request. After identifying potential development needs during conversations with other leaders, Amber and her HR counterparts collaborated on a simple survey asking key leaders to prioritize development topics based on what would be most helpful to their teams. The results provided a clear picture of business priorities, which allowed Amber to see exactly where the talent development team could make the most impact.

But her innovations didn't end there. Each area of her company held an all-hands meeting with leaders at different points during the year. In the past, the HR and TD teams had been invited to these meetings at the last minute and asked to talk about a current initiative or to kick off a learning project. Following her survey about development topics, Amber took a proactive approach, contacted each area's VP, and let them know how they could partner with her team.

"Based on the information shared by leaders across the company," she wrote, "we will be focusing on [an area-specific development topic] as a priority this year. We would love to engage with your leaders around this topic at your all-hands meeting. When is that meeting scheduled?"

Boom. Leader input received. Priorities set. Action plan determined and communicated before the ask was made. No sitting around and waiting to be told what to do.

In this instance, Amber reached out to identify priorities that weren't previously determined, but sometimes priorities are set by others and not communicated directly to the L&D team in a timely manner. SBPs don't let this stop them. Instead, they learn where they need to look for these pieces of the puzzle so they can use them to build their own strategies.

Consider the story of Kacie, the SVP and director of organization development at a small community bank. Her small but mighty L&D team needed to strategically plan how they would partner with the business ahead of time to make a real impact. Initially, she wasn't brought into meetings with each team, so she decided to use a secret weapon: SharePoint, the company's collaboration platform. Each department at the bank records its annual strategic plan in a specific location in SharePoint, indicating which other departments need to be involved in initiatives. For Kacie, this became a strategic goldmine of information.

On the platform, Kacie could filter queries based on words and phrases—such as *organization development*, *training*, or *learning*—and see which departments were planning to include her team in their initiatives. Armed with that knowledge, she proactively reached out to meet with each department leader and started discovery conversations before receiving the directive saying, "It's time to train. Let's bring in the org dev team." This is a perfect example of an SBP inserting herself into new spaces to better accomplish the organization's goals.

Amber's and Kacie's experiences show that you don't need to wait for the perfect plan to come across your desk to begin working as an SBP. In fact, you shouldn't! Learn about the business, collect pieces of the puzzle along the way, and then reach out to discuss plans for a partnership, before other leaders have even discussed involving L&D.

Continuously Adding Value

All learning leaders who successfully become true partners add enormous value when working with others across their organizations. Every project, interaction, request, and action go beyond "just the basics." Even when SBPs say no, they manage to add value to the business. They do this by employing a few simple tactics:

- Asking, "What *can* we do?"
- Adding small "sparks of extra"
- Thinking in terms of scale

Asking, "What Can We Do?"

Strategic business partners focus on every situation with a positive lens. I worked with one L&D manager named Brian who was a master of reframing the most negative situations with optimism. Even when he had to say no to a stakeholder, the person left feeling empowered. How is that possible? I think it comes from the question he asked when faced with any problem: "What *can* we do?" Instead of focusing on what they would be *unable* to accomplish due to limited time and resources, he reminded his team to think about what they *could* do to help.

For example, perhaps you can't create a separate coaching program for managers and supervisors in your contact center, even though your analysis shows that would be ideal. What are other ways you can equip or empower them to develop essential skills themselves? Are there existing resources you can leverage? Are there other people within the company who can help?

Or perhaps you can't pull everyone off the phones for multiple hours of training at the same time (and you know this approach won't be effective). How can you get them the same information using a different modality?

By continuously framing each challenge with the question, "What *can* we do?" Brian encouraged us all to think creatively and respond positively. Remember that there is always something you can do in every situation, even if it's small. You are not required to respond exactly as others define a positive response. You can think differently and still provide value.

Adding Extras

When an SBP receives a request that must be fulfilled, they add their specific expertise to provide a better product than the stakeholder requested. (Yes, even SBPs occasionally have to deliver on orders!) In other words, they go above and beyond.

Stakeholders in most organizations don't understand the L&D team's full capabilities. It's up to us as learning leaders to show them our capabilities, a little at a time, in several different ways. One of those ways is to add a "spark of extra" or unexpected value to every project. By exceeding expectations in small ways every time we work with other leaders, we slowly and gently educate them about what we can do.

Robert, the training manager at a small oil and gas company, inherited the task of coordinating an annual leadership development program from his predecessor. The program pulled in more than 50 leaders from across the company with a curriculum that took place over four days at an off-site location and was led by the CEO.

Robert's directive was to organize and coordinate the existing program, but he knew that having the CEO and executive staff talk at the leaders for four days wouldn't be effective. He couldn't simply say no to this directive, but he could make small changes to improve the overall impact and outcome. First, he broke the curriculum into smaller workshops to allow for more interaction and discussion. Then, he added follow-up sessions spaced throughout the year to reinforce the concepts and foster collaborative conversations. Finally, he took all the PowerPoint slide decks and aligned them to the company brand for consistency, which improved the professional look and feel of the program (not to mention delighting the director of marketing).

The individual changes were small, but together they added up to an effective starting point. And, the impact rippled across the organization. Robert showed key leaders that there was more to learning leadership than sitting in a hotel ballroom for four days with 49 silent colleagues.

Joe, the director of L&D at a midsize automotive supplies manufacturer, calls this type of work "guerilla effectiveness." By this, he means that small, unconventional tactics implemented from the ground level can positively affect the larger business picture. "I know that a training class in communications isn't going to move the needle on what the stakeholder is asking for," Joe says, "so I ask myself what I can sneak in that will make a difference."

Quite often, one of Joe's unconventional tactics is to slightly expand the scope of the request so he can do things he knows will make a better measurable impact. For example, he might add components to the communications curriculum that will have a direct impact on turnaround times or other metrics already measured by the business.

Can you think of any small ways that learning leaders who have collaborated with you as SBPs have added value beyond the ask? They might have been given fairly rigid parameters—like the banks of a river—for what needs to be accomplished, but they took control of the route they would swim within those banks to create a more effective and meaningful journey.

Thinking About Scale

Strategic business partners rarely take on a project that will affect only a small number of people within their organization. They always think about how their work can scale and increase its impact. They continuously question whether a particular project can be used by others as is or with different marketing or slight modifications.

Adam, an organization development consultant in a large healthcare system, received a request to train every physician, pharmacist, and clinical staff member at a single hospital within the system. "Why wouldn't we include this training for all six hospitals?" Adam asked quickly. "We're looking to maximize the impact of L&D through efficiency and scale. Why train a few when we could train many?"

Nate, the senior manager of talent management design and leadership in a large outdoor retailer noticed that the majority of the company's leadership development programs were high touch and focused on 15 leaders in the company's home office. While the participants in the program loved it, the organization's 1,500 other leaders weren't benefiting. Nate started asking questions, including, "How can we change this program so it works for *all* of our business's leaders throughout the world?"

Jenn, the director of program management and organization development at a midsize biotech company, likes to think about programs using an 80/20 lens to allow for nuance between departments. When her team is building a learning solution, she asks them to think about the core 80 percent of the program encompassing the things that *everyone* can benefit from—and that becomes the basic design. The other 20 percent is flexible. This part of the program can be customized or adjusted to fit different organization areas or roles.

Whether they are asking questions about how to expand company reach or how to create a multipurpose learning solution, these leaders aren't accepting any request or program at face value. They aim to improve the performance of as many people across the organization as possible, even if their L&D team is small. In other words, they are adding value through scalability.

Truly Collaborative

Learning leaders who are working as SBPs don't just cooperate; they collaborate. When we cooperate, we each do our part to complete a task. We share information in a transactional manner, passing it along from one person to the next. In a traditional L&D project, this often happens between a designer and a SME. Order takers are excellent at cooperation.

Collaboration, on the other hand, stresses that each person in a project brings different expertise, and all expertise is equally needed, valued, and used. The result of effective collaboration is the creation of something new that no one person could have created alone. True collaboration creates a partnership between all the minds in the room, changing and morphing ideas and outcomes based on each person's individual expertise.

As an SBP, you will be well aware that you bring expertise in L&D to every project. You will also expect others to bring their expertise, and as a result, the project will be different, more robust, and more effective. SBPs approach their work collaboratively by:
- Engaging others' expertise
- Sharing the responsibility of learning
- Busting silo walls

Engaging Others' Expertise

We usually need all the available expertise to create something fresh that no one could have created alone, and as SBPs, we show up believing in our own expertise as much as we believe in the expertise of the others in the room. We see our value, and we see others' value.

Adam, an organization development consultant at a large healthcare company, isn't shy about sharing what he and his team bring to any project. He calls out the expertise of others and then shares his own. His initial conversations go something like this: "You are the product owner of the widget business. That means you are the go-to person for widgets. I'm grateful for that, and we will lean into your expertise in that area throughout this project. I'm the person behind the curtain for all the knowledge when it comes to talent development and how to make learning stick, how to evaluate the learning, and how to do all the pieces that come along with the learning portion of this project."

After this preamble, Adam and the other leaders he is working with dive into the project. They all trust that everyone is bringing expertise into the room, playing their part, and building something together. SBPs believe we need *everyone* to create the best solution possible.

Sharing Responsibility for Learning

SBPs don't hog learning programs in their companies; they do the opposite. Although they are experts when it comes to people development, training, and learning, they don't expect to be the only ones performing these functions. They acknowledge that everyone in the organization might potentially play the role of *trainer* or *coach* as they help someone else develop or learn a new skill. They see a large part of their role as helping equip others to do that work well.

For example, Sarah, the learning and organization development manager at a midsize retail company, had a small team. She knew they couldn't design learning content for everything everyone needed in every location. She recalled one operations meeting when someone said, "We need more training on how to cut keys." Once the word training was mentioned, all eyes in the room instantly turned to her. But she quickly responded, "I don't know how to cut keys. I'm not the person to teach everyone how to do this in every store. But I can train trainers on how to do this. I can train trainers, but I cannot be one."

Many organizations have initiatives to help employees understand the best ways to train and develop others. They are often anchored by the L&D team, scaling learning expertise throughout the organization through shared responsibility.

Busting Silo Walls!

There's another superpower those who work as SBPs employ every chance they get. It's often unique to L&D but doesn't necessarily have anything to do with learning. This superpower is the ability to bust through the silo walls between departments and business units to help people connect, collaborate, and become more productive.

Silos form gradually, over time, as team members focus on their own work. They genuinely think they are doing their best, but the more they put their heads down and bury themselves in their daily tasks, the higher the walls become, separating them from effective collaboration and larger organizational goals. As silo walls strengthen and grow, they create inefficiencies, duplication, and misalignment.

Because SBPs live outside these siloed teams, they have a broader view. Like those sitting in the press box during a sporting event, they can see the gaps and missteps that players on the field miss. Their unobstructed view provides unique and powerful potential for learning leaders to help organizations collaborate effectively and achieve their overarching goals.

Elizabeth, the head of learning and leadership development at a large global manufacturing company, calls her silo-busting skill "playing pharmacist." She isn't formulating drugs or handing out prescriptions, but she is watching for interactions that could make the company better or unintentionally lead to damage. She came up with the name because a pharmacist who receives two prescriptions for the same patient from two different doctors must look closely to determine whether the combination of prescriptions could have a negative effect, including serious illness or even death. (Thank goodness we have pharmacists to identify that possibility!)

When Elizabeth is playing pharmacist in her role as an SBP, she isn't calculating life, death, or serious illness; instead, she is listening for overlap or conflict. Because she is talking with different business units, she sees beyond the silo walls and can point out when two areas of the organization are attempting to do the same thing independently of one another. On the flip side, she can let leaders know if their teams are sending conflicting messages that could lead to misalignment and confusion down the line. By playing pharmacist, Elizabeth often encourages—and sometimes facilitates—fruitful collaboration among people from different areas in the organization.

SBPs understand how to work collaboratively by valuing the expertise of everyone in the room, including their own. They don't own the work of learning throughout the organization, but they do help others accomplish goals effectively. They also use their superpower, sitting outside the team and looking in, to bust silos and encourage collaboration.

It's time to draw a new road map for the way we work as L&D leaders, a map to help us move from believing we must always settle for a supporting role to seeing ourselves as SBPs. Others in our organizations will notice this shift based on our collaborative conversations, our respected work and solid relationships, and our early involvement in initiatives.

The creative thinking behind this new road map will take place on the inside, as we shift our mindsets and approach our work differently. We will believe and act as if we are an important partner to the business, work proactively, continuously add value, and collaborate effectively.

As we hit each internal benchmark, we will begin to get unstuck. We will start moving from an environment in which we only take orders to a place where we work as SBPs.

In the next two sections of this book, I'll expand on these approaches to help you move step-by-step into the SBP role, first by building the necessary foundation and then by developing and executing a plan for your work within your organization. But first, take a few moments to reflect on your situation using Tool 3-1 at the end of this chapter.

Summary

The work of an L&D strategic business partner has little in common with the work of an order taker. Becoming an SBP requires shifts in mindset and approach. SBPs see themselves as important contributors to their organizations, not as a support function. You can spot an SBP because they always exhibit three key behaviors:

- Collaborative conversations
- Positive rapport, reputation, and relationships with others
- Early involvement in key initiatives

Beyond these external behaviors, the work of becoming an SBP—including several key mindset shifts—happens within each learning leader. Generally, SBPs are:

- Business focused
- Proactive, not reactive
- Continuously adding value
- Truly collaborative

Tool 3-1. Assess Your Strategic Partner Mindset

Do you approach your work with an SBP mindset? Fill out this assessment to understand where to best focus your work going forward.

Take a moment to put your thoughts on paper. How often are you able to approach your work by applying the following action? Using the simple scale—0=never, 1=rarely, 2=about half the time, 3=almost always, 4=always—note the degree to which each of these scenarios describes your mindset. Then, total your score and record it at the bottom of each table.

Business-Focused Actions	Rating				
Functioning like the rest of the business (according to metrics and expectations)	0	1	2	3	4
Thinking about the big picture first and taking small steps second	0	1	2	3	4
Seeing business improvement as the most important objective	0	1	2	3	4
Working within organizational politics and culture to achieve outcomes	0	1	2	3	4
Total					/16

Proactive Actions	Rating				
Inserting yourself across the organization	0	1	2	3	4
Learning by overhearing	0	1	2	3	4
Making recommendations without requests	0	1	2	3	4
Total					/12

Actions to Add Value	Rating				
Asking, "What *can* we do?"	0	1	2	3	4
Adding small sparks of extra to every project	0	1	2	3	4
Thinking in terms of scale	0	1	2	3	4
Total					/12

Collaborative Actions	Rating				
Engaging everyone's expertise (including your own)	0	1	2	3	4
Seeing L&D as something owned by everyone	0	1	2	3	4
Busting through silos to connect different areas of the organization	0	1	2	3	4
Total					/12

Scoring

Which areas have the highest scores? That's where you're approaching your work most like an SBP. Note some specific examples in which you have done this well.

Which areas have the lowest scores? Those are the areas in which you have the greatest opportunity to improve your SBP approach. What do you think is holding you back? It might be helpful to refer back to previous chapters to gain more insight.

Tool 3-2. Assess and Strategize to Become an SBP

The next two sections of this book provide a practical guide to becoming a strategic business partner. Because we are more likely to remember and apply information that relates to our current circumstances, it can be helpful to define those circumstances before we begin to learn.

This tool serves as a reflective personal assessment to determine where you will benefit most from working differently. If you are honest in filling it out, the assessment will reveal your biggest areas of opportunity. Each section corresponds to a specific chapter to help you prioritize your strategy as you read through the rest of the book. Note: Some statements in the assessment include multiple concepts. Do your best to select your answer based on all the combined elements.

How true are each of the following statements for you? Use this scale to respond to each statement as honestly as possible:

- 1 = Not at all true
- 2 = Mostly not true
- 3 = True half the time
- 4 = Mostly true
- 5 = Completely true

After completing each assessment section, add the numbers you circled to get a total.

1. Foundations: Business Understanding (Chapter 4)	Rating				
I can explain to someone else why my company exists, whom it serves, and what problems it is solving.	1	2	3	4	5
I know the current strategic goals and initiatives.	1	2	3	4	5
I have a solid understanding of how my company functions (e.g. revenue, expenses, organizational structure, and work cadence).	1	2	3	4	5
I have a strong understanding of the company culture, including unwritten rules.	1	2	3	4	5
I know how to find the information necessary to learn more about the business.	1	2	3	4	5
Total					/25

2. Foundations: Internal L&D Playbook (Chapter 5)	Rating				
I can clearly articulate the purpose of my L&D team's existence in the organization.	1	2	3	4	5
Each member of my L&D team has clearly defined responsibilities.	1	2	3	4	5
My L&D team has clearly defined work processes.	1	2	3	4	5
My L&D team measures adherence to standards of work (what good looks like) for each individual team member.	1	2	3	4	5
Each L&D team member understands the team's behavior expectations.	1	2	3	4	5
Total					/25

3. Foundations: External L&D Playbook (Chapter 5)	Rating				
My L&D team has a defined intake process that matches the company culture and is easy for stakeholders to complete.	1	2	3	4	5
My L&D team has a written overview describing our typical projects and what each includes.	1	2	3	4	5
My L&D team has a written overview of the time necessary to complete each type of project.	1	2	3	4	5
My L&D team has a summary of the typical measurable results from each type of project.	1	2	3	4	5
My L&D team clearly defines and articulates the roles and responsibilities for all those involved in a learning project (e.g., L&D team members, SMEs, and stakeholders).	1	2	3	4	5
Total					/25

4. Foundations: Key Stakeholders (Chapter 6)	Rating				
I can easily list every key stakeholder for the L&D function.	1	2	3	4	5
I know why each key stakeholder is important to L&D's success.	1	2	3	4	5
I understand how each stakeholder perceives me in my L&D role (e.g., as an order taker, SBP, or somewhere in between).	1	2	3	4	5
I understand the reason for each stakeholder's perception of me in my L&D role.	1	2	3	4	5
I know exactly what to do to improve each stakeholder's perception of me to that of an SBP.	1	2	3	4	5
Total					/25

5. Daily Practice: Partnership With Stakeholders (Chapter 7)	Rating				
I can effectively navigate within organizational politics.	1	2	3	4	5
My communication with stakeholders is consistent, continuous, and delivered in a way that works best for them.	1	2	3	4	5
I know what's most important to each of my stakeholders.	1	2	3	4	5
I spend more energy on the stakeholders who produce the most positive results.	1	2	3	4	5
I effectively tap into L&D naysayers.	1	2	3	4	5
Total					/25

6. Daily Practice: L&D Strategy (Chapter 8)	Rating				
My L&D team has a clearly defined strategy that is aligned with the organization's most important goals and initiatives.	1	2	3	4	5
My L&D team's strategy is realistic.	1	2	3	4	5
I know how to negotiate with business leaders to gain clarity in strategic priorities and commitment to necessary resources for the L&D strategy.	1	2	3	4	5
The L&D strategy is clearly and regularly communicated to all stakeholders.	1	2	3	4	5
My L&D team is following a clear plan to operationalize our strategy.	1	2	3	4	5
Total					/25

7. Daily Practice: Strategic Yes, Strategic No (Chapter 9)	Rating				
Each time my L&D team says yes to working on a project, it is strategic and intentional.	1	2	3	4	5
My L&D team says no to working on projects strategically and intentionally.	1	2	3	4	5
I know how to do the analysis necessary to determine whether a learning or training solution will solve a stakeholder's problem.	1	2	3	4	5
I know what to do if I discover that a learning or training solution will not solve a stakeholder's problem.	1	2	3	4	5
My L&D team ensures stakeholder commitment and partnership before pursuing a learning or training solution.	1	2	3	4	5
Total					/25

8. Daily Practice: Measurement (Chapter 10)	Rating				
My L&D team has a defined plan for how to measure the results of our work and it includes all three types of measures (efficiency, effectiveness, and outcomes).	1	2	3	4	5
Before designing any type of learning solution, I work to define how it will be measured.	1	2	3	4	5
I know what to do if the business doesn't have any existing performance measures related to the learning solution.	1	2	3	4	5
My L&D team has a repeatable system in place to gather, analyze, and communicate the results of our measurement.	1	2	3	4	5
We communicate the results of measurement in a way that makes sense for each stakeholder group.	1	2	3	4	5
Total					/25

9. Daily Practice: Team Development (Chapter 11)	Rating				
Everyone on my L&D team knows how to work as an SBP.	1	2	3	4	5
As an L&D leader, I continuously share a vision for L&D to work as effective SBPs.	1	2	3	4	5
The name of my team and the titles of team members reflect the vision to work as SBPs.	1	2	3	4	5
Everyone on my L&D team has a foundational understanding of L&D.	1	2	3	4	5
Everyone on my L&D team is actively working to uplevel their skills as an SBP.	1	2	3	4	5
Total					/25

Assessment Section Totals

As you look at the totals for each section, use this explanation as a guide for where to focus while reading the remainder of this book:

- **If you scored 16–25 points:** You're doing well in this area! Feel free to read the corresponding chapter to gain new ideas or affirmation.
- **If you scored 5–15 points:** Spend some focused time on the chapter related to this area, making sure to work through all activities and reflection questions.

If you are struggling or overwhelmed, be sure to read chapter 12, "Find the Opportunity in Every Order." Becoming a strategic business partner won't happen overnight, but there are small things you can do every time you need to take an order for a learning solution that will slowly move the needle.

PART 2
Foundations

CHAPTER 4
Understand the Business First

As a strategic business partner, *business* is literally your middle name. Understanding the business goals and challenges driving your organization is essential to becoming a successful partner. I would go as far as to say it is absolutely critical. The business side of your organization is the foundation for everything that you and others do each and every day. It is the framework within which you develop your programs and the reason your L&D team exists.

Traditionally, developing a deep understanding of the businesses in which we work has been a stretch for many learning leaders. Most of us don't begin our L&D careers with a passion for the intricate details of business. We love learning and people development, not calculating profits and losses. We're looking for light bulbs that signify an aha moment, not dollar signs. While we usually amass some knowledge about how the business side of our organization works along the way, often that knowledge isn't deep. We're busy with our daily to-do lists and tell ourselves we'll pick up what we need to know informally if and when we need to know it. Or maybe we simply aren't that interested.

Whenever we pass up the chance to learn more about the business, we hold ourselves back from becoming SBPs. How can we truly partner with other leaders in our organizations on a strategic level without understanding the inner workings of the business? How can we help solve talent challenges if we don't understand why they emerged? We know how people learn and develop, and this knowledge carries enormous value. But we can never bring our best ideas to the table if we don't understand the full context in which learning and development occur. Why would other leaders trust us as strategic partners if we don't understand the long- and short-term strategies the organization is pursuing?

If we remain ignorant of large parts of the business, we are setting L&D up to become a nice-to-have instead of a must-have function.

In this chapter—in a variation of big-picture, small-step thinking—we examine the big picture of the business and then look at some of the finer details.

Six Questions About Business Basics

When it comes to learning the business basics that will provide context and direction for your work in L&D, I suggest focusing on six questions:

1. **Why** was the business founded?
2. **Who** are the customers or audience the business serves?
3. **What** products or services does the business provide?
4. **What** strategic goals and initiatives are priorities for the business?
5. **How** do the day-to-day operations of the business work?
6. **Where** does the company's culture intersect with business success?

I find it helpful to visualize these essential questions in the form of a funnel, starting with the broadest question at the top and moving down to narrower, more detailed questions with each subsequent level (Figure 4-1).

Let's break these questions down one at a time. In some cases, I'll also suggest further resources you can consult to learn more.

1. Why Was the Business Founded?

The first question you'll need to answer is the most elemental: Why does this company exist? Put another way: What need does the company fulfill?

The company's purpose or mission statement grounds every decision and initiative it pursues, as well as how the business functions. Not all companies have a clearly defined vision, purpose, or mission, but most have at least one or two key public statements. Find them and store them in your memory for later. If you need a more direct reminder, post these statements in a location that's visible to you during your workday.

Figure 4-1. The Business Basics Funnel

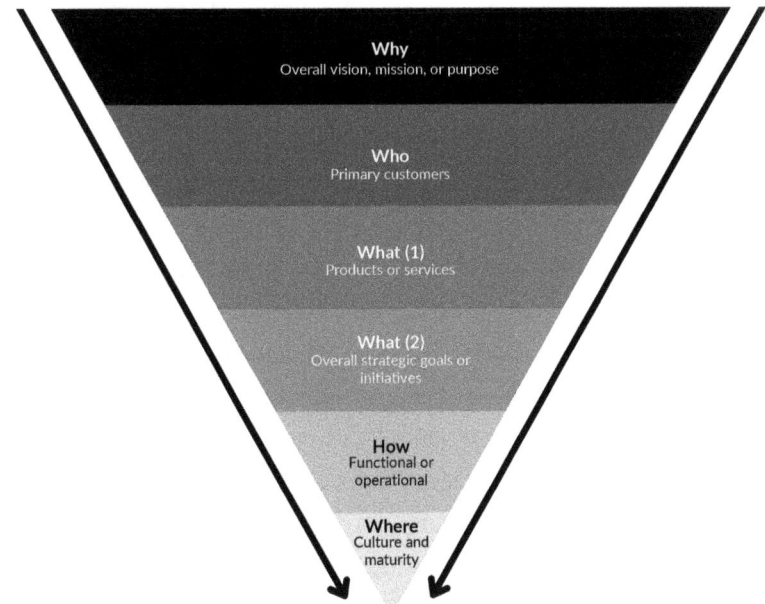

When I worked as a campus tour guide in college, we had to memorize the university's mission statement and share it with parents and students on our tours—and I still remember it today:

> The purpose of Concordia College is to influence the affairs of the world by sending into society thoughtful and informed men and women dedicated to the Christian life.

Years later, I went back to the school to work as the assistant director of student leadership development. The backbone of our program was—you guessed it—to develop leaders to "influence the affairs of the world." Like all good mission statements, Concordia's stood the test of time and helped ground all programs and initiatives across the organization. Your company's mission statement should do the same—grounding the work you and your colleagues do by providing big-picture purpose and direction.

"Why was the company founded?" might be the easiest of the six questions to answer because the vision, mission, or purpose can often be found on an organization's website or as part of the annual report. Chances are you saw your organization's vision and mission during the interview process or onboarding experience or on company correspondence. Search through the website, intranet, and any other information you've received and see what you can find.

2. Who Are the Customers or Audience?

Your organization exists to serve a group of customers or a specific audience. Who are these people? What are they like? Where do they live? What are their pain points or challenges? What makes them unique? How do the products or services your company provides benefit their lives or meet their needs?

When I worked at Discovery Benefits, we had two quite distinct groups of primary customers, and this was often hard to explain and difficult for new employees to wrap their brains around. Our first customer group included HR professionals at companies of all sizes. We helped them administer employee benefits, which, in the United States, can become very complicated, very quickly. The second group of customers included the employees in each of the companies whose benefits we administered. Often, these customer-employees had questions about complex specifications in their benefit plans, and we were available to assist. Our L&D team did our work with both of these customer groups in mind, even if we weren't building education experiences specifically for those customer groups.

One of the best ways to be a strategic partner in your organization is to approach projects by understanding the people who are the most important for the business to serve—and that usually means the customers. While designing learning experiences, repeatedly ask yourself how your work will benefit the business's customers.

Note that you may need to do some legwork to find comprehensive information about your organization's primary customers. In my experience, colleagues in marketing, sales, and other functions that service customers directly tend to know the most about them. Some companies develop *customer personas*, which are detailed descriptions of typical customers and their needs. Other companies may have informal descriptions, but chances are that someone in your organization can tell you a lot if you ask the right questions. Start with these:

- Can you describe our typical, primary customer?
- Is our typical customer a group of people or an individual?

- What is that person or group of people looking for when they work with us?
- When and why do our customers get frustrated?
- When and why are our customers most pleased with our company or our products or services?

3. What Products or Services Does the Business Provide?

Even if you work in leadership development and rarely focus specifically on the tangible products or services your business offers, you need to know how your company makes money, which is directly tied to the products and services it sells. What is your organization offering to its customers or audience?

During my time at Discovery Benefits, we sold both services and products. The services included the administration of plans related to US healthcare benefits in our software system. The products were the plans themselves, including Health Savings Accounts (HSAs), Flexible Spending Accounts (FSAs), Health Reimbursement Arrangements (HRAs), and COBRA Insurance. The first step for any new member of our learning team was to dive in and learn the basics of each product, including:

- What are the components of the product?
- What benefits do they provide to customers?
- How do the products differ from one another?

After defining what products or services your company offers, the next step is to understand each item's *life cycle*. Most companies define a clear process from when a sale is made through the completion of a customer's interactions around that sale. For example, our Discovery Benefits product and service life cycle looked something like this:

1. The sales team sells a product or service.
2. Technical setup:
   » The customer onboarding team ensures proper system setup.
   » The operations team performs customized technical software setup.
3. Ongoing service:
   » The client services team monitors the account, responds to questions and concerns, and upsells additional products.

» The contact center staff answers benefits questions from customer's employees.
» The claims team processes benefit claims according to governmental rules.
4. Customer termination:
» Customer accounts are closed, and information is transferred to a new provider.

This is a simplified life cycle, of course, and there are more complex processes and procedures within each step. When you are first learning about your organization's products, focus on high-level basics, saving details for later when you're working with teams and stakeholders.

In my experience, information about products and services as well as their life cycles is usually found in multiple locations or can be gathered through conversations with multiple people. Start with your company's website or intranet pages and continue asking questions of colleagues who regularly interact with those products and services. This may include sales team members who need to explain the products and services to potential customers and operations leaders who are making sure they are managed well.

4. What Strategic Goals and Initiatives Are Priorities?

An organization's strategic goals and initiatives are the top priorities it will pursue to help continue advancing toward its mission or purpose. These goals and initiatives are expansive, meaning they require work from many—if not all—business units to make progress and ultimately achieve them. Each unit in the business should be aware of the strategic goals and initiatives and use those to inform their smaller goals and initiatives, describing exactly how the smaller ones will contribute to the larger ones.

If, as L&D leaders, we want to fully partner with the business, what is important to them must also be important to us. We need to be in the same boat, rowing in the same direction, heading toward the same destination. Our strategic goals, aligned with those of the business, are where we should spend the majority of our time and resources.

Many companies determine their overall goals and initiatives via a strategic planning process with top leadership. Some conduct this process every year, while others do it every few years. Often, a timeline for achieving key strategic goals spans three to five years, but this isn't always the case.

In an ideal world, every L&D leader would have access to clearly defined strategic goals and initiatives in their organizations. If that is the case for you, congratulations! You can use this information to determine your team's strategy.

However, many of us must embark on a brave quest into the hidden corners of the business to find what we need. In some cases, companies create and share strategies at town halls or all-hands meetings. In others, the company intranet and shared documents provide a great deal of information. You may need to embark on a fact-finding mission, asking other leaders in the company what they know and how they determined their department's goals and priorities for the year. I have even come across a few companies that haven't defined any initiatives or goals beyond increasing revenue or "being the best in our industry." In these cases, you will have to keep asking questions and consulting with your L&D team for creative solutions to learn more—and then address the answers you discover.

5. How Do Day-to-Day Operations Work?

Now, it's time to immerse ourselves in more details. An SBP knows how the business operates so they can work in ways that are aligned with—not running counter to—business goals. When L&D leaders understand how the business functions, they can build trust and credibility as partners.

I break down the basics of business operations into seven areas represented by the acronym I-RECCOM, which I remember by thinking, "I RECCOMend that you find out these details about how your company works." Unfortunately, the spelling is a little off, but I hope it jogs your brain as it does mine, and that you can recall the words industry, revenue, expenses, cadence, challenges, organization, and metrics.

Industry

Every industry includes common practices, acronyms, certifications, and other things that people "in the know" take for granted. Just think about the L&D

industry! Using ADDIE or SAM, calling our audience *learners*, referring to adult learning as *andragogy*, calling out *Kirkpatrick* or *Phillips* as shorthand for measurement guidelines—I could go on and on. If you've been an L&D professional for a while, you have probably mastered the industry lingo, but what about the language of your company's industry?

Whether your organization is involved in hospitality, automaking, telecommunications, or any other industry, that is the world in which your customers and many of your colleagues spend their days. It's where their expertise lies. You don't have to reach a high level of expertise in the industry to work in L&D, but you should have a basic understanding of it so you are comfortable speaking the same language and designing customized solutions with that specialized knowledge.

I learned early on that the same term often has different meanings in different industries. When I was serving on the board of my local ATD chapter, our bylaws dictated that we have a neutral party review our finances every year. We were a small chapter with minimal expenses and revenues. Double-checking our spending to ensure there was no fishy activity should have been easy, so I wasn't concerned when other members of the board asked me to find someone who could perform an audit for our chapter.

I started reaching out to accountants I knew, asking if they could do an audit. They all reacted as if this would be a major project, not a quick review of simple bookkeeping for a small nonprofit. They all said they had no time to perform the audit.

Surprised by negative reactions multiple times, I finally asked one of the accountants in desperation, "What does it mean to you to perform an audit?" She explained that in the financial services industry, an audit is an in-depth process that follows specific, rigid guidelines. The person performing the audit also needs special training. I took a step back and carefully explained to her what we needed, asking if, in her professional opinion, this constituted an audit. "No," she told me. "What you want sounds more like a *financial review*."

Once we switched our terminology, it was much easier to find someone to help us. I learned from that experience that finding a common vocabulary with colleagues and stakeholders is essential—and not having one can sabotage your goals.

Study your company's industry and learn about common terms, acronyms, and certifications. Visit the industry's association websites (almost every industry has one) and scan for terms you don't recognize. You might even want to sit in on a webinar or two! Make note of your questions and, with an attitude of curiosity, ask business leaders in your company for more information. Keep track of your findings in a way that works for you.

Speaking the same language as others in your company will help you form connections, strengthen relationships, and build credibility. To start, ask these questions:

- What industry is your company in?
- Is there a glossary of terms used in the industry? Do you have access to it?
- Which key industry terms should you include in the learning solutions you create?

Revenue

The importance of revenue isn't difficult to understand. Businesses need to be profitable to stay up and running. The money coming in keeps people employed, the lights on, and the business in business. You don't need to know as much as the CFO about your organization's revenue. You'll just need answers to a couple of questions:

- What are your company's major sources of revenue?
- Are there additional, smaller streams of revenue? What are they?

Public companies must make their earnings public, so you can find basic data in places like annual reports, press releases, and the Securities and Exchange Commission (SEC) website. But, you can also just ask. Remember, you don't need to see the detailed balance sheets. Your goal is simply to gain a high-level understanding. The questions discussed here shouldn't come off as threatening to key leaders in your company. They should indicate your interest in serving as a partner.

All companies—unless they are grossly mismanaged—pay close attention to anything that contributes positively to their bottom line. You should pay attention too.

Expenses

Expenses are on the opposite side of the balance sheet from revenue and are equally important to understand. All business owners know that they need to spend money to make money, but the aim is to spend it wisely, in a way that generates profits. Where does your company spend to operate well?

Money equals impact. As an SBP, you should pay attention to how the L&D team positively affects revenue or reduces expenses. Once you identify your company's major sources of revenue and expenses you should be able to identify how your L&D programs and projects affect them. For example, in many companies, the biggest expense is employee salaries. If an L&D program reduces the time to onboard new employees, you have decreased a nonproductive employee expense.

Generally, information about expenses can be found in balance sheets or other financial documents. You will likely need to ask business leaders for this information. If they won't share the complete report, don't despair! Again, ask for a high-level view. Here are some questions you can ask:

- What are the biggest expenses in the company?
- Are there any expenses the company is actively trying to reduce?

Cadence

The word *cadence* refers to the cycle of the work done in a business. Many companies experience peaks and valleys—times when employees' workloads are heavy and times when the pace slows down a bit. In some companies, the cadence is tied directly to the life cycle of products or services delivered, and in others, cadence depends on an external calendar or key events.

At Discovery Benefits, our work was tied to benefits open enrollment periods. In the United States, employers and health insurance companies designate certain times of the year for employees to enroll in or change health benefit elections. Most open enrollment periods occur in the second half of Q4, and benefit plans start in January, at the beginning of the calendar year. For Discovery Benefits, the curtain went up on our work during open enrollment. We needed to ensure sales and plan setups were completed before that date. We always expected a higher volume of questions from customers during open enrollment, which meant the intensity of work from October through January was extreme and relentless. Overtime was common, and our L&D team knew that planning learning events in this period was impossible because almost no one would participate. If we required participation, the attendees would be distracted. Our planning sessions and regular meetings with business units also had to pause at this time to allow for more urgent work to occur, and we often stepped in to help other units with work overflow. Our knowledge of the work cadence allowed us to be good business partners.

Sometimes, you will find shared documents that describe your organization's cadence, but more often this knowledge isn't written down. That means, your best bet to find the cadence is to ask someone who has been around for years.

You should also be alert to the fact that different teams may have different cadences. In my Discovery Benefits example, the sales and setup teams needed to be ready before open enrollment, but the contact center was busier after open enrollment was complete, when participants started to use the benefits they had selected. Start with finding answers to these questions:

- When are the employees in your organization the busiest?
- When might their work progress at a slower pace?
- Are workload volumes cyclical? If yes, what determines the cycle?

Challenges

Every company faces challenges. Some are persistent and internal; others are the result of external factors like economic cycles, world events, or cultural trends. Some challenges are small and easily tackled and resolved, while others require a consistent, widespread effort to address.

L&D can and should work as a strategic partner to solve business challenges, but to do that, L&D leaders need to understand those challenges. Pervasive challenges should inform our L&D strategies so we can work proactively, rather than reactively, helping to develop solutions before we're asked.

There are some significant challenges companies I've worked with have faced over the years. Some, such as rapid growth and adding new products, are positive situations in the long run but present as challenges because they

require new ways of thinking, new processes, and creative problem solving. Your organization has probably faced some of these challenges too:
- Mergers and acquisitions
- Adding and integrating new product lines
- Increasing customer demands and complaints
- Rapid growth, requiring continuous hiring and onboarding
- Clunky and outdated technology or implementation of new technologies
- Inefficient processes
- Leadership turnover and lack of depth in the leadership pipeline
- Data breaches
- Lockdowns as a result of the COVID-19 pandemic

Can you identify the current most pressing challenges your company faces? Other than directly asking, one of the best ways to find out is to pay attention when sitting in on meetings and ask yourself these questions:
- What are the themes that leaders are consistently talking about or sharing?
- What situations seem to be adding stress or occupying a lot of conversational space right now?

Organization

When I refer to business *organization*, I'm talking about how your company is structured. Most companies are organized into multiple business units or functions that define who does what and where they sit within the company hierarchy. We've all likely seen this hierarchy visualized through a multilevel organizational (org) chart.

An org chart provides a high-level overview of business units like marketing, sales, service, finance, and human resources, but to find out what each unit really does, you'll need to ask the people who do the work. I recommend embarking on a learning tour to conduct short interviews with key individuals (usually midlevel leaders) in each business unit to ask about their teams' day-to-day work, their scope of responsibility, and other information. You can also sneak in other questions related to day-to-day knowledge like cadence, challenges, expenses, and how that team contributes to revenue. If I'm new to a role, these interviews are the first things on my agenda, but even if you've been in your position for a long time, a learning tour is worthwhile to reacquaint yourself with the lay of the land.

You can usually find org charts on your company intranet, in shared documents, or by simply asking colleagues. Keep the most up-to-date org chart nearby to determine the right person to go to when you have questions.

Metrics

Most companies use a variety of metrics to measure the performance of individuals, teams, and the company overall. This quantitative data is also used to determine areas of need, create goals and initiatives, and inform decisions about investing resources.

Find out what metrics are most important to the business as a whole and to individual units. Understanding individual business unit metrics is especially important if you regularly work with a specific unit because they can give you a heads-up on areas of concern that L&D might be called in to help fix. If you understand the metrics involved in any request, you can ask more well-informed questions and build an appropriate L&D strategy.

You may also want to use some of the data in the measurement strategy for L&D initiatives. Ask yourself a simple question: "If the numbers that the business cares about start to dip, how can L&D partner to help raise them?"

We will discuss measurement strategy more in chapter 10, but your best starting point is a solid overview of the metrics that are important to the business as a whole. Unfortunately, getting access to metrics can be one of L&D's biggest struggles. In smaller, less mature organizations, the metrics may not exist or may not be organized or shared in a readable format. Do your best to find key metrics by asking questions, listening in on meetings, and scouring the company intranet, but if you don't make progress, don't worry. Just keep asking!

If you're able to gather information about all the items included in the I-RECCOM list, you will have gone a long way toward a basic understanding of how and when work gets done in your organization, major challenges, and what's most important to the business's health based on data.

6. Where Does the Company's Culture Intersect With Business Success?

The last aspect of business basics, company culture, is more art than science. You'll find very few artifacts, neatly typed documents, intranet pages, or well-articulated statements from stakeholders to guide you because a company's culture is about the unwritten practices that determine the way work is done. Most of these practices develop over time, based on human interactions, quality processes, and continuous improvement.

Culture refers to shared values and accepted behavioral norms. Most people begin to understand a company's culture after spending considerable time in it and observing their colleagues. As an L&D professional, if you understand your company's culture, you will be better able to adapt to the organization's politics and create solutions that align with unwritten rules. Consider four categories of company culture as you try to better understand its influence on the business: unwritten rules, values, acronyms, and maturity.

Unwritten Rules

Unwritten rules are the least clearly defined area of company culture but perhaps the most important. These rules of engagement determine how we show up each day ready to work and what behaviors are acceptable or unacceptable in the workplace.

Unwritten rules can include the level of formality in our dress and communication, how we resolve conflicts, how often we communicate, and how we conduct meetings, to name a few. For example, does your company expect that all correspondence will start with "Dear" or a casual "Hi"? Or is it acceptable to jump into the content with no greeting at all? Is small talk included in business emails? When addressing a conflict between employees, do managers call it out immediately or do they wait for a quiet meeting behind closed doors? Does everyone respond to every email message with "Thank you," or do most people just leave it open ended? Is there an acceptable window of time in which to chime in?

My L&D team was caught off guard by unwritten meeting rules when another company acquired Discovery Benefits. Soon after the acquisition was finalized, everyone from Discovery Benefits received an onslaught of meeting requests. Our calendars were flooded, and we were confused by the topics. We accepted them all but were only more confused when we showed up. We had no idea how most of them related to our roles—or even what some of the topics were.

Eventually, through casual discussions and questions, we realized that the unwritten rules of calendar invites had changed. At Discovery Benefits, we were only invited to meetings if our attendance was needed. Thus, if we were invited to a meeting, everyone expected that we would accept. In contrast, our acquiring company invited not just those who truly needed to attend, but anyone who might benefit. Each invitee was then expected to decide on their own whether to attend or not. This is a great representation of how unwritten rules can lead to confusion.

If you want to navigate the politics of your organization successfully as an SBP, pay attention to, and do your best to follow, the unwritten behavior rules. Of course, because these rules are unwritten, they can be more difficult to determine. Watch and learn how others successfully navigate their daily work and communication. As you observe, opt for curiosity instead of frustration about what works and what doesn't. Don't be afraid to ask questions. At Discovery Benefits, we only discovered these new-to-us unwritten rules by reaching out and directly asking about the purpose of the calendar invitations and the expectations for attendance.

Values

Company values can be easy to find because they are often embedded within or written alongside the mission or vision statements. Values are formal declarations that represent the foundational principles of the company and guide the spirit in which the work is done.

If stakeholders and employees agree certain company values are important, L&D programs should reiterate and reinforce them regularly. I have worked in companies where the core values provide the foundational components of the leadership development program, the onboarding program, and the systems for rewards and recognition.

Acronyms

Acronyms become key aspects of company culture when they are common internal vernacular that someone from outside the company wouldn't necessarily understand. Other acronyms like HR, P&L (profit and loss), and KPIs (key performance indicators), are commonly understood across a variety of industries. Acronyms used throughout a particular industry are not necessarily part of a company culture.

Discovery Benefits had what often seemed like an endless list of acronyms, including *PS (participant services*; the area that serviced employees of other companies) and *CS (client services*; the area that serviced our HR administrator clients). From the point of view of an outsider or a new employee, those acronyms could have represented many different things, so getting to know our company culture meant memorizing these specific meanings.

Maturity

Companies operate at various levels of maturity, which change over time. A company's maturity is reflected in its culture, the quality of the operational and strategic processes, and the degree to which it focuses on continuous improvement. Several models, such as the popular Business Process Maturity Model (BPMM), the Process and Enterprise Maturity Model (PEMM), and the Capability Maturity Model (CMM) outline business maturity levels and could be helpful if you like to study theories to create clarity. For L&D, company maturity is important because it will dictate the readiness of the company to take on certain learning initiatives.

A lot of people in the L&D community think creatively and have big dreams of creating change and having a significant influence in the organizations they work for. But if a company isn't mature enough to handle those changes, most ambitious initiatives will fail.

To understand whether this is the case, start by observing accepted quality and decision-making processes, as well as colleagues' existing knowledge of L&D topics. If you can see that it would be a stretch for most people in the organization to wrap their heads around a certain topic, or even understand the reason behind a novel approach, determine to what degree this is the case. Much like the *zone of proximal development*—in which we gradually expand the ability of learners to perform tasks on their own—we need to gradually expand the understanding of those in the organization beyond their current level of maturity to accomplish some of our goals.

For example, Colin, the learning and organization development manager for a midsize manufacturing company, had to go through this when he implemented a new performance development process in his organization. The maturity around the performance development process at his company was low, meaning most employees and leaders didn't understand what a performance development process was or how to do it well. So, instead of asking everyone in the company to develop SMART goals, log them into the human resource information system (HRIS), and monitor them regularly throughout the year, Colin's team started by asking everyone to create one goal. They didn't care about the quality; they only cared that each person had a goal. If someone talked about their goal with their manager throughout the year, that was icing on the cake. Colin called this "level 1 performance development."

The ultimate vision was for everyone to create SMART goals and use those as key indicators of performance development in a defined and effective process, but Colin's team accepted that the organization's maturity level wouldn't allow them to start there. Throughout the year, the team collected strong and weak examples they could use the next year to coach leaders on creating more effective goals and bring the company up to the next level of maturity.

My advice to any L&D leader is to match your initiatives to the company's current maturity level, as Colin did. Don't ask people to jump to a level they aren't ready for.

On a final note, I have yet to meet an L&D professional who received a complete overview of all these business basics upon entering a leadership role. Don't put too much pressure on yourself to know them right away. Instead, work to collect information in bits over time, putting together the business puzzle to eventually see a complete picture.

That said, I'm guessing you already know more than you think. You may have even skipped or skimmed some sections in this chapter for that reason. If you figure out where your biggest gaps are when it comes to business basics, you can plan to go forward from there. Use Tool 4-1 at the end of this chapter to assess your knowledge of each business area. Pat yourself on the back for the ones you are already familiar with and set a goal to learn more about the others. In the next section, I suggest a few more practical approaches to finding the information you lack. Read on to learn more.

Seven Ways to Learn More About Business Basics

Based on my own experience and what I've learned from the L&D leaders I've interviewed, there are seven highly effective ways to find information about business basics: scouring digital sources, asking someone directly, inserting yourself into meetings, listening strategically, finding a mentor, going to the *gemba*, and reflecting on and learning from every project. You'll find you can enhance each method with a healthy dose of curiosity and by adopting the attitude of a keen detective who's searching for clues.

1. Scour Digital Sources

Chances are, you have access to more information than you think. Scour your company's digital sources, including the official website, intranet, knowledge base, and shared files. Don't be afraid to click on sources you haven't seen before to learn more.

2. Ask Directly

Want to know more about the business of your organization, including reports and metrics? It seems too obvious to say, but—just ask! Sometimes, all it takes is directly asking to be copied on quarterly reports and strategic planning documents, but you might need to ask more than once. You should also be prepared to explain why you're interested; you could say something like, "I want to learn as much as I can about our business so I can be a partner who helps to proactively solve talent challenges."

Unless there is a good reason or a clear cultural norm for not sharing this information, most people will find it difficult to deny a colleague who is trying to learn more to improve the business.

3. Insert Yourself Into Meetings

One of the key differences between the average order taker and SBP is that SBPs don't wait for invitations. They insert themselves into meetings and other situations in which they believe they have something to learn or contribute.

Ask for an invitation or virtual meeting link using the same justification I suggested for learning more about reports and metrics. Emphasize the truth—that you simply want to learn more about how the business works. You can even offer to take notes for the group if it gets you in the door.

4. Listen Strategically

Strategic listening goes beyond simply listening to learn or understand. When listening strategically, you are actively seeking information that will help you put together the big picture of the business puzzle. Whether you are in a large company meeting or a one-on-one conversation with a stakeholder, look out for clues about how the business operates. Listen for definitions of new-to-you acronyms, insights into the organization's biggest challenges, allusions to unwritten rules, and nods to the ups and downs of revenues and expenses—all information that can help you fill in gaps in your knowledge.

> **Talk Less, Listen More**
>
> Mechelle, the director of L&D at a small community bank, told me that she aims to listen more than she talks in every meeting she attends. "My lips should be closing, and my pen should be moving," she explained. "While other people get coffee, I'm writing down acronyms I don't understand."
>
> As she puts together the pieces of her big picture puzzle, Mechelle also notes anything she didn't understand so she can ask about it later. In other words, she listens strategically.

5. Find a Mentor (or Two!)

I have benefited enormously from relationships with business mentors throughout my career, and I heard praise for mentors from the learning leaders I interviewed. A business mentor is someone outside your HR and

L&D departments who meets with you regularly to help you gain insight into how the organization operates as well as top business challenges, pressures, and goals. A mentor can also amp up your business acumen and answer your questions about how to navigate the company's political landscape. One thing my research revealed quite clearly was that leaders who worked as SBPs consistently leveraged mentoring to learn more about the business.

> **Finding a Business Mentor**
>
> Finding mentors doesn't need to be difficult. Often, L&D leaders form mentoring relationships with key stakeholders who understand the potential of a well-run L&D function. You might start meeting with a stakeholder for another reason and later take advantage of your good relationship to ask business-related questions. In other instances, you might develop a mentoring relationship after working on a collaborative project.
>
> When looking for a business mentor, you can use a high-level focus to gain general business knowledge or get more granular and find someone who fills a specific gap in your knowledge or skills. For example, you might need help reading company balance sheets or unraveling the details of international trade.
>
> You need not identify a mentor through a formal program, although that can be a good option if its available at your company. Sometimes, you'll be able to work with a supervisor to identify a good fit, especially when it comes to filling a specific gap in knowledge.
>
> In your initial outreach, let the person know you are trying to learn more about the company. If appropriate, ask if you could meet regularly (monthly, bi-monthly, or quarterly, for example) and say that you'll bring specific questions. A mentoring relationship can persist over a long time or can serve a specific purpose that is completed in a couple meetings.

6. Go to the Gemba

Gemba (also spelled *genba*) is a Japanese term that means the "actual place" or "the real place." In business, "go to the gemba" or "do a gemba walk" usually means visiting locations where value-creating work is done, such as factory floors, restaurant kitchens, sales calls, or office desks. In L&D, we often want to go to the gemba to observe work being done. Nothing is a substitute for seeing employees completing work tasks in real time, either in person or remotely. We can observe real-life challenges, unwritten processes, methods used only by top performers, and more.

Regularly going to the gemba will help you to see work firsthand and give you an enhanced understanding of daily life around the business. One of my colleagues made it a practice to go to the gemba to observe once a month for just half a day. I have taken a few hours to observe sales presentations or listen in on some phone calls in a contact center, and I learned more about the business in those few hours than I did in most of my conversations with employees and stakeholders. Where's your gemba?

7. Reflect On and Learn From Every Project

Every project you do is an opportunity to learn more about essential business basics. I find it helpful to set aside dedicated time during and after every L&D project to reflect on the business basics it illuminated. During this time, ask yourself:

- Did you learn more about business cadence or challenges?
- Do you have a better understanding of performance metrics as a result of something that happened during your most recent project?
- Were some of the organization's unwritten rules revealed?

Reflection is one of our most powerful learning tools. It helps us make sense of the information coming our way and organize it into meaningful buckets. It can help you as you work on assembling the puzzle pieces of the business into a clearer picture.

You can't learn everything you need to know about your business in a day or a week. Depending on your access to various stakeholders, business functions, and reports, your business education may take many months. You will continue to learn little pieces of information that gradually fill in gaps throughout your time at a company, but the best place to start is by identifying areas in which you need to deepen your understanding and gather information in each category we've just discussed.

Watch and listen to those around you! As you gain more experience, your knowledge of the business will improve, but that isn't the only foundational element to becoming an SBP. While learning business basics, you also need to clarify how you run your L&D business—and this is what we will cover in the next chapter.

Summary

A comprehensive understanding of the business you work for is critical to what you will do as an SBP. You can understand the business by answering six questions:

1. **Why** was the business founded? In other words, what is its overall vision, mission, and purpose?
2. **Who** are the primary customers or audience?
3. **What** products or services does the business provide, and what is their life cycle?
4. **What** strategic goals or initiatives does the business prioritize?
5. **How** do day-to-day operations work?
6. **Where** does the company's culture intersect with business success?

When examining how business operations work, you should dig deeply into issues represented by the acronym I-RECCOM: industry, revenue, expenses, cadence, challenges, organization, and metrics. Most L&D leaders have to search diligently for this information.

We are all in a perpetual search for more relevant, useful business information. Some helpful strategies for intelligence gathering include scouring a variety of digital sources, making direct asks, inserting yourself into meetings and conversations, listening strategically, finding a business mentor, "going to the gemba," and reflecting on and learning from every project.

Tool 4-1. Grade Yourself on Business Basics

After reading this chapter, take a moment to put your thoughts on paper. Use the following scale to grade your knowledge of each business basic:

A = I have a full understanding.
B = My knowledge is very good, although not yet complete.
C = I have a moderate amount of knowledge.
D = I know only a little.
F = I have no knowledge of this.

Business Basics	Grade				
Overall vision, mission, or purpose	A	B	C	D	F
Primary customers	A	B	C	D	F
Products and services offered	A	B	C	D	F
Product, service, or customer life cycle	A	B	C	D	F
Strategic goals and initiatives	A	B	C	D	F
Industry basics	A	B	C	D	F
Revenue sources	A	B	C	D	F
Largest expenses	A	B	C	D	F
Work cadence	A	B	C	D	F
Biggest current challenges	A	B	C	D	F
Reporting structure (org chart)	A	B	C	D	F
What each business unit does	A	B	C	D	F
Most important metrics	A	B	C	D	F
Unwritten rules	A	B	C	D	F
Values	A	B	C	D	F
Company-specific acronyms	A	B	C	D	F
Process maturity (what is acceptable and what would "stretch")	A	B	C	D	F

How did you grade your knowledge of each business basic? Focus on learning more about the ones you don't know as much about.

CHAPTER 5
Build Your Internal and External L&D Playbooks

The recommendation to "get your own house in order" before focusing on the problems of others is advice that, all too often, L&D leaders don't follow. We build our careers solving other people's problems but tend to ignore those right under our noses. We fail to define our L&D team's purpose, roles, and responsibilities; may have unclear or poorly documented processes and expectations; don't adequately track team member workload, capacity, and performance; and may not know our key partners in the organization. If we don't excel in these foundational categories, we can't expect our teams to work confidently and effectively—and the result will be poor working relationships with other business functions.

When it's time to do difficult things as an SBP, like pushing back on a stakeholder request to align projects with strategic initiatives, we won't succeed if we haven't laid a strong foundation with our team. An effective, well-supported team also decreases conflict and increases job satisfaction and retention. Who doesn't want that?

Getting your L&D house in order by building strong internal and external L&D playbooks is essential for your work as an SBP. Your internal playbook guides your L&D team operations, and your external playbook defines how your team works with the rest of the organization. These playbooks can take several forms—a series of key documents, an intranet site, a group of checklists, or a full-scale digital book. The format will vary depending on what works best for your team and your stakeholders.

In this chapter, we will first cover how to develop your internal playbook using a six-step pyramid, and then we will discuss how to assemble the four parts of your external L&D playbook.

Develop Your Internal L&D Playbook in Six Steps

Your internal L&D playbook is your team's foundational document, and the process of building it step-by-step will help you work confidently and effectively with every other part of the business. This needs to be a priority for any L&D leader. I use the internal L&D playbook pyramid to guide the building process (Figure 5-1).

Figure 5-1. The Internal L&D Playbook Pyramid

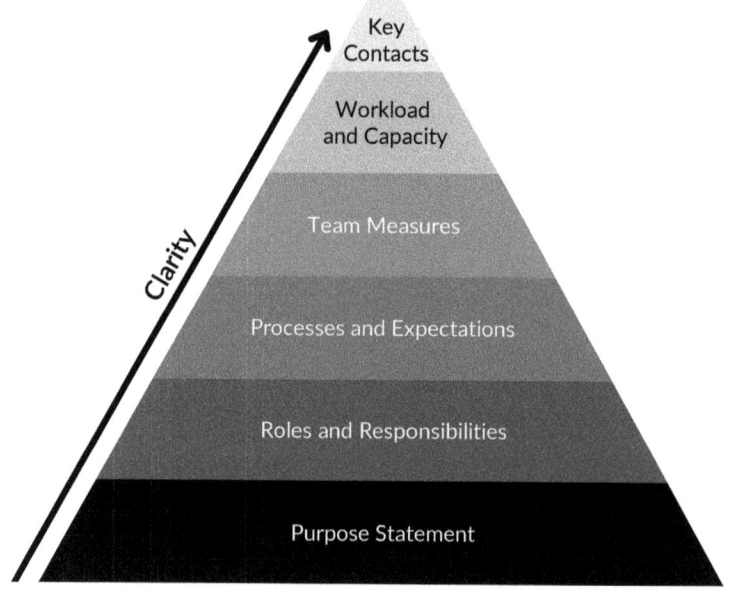

The internal L&D playbook pyramid has six different levels or steps. As with any pyramid, it's best to start at the bottom, with the most foundational elements, and work your way up. From bottom to top, the steps are:

1. Create a clear purpose statement.
2. Clarify roles and responsibilities.
3. Define internal work processes, standards, and behavioral expectations.
4. Determine performance measures and track accountability and improvement.
5. Track team members' workload and capacity.
6. Define key contacts in the business.

Once you have taken all the steps up the pyramid, you will have everything you need for an effective internal L&D playbook. Then, you can format it as the type of document you prefer and make it available for your team to reference as needed.

Although it would be great to begin building your internal playbook while forming your team, this is impractical or impossible for most L&D teams. You don't need to be a brand-new L&D leader with a brand-new team to start this process, and you don't need to pause all your operations to create a playbook.

Most L&D leaders will develop an internal playbook a little at a time while continuing their daily work and current projects. Some elements will take longer and involve more intensive work than others. On the other hand, many leaders will have worked on some of the components of the pyramid already and will simply need to document them.

In the pages that follow, I suggest questions and activities to help you carefully and deliberately work through all six steps of the pyramid. You might decide to work on multiple steps simultaneously or in a different order. Use this chapter as a guide and adapt the steps to your team's circumstances.

1. Create a Clear Purpose Statement

When you can clearly define and articulate the purpose behind your L&D team's work so it aligns with the larger organization's purpose, your team will have a clear focus that highlights their impact and helps them understand their role in the bigger picture. When deciding whether to take on certain projects, it can be helpful to ask, "Does this align with our team's purpose in the organization?" If the answer is no, that project might not be worth the time and effort.

A clear purpose grounds and informs all the work you and your team do. To define your team's purpose answer two questions:

1. Why does your L&D team exist?
2. Who is your primary audience?

Why Does Your Team Exist?

You should be able to explain the reasons your business keeps funding your team, projects, and work. In his 2012 book, *The Advantage: Why Organizational Health Trumps Everything Else in Business*, Patrick Lencioni suggests this question can be used by all organizations seeking clarity of purpose.

Yes, it's a big question, but it isn't meant to be philosophical or inaccessible. It's highly practical. Businesses don't maintain and fund departments, teams, or roles for kicks. Your L&D team is a vital part of your organization, which expects you to do something and add value that moves the business forward. What is that value?

Spend some time brainstorming your answers, ideally with team members. After brainstorming, you should be able to narrow your answers down to what you believe is the highest priority and best answer.

Who Is Your Primary Audience?

The answer to this question is a little more cut-and-dried than the first. Our work is not designed to serve ourselves. In L&D, we serve an audience, or multiple audiences, in our organization. Who are they?

Some L&D teams are dedicated to an entire company, but others have a more limited or specialized role. Your team may focus only on onboarding while another serves just the needs of leaders or a specific area of the company, such as operations or the contact center. Defining your audience as clearly as possible will lead to the most useful purpose statement.

After determining your answers to both of these questions, you are ready to write a purpose statement that clearly articulates why your team exists and the audience you serve. The sample statements in the sidebar should help to inspire you.

Sample L&D Team Purpose Statements

To help you get started, here are a few of my favorite L&D purpose statements. Note that each includes answers to both key questions.

> The learning experience team exists to help team members throughout our company get better at their jobs. We help people improve their individual performance so they can simplify the complexity of health insurance for our customers.
>
> The leadership development team exists to improve leadership skills and capacity throughout the organization, from individual (self) leadership to those leading teams for the first time to experienced leaders and executives who desire to make a bigger impact.
>
> The new-employee onboarding team exists to provide each new employee with a positive and practical experience from the moment they accept a position through when they are in full production. This includes viewing the company in a positive light, experiencing a positive corporate culture, and learning the basics of success in their role.

YOUR TURN

Create Your Own L&D Team Purpose Statement

Brainstorm answers to the following questions with key team members, or your entire team:
- Why does your team exist? What is the reason the business keeps funding your projects and members?
- Who is your primary audience?

Write down your purpose statement, share it with others on your L&D team, and ask for feedback. When you have finalized your statement, save it in a place that your team members reference often.

Here are a few other ways to help your team members keep the statement top of mind:
- Add the statement to the top of your team intranet page.
- Include the statement on all team meeting agendas and project templates.
- Put the statement in your email signature.
- Post the statement in a visible location.

2. Clarify Roles and Responsibilities

Each of your team members' roles and responsibilities need to be clearly and concisely defined. Ask yourself whether you would be able to give an outsider a snapshot description of each person's work. Could each team member describe their role and those of their colleagues? Do they know where their role ends and someone else's begins?

Not a Job Description

An internal playbook's roles and responsibilities section is not a collection of job descriptions. You probably have job descriptions for each team member that include a list of responsibilities. However, I rarely find these helpful after hiring. Job descriptions often become outdated due to organizational changes, so they are only accurate on the day someone begins a job—not afterward. Even if the job itself doesn't change, companies often fail to include enough information about the role, glossing over what really happens day-to-day. This can create problems because leaders find it difficult to hold team members accountable for responsibilities that are not fully described or explained in a job description.

After a company reorganization at Discovery Benefits, I inherited a new team of trainers who were responsible for training operations specialists. They were called *trainers* but were actually SMEs who had previously held the title of *operations specialists*. The company frequently tapped these folks to train new team members one-to-one, although they lacked formal experience and expertise in L&D. Their job descriptions said they were responsible only for training new employees and updating training materials. Problems arose immediately after the reorganization put them on my L&D team.

Do you remember an awful group project in school? One where you felt like you were doing all the work and ended up resenting your other team members? That happened. Not only were the new trainers lacking essential L&D skills, but one person on the team was underperforming. We had no way to hold the underperforming trainer accountable or to create a performance improvement plan because, technically, he wasn't solely responsible for any one part of our work. We were all using all the materials, making it almost impossible to tell who had contributed updates and who hadn't. Morale began tanking fast.

True collaboration, one of the approaches to work that distinguishes SBPs, was also absent from our team in this transition period. For collaboration to be truly effective, everyone needs to bring their expertise to a project, but there wasn't an opportunity for anyone on the team to develop expertise distinct from anyone else's. We needed a solution, fast.

To strengthen our internal playbook and level up teamwork and accountability, we split up the workload by separating and distributing high-level responsibilities so everyone owned a portion. Assigning specific tasks to each team member allowed us to accurately assess individual progress and performance. The more clearly defined responsibilities also allowed team members to become experts in areas they owned. When your team members own portions of L&D's work and develop expertise, the other team members and the organization as a whole can tap them for that expertise, allowing for deeper collaboration and teamwork. In our case, another benefit of this change was that morale started to improve almost immediately.

Clarifying team roles and responsibilities can be a complex process or as simple as writing down the items and areas of expertise that each person is spending their time on each day. The purpose isn't to define responsibilities on a microlevel but to provide a clear picture of who does what on the team and allow for ownership, expertise, accountability, and more effective collaboration.

One of the ways we communicated roles and responsibilities more effectively than job descriptions was by using a simple, internal org chart and adding an additional sentence or two listing key responsibilities and strengths. Each team member understood their place on the chart, and we shared this tool with my boss but didn't share it externally.

Figure 5-2 shows a partial sample of our chart to give you an idea of what yours could look like.

Figure 5-2. Sample L&D Team Org Chart (Internal-Only Version)

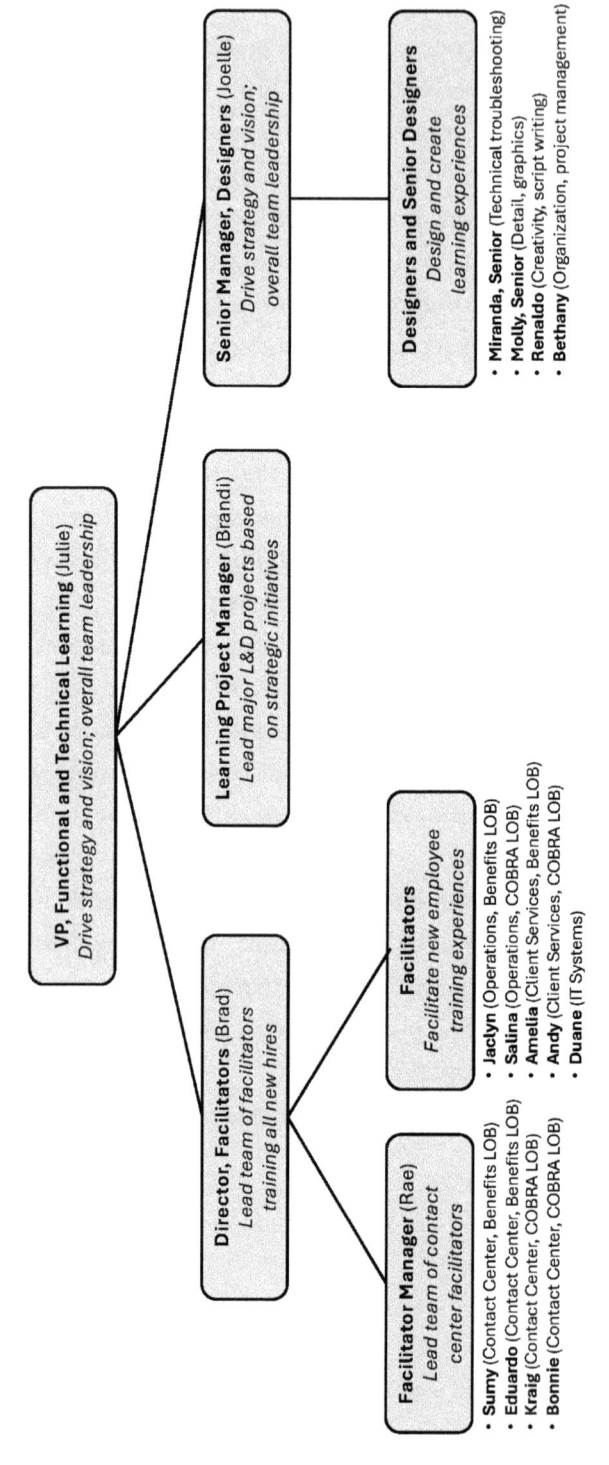

96 | Chapter 5

On our chart, we defined responsibilities according to the area in which each person trained and the line of business (LOB) or product line. Designers had a variety of design projects that weren't based on lines of business or training areas, so we listed their specialties (strengths) on the chart. (Their assignments were tracked on a separate spreadsheet.) Each team member was responsible for specific areas of their design projects, but if they needed help, the org chart showed whom to call. For example, Miranda could troubleshoot technical glitches, Molly made the most beautiful graphics, and everyone knew Renaldo wrote terrific scripts that were conversational and informative. We posted a full version of our internal org chart on our team's intranet site for quick and easy reference.

At the time, our L&D team was divided into two locations, but everyone worked in an office and knew one another well. People reported on their projects at meetings to familiarize others with their areas of expertise. Today, due to the nature of remote work, organizations may need to do this kind of exercise more often to enhance personal connections and knowledge for employees who work from a variety of locations.

YOUR TURN

Clearly Define Individual Team Members' Roles and Responsibilities
To create your own internal org chart, start with these essential steps:
1. **Brainstorm a list of the team's responsibilities that would be most helpful to clearly define.** These may be responsibilities beyond a job description, and they may point to team member strengths and areas of individual expertise.
2. **Define each team member's individual role and their responsibilities or area of expertise.** Ensure that you and other team members know whom you should go to with questions and where to point stakeholders for answers.
3. **Create a document or visual tool that indicates team members' responsibilities.** Share it among your team members and with your supervisor.

Optional: Create more buy-in and discussion by extending this exercise. Ask each team member to define their key responsibilities while you also define those responsibilities separately. Come together for a conversation in which you share perspectives to see where your ideas align and diverge.

3. Define Internal Processes, Standards, and Behavioral Expectations

When we talk about internal team processes, standards, and expectations, we aren't talking about how people work with the rest of the organization or common business processes like turning in time-off requests and timecards. Internal work processes, standards of work, and behavioral expectations are internal to your L&D team and your L&D team only. Are all these things clear to your team members? We'll break down step three into three areas:

- L&D work processes
- L&D standards of work
- L&D behavioral expectations

L&D Work Processes

Think about the work that your team does internally to complete projects and daily tasks. How is it organized? Where is information stored? How long should it take to complete a project? Is time tracked by the project? What data is each team member responsible for tracking? How frequently is content reviewed for accuracy? Do you have quality control or branding standards?

Depending on complexity, processes can be described in-depth or as high-level overviews. There are a lot of processes you could document, but I encourage you not to go overboard. You have other work to do! Most L&D teams can't drop everything to document processes, and not every process requires documentation. For example, you probably don't need a detailed document on how to log in to the learning management system (LMS), but you may need an explanation of how to upload a new course.

The goal of process documentation is to create resources and clarity where needed. Sometimes, all your team needs is a basic checklist, a task timeline, an annual calendar, or a link to an online video. Ask yourself: *What is the minimum amount of information someone needs to clarify this process or task?*

When I oversaw the learning function at Discovery Benefits, the design team had mastered the art of clarifying team processes. This was in large part due to their manager, Jodi, who was keen on clarifying success standards and creating consistency. She was an operational expert who encouraged continuous improvement and regularly iterated team processes as they found better ways to do their work. The design team didn't have a master document full of detailed processes but used simple checklists, notes, and other tools that worked for them. Here are the key processes Jodi's team used, along with the format of each resource.

Project Review

The team member creating a new learning solution reviewed it first for grammar, technical glitches, and adherence to brand guidelines. Then, two other team members reviewed the same items before sending anything to a business stakeholder or SME for review. This ensured that the first time a stakeholder or SME reviewed the project, they could concentrate on the content without distraction. As each internal review was completed, it was tracked in a master Excel spreadsheet that guided each team member on what to review (such as grammar, technical glitches, or brand guidelines).

Adherence to Company Brand Guidelines

Marketing provided the brand guidelines document and Jodi's team linked to it from their review-tracking spreadsheet. Company brand guidelines could also be easily accessed via links from key documents and the team's shared files.

Time Tracking

Team members tracked time spent on each project so they could determine an average number of hours for various project types and calculate project costs. These hours were used to determine the return on investment (ROI) for various projects. Each team member tracked their hours and turned them in to their manager regularly.

Project Templates

Team members used templates for every project. While the team occasionally included design templates, they always included templates for key project documents like contracts and meeting agendas. The templates were housed in a specific team folder.

Project Process

The team had a checklist for each project that provided a few details about each step required to run a design project with a stakeholder. It included everything from when to email stakeholders and SMEs to how to deliver and document a completed project. It also held links to relevant templates.

Content Review Cycle

Jodi's team asked SMEs to review content annually to ensure accuracy. They used a calendar listing to notify them when each piece of content was up for review.

> **YOUR TURN**
>
> ### Identify and Create Helpful Team Process Resources
>
> Chances are, some of your team processes are already defined, but you will need to create others from scratch. Start with what you have and slowly fill in the gaps as you complete other projects. Create a few goals for when you want to finish these resources or ask your team to document processes as they are completed.
>
> 1. **Take inventory.** Note what processes are already defined. Feel free to involve your team for assistance as needed. Here are a few questions to ask:
>   » Are there any key documents or artifacts that inform your team processes? Create a list of what is currently available.
>   » Are they stored in a place that is easily accessible?
>   » Are they up to date and accurate?
>   » Are they used regularly? If easily accessible documents aren't used regularly, it's a sign they may be outdated or irrelevant.
>   » Where do you need help?
> 2. **Determine which areas need a clearer process.**
>   » In what areas do team members frequently trip up or get stuck?
>   » In what areas do errors occur most frequently?
>   » In what areas is work most inconsistent?
> 3. **Determine how your team could create clarity in a process to ensure success.** What's most important for the team function?
> 4. **Create your process.** Look at the tasks you have outlined in the first two steps—those that already exist and those that indicate you need a clearer process. Then, you should:

- » Rank all tasks according to what is most important to your team function or where clarity will help your team be more successful. Start at the top and work your way down the list over time.
- » If an important task already has a process, ensure it is accurate and easily accessible.
- » If a process is needed, is there a project currently using that process or will there be one soon? Add a task to that project requiring team members to create the process.
- » If a process is needed but won't be used soon, determine when it will be used. Plan to complete the process before the need arises, if possible.
- » Begin building your own new-employee onboarding plan with these processes.
- » Determine the best place to store these resources.

5. **Create a common location or system to house all team process resources.** Everyone on the L&D team should know where to find resources for easy reference. Your system can look like a set of checklists, templates, or process documents, as long as they are easily accessible.
6. **Develop a plan for maintaining existing resources and creating new ones.**
    - » As your team grows and changes, ask members to create their own resource documents about new processes as they complete them.
    - » Ask them to help improve and maintain existing resources as they are used.

L&D Standards of Work

Consider the work standards you want your team to strive for. What are your standards for quality, timeliness, and accuracy? How do you define what good facilitation looks like in a classroom setting? How do you define what a good e-learning module includes? A good video? A good knowledge base article? A good job aid? Other L&D products and resources?

Teams outside L&D have specific standards they are working to achieve. For example, a contact center may have a standard for each employee to achieve a specific quality score or resolve a customer issue within one phone call lasting less than five minutes. Well-defined standards help employees know what to aim for and how to succeed. Have you defined what good looks like for the L&D team?

The L&D team's standards of work are simply written expectations for each team member to achieve in their work. These are different than behavioral expectations in that they should be easy to measure. The standards tell employees: "This is what *good* looks like."

A well-defined work standard will be within each team member's control, not dependent on others' actions. For example, a facilitator can control the time at which they start and stop a class, but they cannot control whether every participant arrives on time.

Standards will vary according to each role within the L&D team. For example, a designer will have very different standards than a facilitator or LMS administrator, content expert, or project manager.

In my last L&D team, we defined standards for the two main roles on our team—designers and facilitators. For the designers, the standards were all about quality and timely project completion; for the facilitators, they focused on running engaged, organized classroom training sessions. Here are some sample L&D team designer standards:

- Set realistic deadlines that allow the project to be completed on time.
- If deadlines cannot be met for some reason, create new deadlines, and document the reason for the delay.
- Complete all projects without grammatical errors.
- Complete all projects in adherence to company branding guidelines.

And here are some sample L&D team facilitator standards:

- Start and stop facilitated classes on time.
- Engage the class, at minimum, once every six minutes with some type of interaction or activity.
- Answer all participant questions during the class or follow up afterward.
- Engage participants in at least one knowledge-check activity, formal or informal, before the end of class.
- Ensure each class is prepared for a back-up facilitator, if needed, with well-defined learning outcomes, a script or talking points, and instructions to lead each activity.

> **YOUR TURN**
>
> **Define Standards of Work for Everyone on Your Team**
> For each role on your team, brainstorm the answer to this question: What does good look like?"
> - Involve people in each role in the conversation.
> - **Determine whether the ideas you came up with are under each team member's control.** If they are not, is there a way to rewrite the standard so it is under the team member's control? If they can't control the standard, throw it out.
> - **Make a list of new standards for each role.** Ensure you communicate them clearly to team members and discuss them often. You will also need a way to measure them, which we will discuss in later in this chapter.

L&D Behavioral Expectations

Many inefficient or ineffective teams have unwritten behavior norms. When someone starts a new job, they have to figure out on their own what it looks like to be a good team member and what to expect from the team leader. Without written expectations, this becomes difficult.

In the worst-case scenario, people are judged based on expectations they didn't know existed and feel like they were set up to fail. Sadly, this happened in a company I worked for years ago, resulting in widespread frustration and a huge dip in team morale just a month before the annual performance reviews were conducted. My team's leaders and I had worked hard for several years to set clear expectations for behavior. The expectations were well-known, written down, and discussed regularly. We had a "no surprises" policy, especially around performance management, so team members knew where they stood at all times and how to improve.

After our company was acquired, things changed. When I turned in my performance reports, HR told me the format was not acceptable—they expected me to modify all the ratings and the report to align with the new company's expectations. As you may have guessed, I had no idea what the new expectations were, and they weren't clearly outlined anywhere. My team and I were being judged according to expectations we didn't know existed.

After a long conversation with my new boss in which she explained the new expectations and rating system, I returned to my team to share the disappointing news that we would all be rated according to different expectations than we had discussed all year—and that this would negatively affect raises and bonuses. We were all deeply frustrated, to say the least.

Every couple years, I led an expectation-setting exercise for my team, which we did both in person and in a virtual setting. I asked everyone to answer three questions:

1. What makes a good team member?
2. What makes a good facilitator, designer, or producer?
3. What makes a good leader?

We broke into small groups to brainstorm responses. Team managers brainstormed separately so they wouldn't influence the team members. Once all the responses were shared, leaders categorized them into common themes, integrating their ideas, and then sending a survey to all team members asking them to prioritize expectations.

Each time we did this activity, the leaders added very few new ideas because the team members always had such a clear vision of how they wanted to work with one another, how to be successful in their roles, and what they desired from leaders. After all the input was shared, we solidified the highest priority expectations and communicated them to the team. By the end, everyone had a list of important behavioral expectations that were set by their peers, and each leader had a similar set.

Here are some sample expectations for learning experience team members:

- **Choose a positive attitude.** Be optimistic and assume positive intent from one another, leadership, and the rest of the company.
- **Be open to changes.** Changes come with the territory on our team and in our business. Be flexible, adaptable, and willing to navigate those changes.
- **Communicate openly, transparently, and respectfully with team members, leadership, and other departments.** Have tough conversations and work to find common ground.

- **Practice continuous learning.** Be adamant about increasing your knowledge and skills in the learning profession. Provide and accept forward-focused feedback as an opportunity to learn.
- **Strive for continuous improvement in your work.** See problems as opportunities for creative thinking and improvement. Be willing to think outside the box and not limit yourself to the same solutions, accept ideas from others (brainstorm), and ask questions instead of making assumptions.
- **Be a stellar team player.** Tap into the expertise of others on the team, be supportive and encouraging of team members both professionally and personally, and be ready to back up, help, or jump in when needed. (We're all in this together.)
- **Take ownership of your work.** Keep materials updated, accurate, and accessible so others can confidently and easily use them. Hold yourself accountable to responsibilities and deadlines. Own up to your mistakes and take responsibility for fixing them.
- **Work hard and have fun.** Maintain your sense of humor, let your personality shine, and have fun while doing quality work.

And here are some sample expectations for learning experience leaders or managers:

- **Be understanding and supportive of team members.** Connect with team members as people. Have compassion for team members professionally and personally. Provide recognition for a job well done. Regularly check in on the team's pulse.
- **Be accessible, accountable, and reliable.** Be available for team member questions, admit mistakes and work to correct them, and follow through. (If you say you're going to do something, then do it!) Be ready to jump in and help when needed.
- **Encourage and empower team member growth.** Invest in the growth of each team member by nurturing their unique strengths and skill sets, providing new project or content opportunities and stretch goals, giving forward-focused feedback, and engaging in conversations about professional and career goals.

- **Hold team members accountable while providing autonomy.** Ensure accountability in work, projects, and deadlines while trusting team members to take ownership of their work and follow-through.
- **Communicate clearly, openly, honestly, and transparently.** As much as possible, share information about team and company changes, strategy, goals, and vision. Set and communicate clear expectations. Have tough conversations and deliver feedback in a timely manner. Aim for no surprises in performance reviews.
- **Practice big-picture, small-step thinking.** Stay in the big picture enough to see other perspectives while also understanding how the team fits. Represent and advocate for the team in meetings with other departments.
- **Learn continuously.** Be adamant about increasing knowledge and skill in the L&D profession. Ask questions instead of making assumptions to learn from others. Stay curious.
- **Maintain a solutions focus.** Focus on solutions rather than friction or obstacles when it comes to people, projects, and goals. Assume positive intent, asking, "What can we do?" Help to resolve conflicts and provide guidance. Practice creative problem solving.
- **Work collaboratively across the organization.** Build and maintain relationships with leaders and departments across the organization, working collaboratively to increase effectiveness and impact.

Team members were encouraged and coached to hold each other accountable, and adhering to these expectations became one of our performance goals each year.

YOUR TURN

Create Clarity in L&D Team Behavioral Expectations

Set aside time to clearly outline team member behavioral expectations. You can use the exercise in this chapter or another activity you create.

I recommend involving other team members in this exercise. They will appreciate knowing that they have a voice in creating expectations rather than simply being told what those expectations are.

4. Determine Performance Measures and Track Accountability and Improvement

Most areas of any business are held accountable by providing metrics that indicate team and individual performance, as well as places for potential improvement. The L&D team should be no different.

Some measures will be related to your L&D measurement plan, which we'll discuss in more detail in chapter 10. Here, let's focus on what data you can use to determine whether your team is performing well. If you've defined your team's standards of work (step 3), then you already have a head start!

The cardinal rule is that team performance measures should align with team standards of work. These measures can then be used to hold each team member accountable, but they can also be used to identify what may or may not be working.

You want your team members to be good at their jobs and achieve success. If one team member can't meet a standard, that situation will require coaching. If *none* of your team members can manage a standard, an investigation is warranted, and the standard may need adjustment. What's holding them back from achieving this standard? Why isn't the standard realistic at this time?

In Table 5-1, you'll find team standards for design and facilitation roles from one of my previous L&D teams, as well as the type of measure we attached to each one.

Table 5-1. Sample L&D Team Standards and Corresponding Measures by Role

Role	Standards	Corresponding Measures
Designer	• Set realistic deadlines that allow for the project to be completed on time. • If deadlines cannot be met, create new deadlines and document the reason for the delay.	• Percent of projects completed on time, according to predefined project deadlines. • Percent of projects completed but needing adjustments to deadlines along the way. • Percent of projects completed on time, according to adjusted deadlines.

Table 5-1. *(continued)*

Role	Standards	Corresponding Measures
Designer	• Complete all projects without grammatical errors.	• A quality score for the work, aligned to grammar mistakes from the final review.
Designer	• Complete all projects in adherence to company branding guidelines.	• A quality score for the work, aligned to branding guideline adherence in final review.
Facilitator	• Start and stop facilitated classes on time. • Engage the class, at minimum, once every six minutes with some type of interaction or activity. • Answer all participant questions during the class or follow up afterward. • Engage participants in at least one knowledge-check activity, formal or informal, before the completion of the class.	• A quality score based on L&D leaders and peer facilitators attending training and ranking a trainer on each standard.
Facilitator	• Ensure each class is prepared for a back-up facilitator, if needed, with learning outcomes, a script or talking points, and instructions to lead each activity	• Percent of training sessions fully prepared for a back-up facilitator according to standard.

> **YOUR TURN**
>
> **Identify Measurements for Your L&D Standards of Work**
> Revisit the standards of work you identified for each role in step 3 of the internal L&D playbook pyramid, and outline how you will measure adherence to that standard. Beware! Sometimes this calls for creative thinking!

5. Track Team Members' Workload and Capacity

If you are going to maximize your L&D team's time and resources, you must have a clear idea of what that time and those resources entail. This means keeping your finger on the pulse of your team members' workload and capacity at all times. Include yourself in the group if you are a leader who also contributes to workloads. The goal is to use a workload capacity tracking system to answer the following questions quickly and easily:

- What is each team member working on?

- How much time should be allotted for each project and task?
- Who has available time for additional projects now?
- When will each team member have available time for projects in the future?

Project tracking software can help. Look for software that allows you to estimate the capacity in use as well as the capacity available for each team member based on workload. Of course, you will need to verify the accuracy of estimates with that team member. It's also important to know if there are outside factors affecting someone's maximum capacity. For example, a project might take more time than originally anticipated or a team member may be experiencing difficulties finding daycare for a while.

The full workload and capacity equation is heart + head or person + data. People are always an integral part of that equation.

A Lesson Learned

I learned how important the human factor is in tracking workloads and capacity when several facilitators on my L&D team began issuing frequent complaints to their manager, saying they were too busy and their jobs were causing extreme stress. We asked what was causing the problem, but the facilitators couldn't articulate anything specific, and we didn't see any trends. In addition, the other facilitators training in the same areas weren't voicing similar concerns. It was time to deep dive into the data.

We had the qualitative stories but needed more quantitative data. What was taking up their time and leading to stress? One obvious data source was their calendars. Every training session was listed, so we could easily pull data on how many hours team members were spending in training sessions each week. We looked at the previous four months, and the results were interesting. The team members who were complaining weren't spending the most time in training sessions, and surprisingly, in a couple of cases, they were spending significantly *less* time training than their peers. If they weren't in classes, why were they so busy?

We went another layer deeper, asking facilitators to describe the prep work needed for each session. One facilitator had significantly more prep work because she had to set up a software test persona for every new employee. We adjusted her workload accordingly.

The two remaining facilitators, on the other hand, were facing different problems—one simply took too many coffee breaks and another was just disorganized. Our conclusion? "Busy" means different things to different people. We decided to address their lack of time through coaching.

This experience led us to track facilitator workload and capacity differently. We set up parameters around the ideal and maximum time a facilitator could train each week and tracked both in a training calendar. We also took a deeper look at the time needed to prep for different training sessions and built that into our overview of workload and capacity. Vacation time and other out-of-office appointments also played a role and we made it a regular practice to review workloads during each manager's one-on-one with their facilitator direct reports. During this review, we were able to determine which tasks might be taking up too much time and explore whether changes could make them more efficient.

The project led to an improved organizational system that made everyone more efficient and used our resources more effectively. Do you have a good idea of your team's workload and capacity? How can you get better?

YOUR TURN

Create a System to Track Workload and Capacity

If you aren't already tracking workloads and capacity, start building a system that allows you to do so. The goal is to determine how much work your team members can take on and how much capacity they have available at any given time.

Combine quantitative data with more qualitative personal information to better distribute work and coach performance as needed. Here are some ideas for how to begin developing your system:

- **Audit team members' calendars.** Take a look at meetings, training sessions (if applicable), and time blocked for project work.
- **Ask team members to track their time for a few weeks or months** (if this feels comfortable to you and your team). Give them a few broad tracking categories, or ask them to define their own (such as project work, project meetings, team meetings, stakeholder meetings, training sessions, administrative work, and training prep). Ask them to turn in their tracking spreadsheets to meet predefined deadlines.

- **Create a spreadsheet to track team members' projects, estimated time to completion, and deadlines.** This is a good first step before investing in project-tracking software.
- **Research whether project-tracking software is already being used in your organization.** Could your team use the organization's existing licenses to track your work as well?
- **Research and purchase project tracking software.** This software can monitor your team's workload and available capacity so you have data at your fingertips at any time. Remember to include any knowledge you have of personal situations in addition to workplace data when assigning work.

Because each L&D team has different key responsibilities and projects and different access to resources, it is important to find and use a system that works for your unique situation. If you can't afford to purchase software, use a spreadsheet or two. The important thing is to understand current workloads and capacity so you can better plan how to partner with the business. With solid data on your side, you will be more likely to maximize the use of your team resources without burning anyone out.

6. Define Key Contacts in the Business

It's amazing how much time can be saved if team members don't have to figure out whom to reach out to with specific questions. What if you had a list of key contacts and their areas of expertise at your fingertips? This could help onboard new team members and ease the transition of veteran team members working on new project areas.

If you have been working in your organization for a while, this might be the easiest step of the internal L&D playbook pyramid to complete. Define helpful contacts in the organization's legal teams, communications, marketing, finance, IT, and HR or HR business partner (HRBP), as well as the top leaders in each division or area of the business. You should include the name of the person, their expertise, and why a team member might need to reach out to them. It may look something like this sample L&D contact list:

- Sandro Bertech (legal) reviews and approves all compliance training.
- Lisa Winger (legal) reviews all customer-facing videos and webinars.

- Munich Ibaro (IT) handles urgent LMS issues if a ticket is too slow.
- Jenni Alberson (marketing) handles brand guideline questions.
- Sumayah Tomlinson (contact center) reviews contact center quality guidelines.

> **YOUR TURN**
>
> **Create Your L&D Team Key Contact List**
> To create your L&D team key contact list, start with these steps:
> 1. Create a list of people you reach out to regularly to answer certain types of questions.
> 2. Ask team members to create their own lists.
> 3. Compile the lists, eliminating any duplicate entries, and put the finalized list in a place where everyone can easily access it, and let your team know where it is.
> 4. Update the list when people change roles or leave the company.

Format and Share Your Internal L&D Playbook

A playbook is not the same thing as the L&D strategy. Your strategy informs the direction your work is going, how it aligns with the greater organization, and where you will spend your time and resources. It is a long-term blueprint for achieving your goals and the business's goals.

An L&D playbook, on the other hand, is highly tactical. It includes specific actions your team will take to make the strategy successful and explains why and how you and your team do your daily work. An effective internal L&D playbook allows everyone on your team to know what they need to do to be successful and the importance of their work to the larger organization.

Your internal L&D playbook helps you operationalize and lead your team well. It also provides the direction needed for ordinary daily tasks so you can focus on the bigger tasks.

Where Your Internal L&D Playbook Lives

Your internal L&D playbook is there for you and your team to reference regularly. On rare occasions, you may share parts with the greater organization, but overall, it is just for L&D.

The playbook's format is up to you. I wouldn't spend a lot of time creating something pretty or expensive. You don't need to print, bind, or laminate it. The components don't even need to be in one document or a single format. It can be a combination of lists, visuals, checklists, templates, spreadsheets, and process documents. Most important:

1. It should communicate clearly and make sense to the team.
2. All components should be in a place that is easily accessible to you and the L&D team, such as on the company intranet or in shared files.

Let me reassure you: This playbook doesn't need to be perfect! You don't need to halt all work to create it. My team certainly didn't. We created our playbook a little at a time, over a few years. Sometimes we worked on a particular component because it was needed for a current initiative, sometimes we knew a certain component could provide a quick win, and sometimes we created components as part of a team retreat. Try to complete each piece within a timeline that works for you, whether that's a month or a year. You will eventually have a rock-solid internal L&D playbook and a team primed for success!

Internal L&D Playbook Checklist

L&D team purpose statement:
- Why does your team exist?
- Whom do you serve?

Team roles and responsibilities:
- Include more individualized information than a job description.
- Define specialties and expertise for each person.

Internal team processes, standards of work, and behavioral expectations:
- Aim for minimum processes needed to create clarity where it is most needed.
- Standards of work should answer, "What does good look like?" for each role on the team.
- Include behavioral expectations to clarify unspoken, unwritten norms.

Team member performance measures:
- Align performance measures to standards of work.
- Focus on items within each team member's control.

Team member workload and capacity:
- Track team member workloads and current capacity at all times.
- Combine data and personal situations for maximum accuracy.

Key business contacts:
- List key contacts for the L&D team's work.
- Include their role and when to reach out.

Build Your External L&D Playbook in Four Parts

The best leader I ever reported to in more than 25 years working in L&D—I'll call her Carmen to protect her privacy—was famous for saying, "We need to train the business how to do business with us." She had a unique perspective because she didn't start in L&D or HR; she came up through the ranks of business operations. When she was promoted to oversee a division that included the learning and training function, she was still wearing her strategic and operational hat.

While I was first working with Carmen, key stakeholders regularly came to me saying they had a problem on their team and needed at least 90 minutes of classroom training to solve it. I knew by then that classroom training was only part of a learning solution and sometimes wasn't needed at all. Because of the incredible number of resources required to create and facilitate an interactive classroom experience, and the failure of most classroom training to change behavior, I usually viewed this modality as the last resort.

"No one comes out of a classroom with a bow on top," was how I usually expressed my frustration to Carmen. It seemed to me that none of the stakeholders truly understood what it took to create a robust, well-designed, interactive classroom training course—or any other learning experience, for that matter. They thought we had a magic wand that made the training course magically appear!

I was sharing some of my concerns when Carmen first told me we needed to "train the business to do business with us." Immediately, I felt my perspective start to shift. I recognized that my frustrations had blinded me to the reality of the situation. I was playing the victim with the words, "They just don't understand!" running through my brain.

Carmen was incredibly smart and a visionary. She saw the value that a robust learning function could bring to the business. She also knew, from her years in the trenches, that the rest of the business's leaders didn't understand the value of L&D because the learning team wasn't providing them with any guidance.

She helped me see that I needed to ask new questions:
- Are the stakeholders aware there are different, more effective ways to administer a learning solution?
- Have I demonstrated that we can do more than take and deliver on requests?
- Have I been clear on the time and resources it takes to create a robust solution?

I realized that I was annoyed with the stakeholders because I was making it about me. I was blaming them, but I hadn't considered their perspective, which was simply that they didn't know how to do business with the learning team effectively. We hadn't taught them how, so the cycle of taking orders, feeling frustrated, delivering on orders, and feeling more frustrated, kept repeating.

My conversations with Carmen convinced me that it was time to start training the business to do business with us. I rallied the managers on my team, and we started to build a new type of playbook with the stakeholder audience in mind. Our stakeholders didn't need to know our internal team performance measures, processes, and standards; they only needed to know how to work with us successfully. I called it our external playbook, and it included four parts: the intake process; key definitions; typical projects, timelines, and results; and project roles and responsibilities. Let's discuss each part in more detail.

1. The Intake Process

When learning pros debate what makes an effective intake process, the central questions usually focus on whether the team should use a form to gather information and what should be on it. But a form is only one example of a tool that can help with receiving inquiries and requests. I've heard of intake happening via a good old-fashioned email exchange, inside fancy project management software, and through other more novel options. The tool is less important than the process itself, which should fit the company's culture and maturity and provide the learning team with the information they need to take the next steps.

Simply put, the intake process needs to make sense and work for your stakeholders, first and foremost. If it's too difficult for them to use, it won't be worthwhile. There are three questions you should ask when designing or revamping your intake process:
- What is the minimum amount of information you need to determine whether to act on a request?
- What processes are commonly and successfully used by teams to gather information from one another internally?
- What is your stakeholders' tolerance or preference when it comes to providing information?

Minimum Information

What is the minimum amount of information you need to determine whether to act on a request? Think about your team's process to determine whether training will solve a problem presented by the stakeholders and how your resources are allocated across the learning team and potentially across the company.

Travis—the SVP of talent at a rapidly growing midsize insurance, financial services, and HR consulting company—noticed his team was getting hit from all sides with requests for new training initiatives. He knew they couldn't say yes to all of them. His L&D team needed to focus on projects aligned strategically with current organizational objectives. He also knew that the learning team only had enough bandwidth to work on the key, large-scale projects, which meant they needed additional information to indicate whether a request would make the cut. So, they included three new questions in their intake process.
- Which current organizational objective does this request support?
- Who is the executive sponsor for this request?
- How many people will be affected by this project?

The team could then use the answers to determine whether and how the request tied to a larger organizational initiative. All large-scale projects had an executive sponsor, so that was a way of checking that box. If any of the responses didn't meet L&D's criteria, it was much easier to deny the request or point the requester in a different direction.

Travis told me that "little pet projects just went away" as soon as they added these questions to the intake process.

As part of your thinking about the minimum amount of information you need to act on a request, you should also consider the information you *don't need* at the outset. For example, do you really need to ask about learning outcomes as part of the request? A better question might be, "What performance problem are you hoping this project will solve?" or "What performance problem led you to come to us with this request?"

Your intake process should gather the best information to determine whether training is a viable solution. At a minimum, start a conversation about whether training will solve the problem your stakeholders are describing and if it is worth the resources.

Existing Processes

What processes are commonly and successfully used by teams to gather information for one another internally? This question prompts you to look for processes that your company's teams are currently using to gather information internally. If you can align or mimic current processes, your intake has a better chance of success. The learning curve for building on something that already exists is much less steep than the one that requires people to learn something completely new. Remember, this intake process is one aspect of training the rest of the business to do business with you, so build on familiar structures. Find out the answers to these questions:

- Where do people currently go to request information from one another?
- What software do they use, and is there a ticketing system?
- Can you use that same system or process to start your intake?

Laurel, the senior director of learning experience at a large global multinational technology company, built her team's intake process into the company's existing project management software. Every team in the company was expected to input internal project requests into this software, and the requests were then funneled to the appropriate project team. Laurel realized that the learning experience team could be positioned at the end of one of those funnels. In doing so, the process to request a learning project or to request that learning be part of a project became no different than any other.

Laurel also discovered another huge bonus to using existing software: visibility. Because all the requests lived in the same space, regardless of team, it was easy to determine whether the request or the work was duplicative, saving the time and resources that would have been used to create something redundant otherwise. For example, if a request came in for Salesforce training, Laurel's team could quickly check to see whether a similar project was in process or had been completed by company trainers somewhere else in the world. If so, the teams could collaborate, or Laurel's team could tap into the existing resources. A huge efficiency win for all!

Stakeholder Preferences

What is your stakeholders' tolerance or preference when it comes to providing information? This question requires you to think about your audience and your company's culture and maturity level. Are people used to filling out long forms with in-depth information, or will they see the questions, click out of the form, and send you an email instead?

If you know that the company culture is more conversational and less form-driven, don't put all your time and resources into creating a form. The goal is to get the information you need to determine the next steps, not to make your stakeholders jump through unnecessary hoops.

Let's go back to Travis, the SVP of talent at the midsized insurance, financial services, and HR consulting company. When revamping the intake process, his team insisted on creating a form that all stakeholders would fill out. Travis knew the stakeholders might not be keen on doing this because he'd seen a lot of blank forms returned throughout his career.

"I don't want to break your heart," he told his team, "But nobody cares about your form. They just want to know if you will create training programs for them. Here's the thing. We don't need everyone to fill out the form—we can use the questions to have a conversation."

He instructed his team to respond to any request for training, whether via email, instant message, or a partially completed form, within 24 hours to schedule a consultation over the phone. During that conversation, Travis's team member would use the form as their intake guide. They could usually start the conversation by saying something like, "I've already been able to fill out some of the fields on our form based on your email. Let's fill out the rest together." As a bonus, every time a team member pulled up the form and walked through it with a requester, it helped educate that requester about the process.

In short, your intake process can be a training tool for those throughout the organization who want to know how to work with you, but the process must match the company culture and maturity level, making it easy for stakeholders to engage. In addition, it should be limited to collecting the minimum amount of information needed to determine next steps.

2. Key Definitions

All learning teams operate with a set of commonly used terms. Understanding these can be helpful for stakeholders working with you on a project. Consider the terms you use regularly and include their definitions in project plans, an internal intranet page, and other locations where stakeholders may look when working with you.

Some of L&D terms I've used in external L&D playbook documents include learning outcomes, stakeholder, subject matter expert (SME), executive sponsor, e-learning, knowledge base, job aid, learning management system (LMS), and learning experience platform (LXP). Use this list as a starting point or create your own. Pay attention to questions stakeholders ask and any points of confusion, and then add clarifying definitions to your list. You don't have to create an extensive glossary. If another term is used frequently in the business to describe something you do, use that! For example, some teams use *shadowing* to describe their on-the-job training process. Use their language if it helps them understand.

3. Typical Projects, Timelines, and Results

Your stakeholders need to know what they can expect when working with you, and this item most directly addresses that need. Remember the frustrations I mentioned at the beginning of this chapter about stakeholders not understanding when to use a formal training solution and how long it takes to create that type of solution? Including typical projects, timelines, and results in your external L&D playbook will help resolve those frustrations.

If you've started developing an internal L&D playbook, you already have some in-depth information about projects, timelines, and results. If not, there's no time like the present to start creating them! Stakeholders need to know what your process means for them—not all the back-end details. Essentially, you are outlining what your customers can expect when working with your team from beginning to end. If you don't do this, those customers (stakeholders) will fill in the gaps on their own, based on past experiences—and that's when the frustration sets in.

I remember listening to presentations from college interns who had spent their summer working at a nonprofit. They were sharing final reflections on what they had learned. One intern, Laura, shared a lesson in communication from working with her mentor, Rob. "Things got easier when I realized Rob was thinking in full sentences and talking in half sentences," she said. "I learned to ask more questions and try to get more clarification from him up front because I couldn't read his mind."

I'm sure we've all worked with people like Rob who didn't share all the information we needed. Lack of information can lead to inconveniences, conflict, and extra work later on. The big question is: When it comes to working with stakeholders, are you a Rob? Do you have elaborate thoughts about how you would like stakeholders to work with you, but only tell them half the story? Perhaps, you don't know how to articulate all your ideas, but you often notice that people are not meeting the unexpressed expectations in your brain.

Without clarity around expectations, people always fill in the gaps on their own, falling back into old patterns of what they've done in the past. If you are attempting to move past transactional order taking, you need to lean into asking more questions and becoming a successful partner with others—as Laura did. Working as an SBP means making it easy for others in the organization to know how to work with you.

Before we can begin communicating our expectations and processes to the broader organization, we need to define them for ourselves to ensure we have an effective external L&D playbook.

Ask Yourself Questions to Define Your Expectations

Consider the following questions alone or with key members of your L&D team. Keep your stakeholders' experience in mind. Your answers will define your expectations so you can articulate them clearly to people beyond your team.

- **What can stakeholders expect when working with your L&D team?** Start thinking about how your team currently operates when working with stakeholders and how you would like it to operate differently. Put yourself in your stakeholders' shoes. What should their experience be like?
- **When working with a business stakeholder, where do you start? What questions will you ask and why?** Be sure to include whether you will need specific information to move forward, like a tie to strategic initiatives or an executive sponsor.
- **What potential pathways might you recommend as next steps and why?** Your answers should include the options that may come out of initial conversations, such as conducting a needs analysis, directing stakeholders to existing resources, asking them to collaborate with another business area working on the same type of challenge, a recommendation to outsource the project, or providing direction or support to equip them to complete work on their own.

What Products and Services Will You Provide and When?

Clearly define the type of work your team typically does and how long it takes to complete. Your answers don't need to be so specific that they cannot be adjusted based on individual stakeholder circumstances, but they should paint a clear picture of your typical processes.

Without this information, stakeholders make assumptions based on what they have seen in the past, and this is probably limited to formal in-person or e-learning products. They may not know that you can tie learning needs to internal knowledge base videos and articles, create job aids, or recommend coaching, for example. This is your chance to explain.

You will also need to add a typical timeline for each type of work you do. How long does it take you to perform a needs analysis? How long does it take to create an immersive classroom experience? An online work simulation? A typical e-learning module?

Ensure that you're all on the same page by answering these simple questions:
- What outputs do you typically provide?
- How much time does each output typically take to create?

If you have started working on your internal L&D playbook, you may be able to refer to some of the information related to tracking capacity to determine how long various types of work take. If not, start tracking time now, gathering the data you need to build your timelines as you go.

To give you a baseline starting point, take a look at Table 5-2, which represents the results of a 2021 study by L&D expert Robyn Defelice.

Table 5-2. Average Unit Length and Time to Develop Instructional Product

Training Product Description	N	Average Module Length (Minutes)	Minimum Time to Develop (Hours)	Maximum Time to Develop (Hours)	Average Time to Develop (Hours)
Instructor-Led					
Classroom	197	23	43	141	67
Online or virtual	200	25	35	85	55
E-learning					
Passive (page turners)	140	20	38	79	48
Partial engagement (drag and drops, roll overs, simple animations, or gamified elements)	138	26	65	115	84
Moderate engagement (some games, scenarios, or simulations)	129	20	74	194	116
Full engagement (many immersive games, scenarios, or simulations)	59	17	70	694	155
Microlearning					
Infographics, podcasts, videos, or e-learning	151	6	10	31	18

Source: Defelice 2021

This data will continue to morph and change as we produce and work with new technologies and tools, like AI, to help with product development. As

L&D leaders, we need to pay attention to how long each of our typical projects takes as part of the internal data we collect from our teams.

At Discovery Benefits, my learning design team created a simple document with information about various instructional products that we typically completed. The document included a basic definition of each product type and the time needed to create it. We listed different levels of work similar to those in Table 5-2. Our top-level work was a fully immersive online software simulation created in-house with all the bells and whistles. Our lowest level was a PDF job aid that could be integrated into a team's knowledge management system. E-learning courses of various kinds fell in the middle.

We used this document in conversations with stakeholders, sometimes sharing it during our first conversation. The details were most helpful for especially demanding requests and stakeholders who truly saw us as only order takers. When we began working with people as SBPs and were able to conduct more analysis up front to determine whether learning was needed, we shared this document after the fact, while presenting the results of our findings and working to define the best learning solution.

There are other ways to explain the work we do. For example, Jenn, the director of learning and development at a midsize biotech company is a fan of simple timelines with milestones that show projects from start to finish. Adam, a learning project manager at a large communication company, created an "expectations document" with the time spans needed to create training for major rollouts. He started sharing this document with stakeholders at the beginning of each project, explaining the timelines and reasons behind them. He told me this helped colleagues understand that although the training was the last part of each project created, it didn't mean he could collapse timelines.

"We don't have a tree full of elves in the backyard standing by to design, develop, and deliver training overnight," he told people. "If you want training to stick, we can't keep collapsing our window to create it and expect the same result."

My experience has led me to conclude that once you have something to show stakeholders that explains a little more about the work required to create their desired output, they become much more understanding and are more likely to work with you on alternatives if the timeline doesn't meet their needs. Again, this is part of training our business partners to do business with us.

Describe the Typical Results of Your Work

When creating your external L&D playbook, include the typical results of the work you are doing throughout the company. You will need to have some measurements in place and a basic summary you can easily share. (You'll find more information about measurement in chapter 10.)

Use these questions to help determine what to share:
- What were the measurable results of past projects?
- What are the most common measurable results for each type of output you provide (such as onboarding, e-learning, software simulation, or leadership development)?

Your goal here is to be able to quickly share what has happened in the company as a whole based on past L&D projects. This builds your credibility with stakeholders and helps make the case for a particular approach, if needed.

For example, based on the measurement strategy we had for our onboarding programs at Discovery Benefits, we knew that if we followed our typical process, we could shorten the time from the start date to production for most teams by 50 percent, and we could relieve the training burden for managers by a minimum of 30 percent. Both the confidence and competency levels of new employees participating in our program significantly increased. We shared these numbers with other teams within the organization, especially when we were talking about moving away from a traditional, classroom-intensive model of onboarding to one that stakeholders didn't quite understand.

4. Project Roles and Responsibilities

The fourth and final part of your external L&D playbook explains the roles and responsibilities of everyone involved in a learning project. Again, your goal is to clarify and communicate expectations regarding what it's like to work with L&D.

In many cases, the L&D team expects stakeholders and relevant SMEs to be involved in each project. In other cases, stakeholders expect minimal involvement once they hand off learning projects.

Joe, the director of L&D for a midsized automotive manufacturing company, conducted a voice-of-the-customer survey for every people leader in the organization. He realized he needed a baseline understanding of current perceptions the people leaders had about L&D before starting his quest to make L&D a strategic business partner. The survey results clearly showed that no one clearly understood L&D's roles and responsibilities. Multiple people blamed or gave credit to L&D for things they had no responsibility for creating. One comment said L&D needed to understand how something worked before creating a process for doing it, but L&D's role only involved creating training and onboarding for an existing process—not creating the process itself!

Clarifying roles and responsibilities can be straightforward. You can explain them in initial conversations or put them in writing to review at project kick-offs. In a typical learning project, what are the roles and responsibilities of each of the following people? Create a short definition you can share.

- L&D team member
- Project stakeholder
- Subject matter expert
- Executive sponsor (if applicable)
- Additional support staff members, such as IT or legal experts (if applicable)

At Discovery Benefits, we started discussing these roles and responsibilities during our first conversation with a stakeholder about a potential project. We then asked for the names of anyone who would be included in each role and didn't kick off a project until all necessary roles were filled. The designer or project manager then filled out a project template detailing the project purpose, goals or outcomes, scope, success measures, timeline, and the roles and responsibilities of everyone involved—with names attached. At the kick-off meeting, the designer or project manager walked through the document, describing each role and its responsibilities, and naming the people filling each role. Each person named was in attendance. After the meeting, key stakeholders or executive sponsors had to sign off on the document, indicating their understanding. This careful process ensured the terms of the project—including all roles and responsibilities—were clear.

This approach may or may not work in your company, but providing clarity on roles and responsibilities is an important part of defining the expectations of what it means to work with the L&D team and helps you become a better business partner.

Now it's your turn to create an external L&D playbook. Like the internal L&D playbook, it doesn't have to be a single document; it just needs to be easy to read and understand. Do what works in the context of your company's culture.

> **External L&D Playbook Checklist**
>
> **Intake process:**
> - What is the minimum amount of information you need to determine whether to act on this request?
> - What processes are commonly used by teams to gather information from each other internally?
> - What is your stakeholders' tolerance or preference for providing information?
>
> **Key definitions:**
> - What terms are essential to the process of doing your work?
> - What terms tend to create confusion for those outside the L&D team?
>
> **Typical process, projects, timelines, and results:**
> - Where do you start?
> - What questions will you ask and why?
> - What potential pathways might you recommend as next steps and why?
> - What outputs do you typically provide?
> - How much time do each of these outputs typically take to create?
> - What are the measurable results of past projects?
> - What are commonly seen measurable results for the different types of outputs you provide?
>
> **Roles and responsibilities:**
> - What are the various roles in each learning project?
> - What are the responsibilities of each role?

Summary

Working as an SBP means running your L&D team like other leaders in the business run their teams—with clear purpose and direction. Continue building a strong foundation for working as an SBP by getting your own house in order with an internal L&D playbook, which is just for your team to define how you work internally.

The internal L&D playbook pyramid provides a guide for what to include:
- Create a clear team purpose statement.
- Clarify team roles and responsibilities.
- Define internal team processes, standards of work, and behavioral expectations.
- Determine team member performance measures for accountability and improvement.
- Track team member workload and capacity.
- Define key business contacts.

Keep the components of your internal L&D playbook in a location that is easily accessible for all members of the team.

To work as SBPs, we need to train the rest of the business to work with us; otherwise, they will fill in the gaps on their own. However, we can't expect our stakeholders to understand how to best work with us if we don't tell them. We need to train them how to best do business with us.

An external L&D playbook defines what it's like to work with the L&D team and includes:
- **An intake process.** Intake is a process, not a form. Ask for the minimal amount of information needed to determine whether to act on a request. Ideally, intake will mimic or add to other processes already used to gather information in the company, instead of asking stakeholders to do something new. It should consider the stakeholders' preference for providing information at your company.
- **Key definitions.** Include definitions for learning-related items, but only if they cannot be explained in other terms.
- **Typical projects, timelines, and results.** Define these and use them when talking with stakeholders about potential solutions.
- **Project roles and responsibilities.** Clearly define the roles and responsibilities of all involved in a learning project.

CHAPTER 6
Determine Your Key Stakeholders

As L&D leaders, we never want to work in a vacuum, a space devoid of people, conversations, interactions, and outcomes. We can't sit quietly in a corner by ourselves and expect to make a difference. We can't do our jobs without interacting with people, including the employees we are developing, our fellow L&D team members, and other leaders and colleagues throughout the organization. But in transforming from order takers to strategic business partners, we aren't just interacting with everyone; we are building strategic relationships with a specific group of people—our key stakeholders.

Who are your stakeholders? Anyone in your organization who has a vested interest in L&D's work. These stakeholders work with L&D leaders regularly, and your *key stakeholders* are the most essential to the work you do. They have the power and influence to move L&D projects forward or completely block progress.

You typically need to tap into the knowledge and influence of key stakeholders at several points during a project and when planning and executing your overall L&D strategy. As an L&D leader, you don't determine the direction of the company or the processes used to get work done, but you bring your expertise to partnerships with key stakeholders to make things happen. Key stakeholders are your connection to the rest of the company, influencers, business experts, and collaborative partners. They help ensure that your work is strategically aligned, help secure the right resources, provide expertise, and bring your work to the attention of the larger organization.

Identifying the key stakeholders whom you will need to work with is a critical first step in becoming an SBP. Although company structures vary, L&D key stakeholders usually fall into five categories: your L&D team, your boss, HR and HRBPs, executives or senior leadership, and frontline or middle managers.

Your L&D Team

Unless you are an L&D department of one, your team will be critical to developing initiatives, achieving goals, and measuring success. At the same time, they can also become one of the biggest barriers to working as an SBP. Confusion, misalignment, and misunderstandings within your team can turn initiatives on their head, making them impossible to complete successfully. As we discussed in chapter 5, you can avoid problems within your team if you have an internal L&D playbook that defines their purpose, roles and responsibilities, processes, standards, and expectations.

Consider the team performance analogy about rowing a boat. When everyone is rowing in the same direction, toward the same destination, and they all know their role in moving the boat forward, it's smooth sailing. But if team members are all sitting in a random seat, not sure which direction to row, the boat will come to a standstill—or start spinning in circles. Some people will grab the closest oar; others will not touch an oar at all. A few people will try to put themselves in the role of captain, and others will decide to do the work of the person sitting next to them without permission. The whole team knows they are not succeeding, even if they don't know what success looks like. Frustration builds, morale tanks, conflict erupts, and people start jumping overboard!

I admit that analogy might be a bit dramatic, but my point is that your team members are among your most valuable stakeholders when it comes to achieving L&D goals. They should understand and buy in to your vision and the plan to achieve it. Team members must clearly understand how they can use their strengths and expertise to contribute to success. In other words, they must know which seat is theirs and which direction to row, so the L&D boat can move forward.

Rose, the director of training and development at a midsize environmental services company, knew the importance of her team as stakeholders the moment she started in her role. The group included four people, and she immediately noted inefficiencies that would stop them from scaling. She was savvy enough to know that she couldn't just walk in and announce the problems. She had to earn the team's trust and, as she put it, get her sea legs. "I needed to win the team before we could work on any deliverables," she said. "If I didn't have their trust, I knew nothing would get done."

After Rose got to know her team, she defined what it would look like to become a high-performing, streamlined team—one in which individual responsibilities were communicated clearly and everyone was rowing in the same direction. She gradually introduced them to a new way of working. Over the next four years, the L&D team grew, became more efficient and effective, and took on more work than Rose could have imagined when she started. "When I look back," she reflected with pride, "I think, gosh, how did we do all this? A few years ago, I would have said there's no way we could have produced close to what we are producing now. But we're doing it!" She knows the success they are experiencing now is because she had the smarts to win over the team before introducing changes.

Robert, the training manager at a small oil and gas company, didn't have a centralized team. His company dispersed people performing a training function into every location, and they all reported to different leaders. This system created inconsistencies and prevented the trainers from acting like a team. Before Robert started, the group had never even been on a call together.

Robert knew that to work as a strategic partner, creating a robust and consistent approach to learning and training, he had to create a team—regardless of the reporting structure. He had to influence them without the authority of being the boss. So, he started by gathering the group together regularly in a simple virtual meeting to discuss what everyone was working on and share ideas. After several months, he sent out an industry report on trends and asked each member of the group to pick one section, read it, and share what they found insightful at the next virtual meeting. His goal was to build developmental knowledge and credibility. He also initiated 15-minute one-on-one weekly check-ins with each member of the group. Finally, he brought everyone together, in person, for team building exercises and to write the mission and vision statements for the L&D function together.

After the in-person meeting, Robert's plan to build a team took a major positive turn. Members started reaching out to one another to share ideas and ask for help with challenges—without involving Robert. He knew at that point that he could begin to build a mission and vision with a team of people who were rowing in the same direction.

Now that you've learned a little more about how others work effectively with their teams, consider these questions:
- Does your L&D team know which direction you are heading?
- Are they all on board and rowing in the same direction?
- What do you need to do to create camaraderie, collaboration, and clarity?

Your Boss

I don't love the word *boss*—maybe because it sounds authoritative and that isn't my style, or maybe because I was accused of being too bossy by my younger sisters as a kid. Whatever the reason, I still use it, because it's a quick, easy to understand way to indicate reporting structure. Your boss is incredibly important because they *tell the story of the work you do* to people in other circles of the business. In addition, they can often remove roadblocks to smooth your way forward.

Your boss needs to see L&D as an SBP, and it's your job to *lead up* to explain that concept. *Leading up* involves guiding people in positions above you in the organizational hierarchy to provide the insights and knowledge they need to work effectively. When we think of exercising leadership, our minds usually jump to leading from the top down, but if your boss has limited experience in L&D or other people development fields, leading up will be essential.

When you are leading down, you are helping to equip and empower people on your team. When leading up, you are helping to equip and empower those at a higher level, like your boss. Pay attention to how your boss prefers to receive information. For example, I had one boss who wanted all information verbally in a one-on-one meeting and another who preferred a regular recap of my team's activities in writing. Another tip for leading up is to think deeply about the person's role. If you had their job, what questions would you want to be prepared to answer about L&D? What challenges might you be facing regularly? What pressures might you be under? What successes would you be excited to share? Think of your boss not just as a boss, but as a person who is also navigating the stresses of work and politics in your company.

As a boss myself, I always loved to tell others about my team's successes. I appreciated it when team members came to me with challenges and either asked for help removing a roadblock or wanted to brainstorm potential solutions. I also hated it when I was caught off guard, especially by those higher up than myself. No boss wants to look like they don't know what their team is doing.

When I lead up, I focus on communicating what I believe my boss needs to know, always asking if additional information would be helpful, and specifically calling on her when I need help removing a barrier. But leading up always varies depending on the situation and people involved.

Laurel, the senior director of learning experience for a large global multinational technology company, found herself reporting to a regional VP of sales who had never heard of the acronym *L&D* and knew nothing about the function. He was open to learning, recognized the brilliance of Laurel and her team, and did his best to tell their story and remove roadblocks. She considered keeping him in the loop on projects—educating him a little at a time about how her team did their work and sharing their successes—to be one of the key aspects of her role.

Laurel belonged to an external network of learning leaders in which members regularly shared stories about their work, including how they overcame challenges and achieved success. One day, she was in the hot seat as the featured speaker and saw an opportunity to lead up. She invited her boss to attend so he could hear her talk about the learning team's story.

After the event, he pulled her aside. "Laurel, that was so cool," he said. "I've heard you tell all those stories before, but to hear you lay it out for others in the profession the way you did . . . it really hit me."

Laurel led up by simply inviting her boss to overhear how she framed the challenges and solutions for others in her profession.

Denise, the training and development manager at a small healthcare technology company, had a completely different challenge. She found herself reporting to a boss who had been promoted from an administrative position to leading the HR function. Although her boss was highly supportive and great at sharing information with others when approached, she wasn't initiating conversations with the C-suite or advocating for the team when needed.

Then, Denise and her team saw an opening that proved to be the perfect opportunity to lead up. In HR team gatherings, her boss regularly asked the team to participate in brainstorming ways to improve the HR function. In response, Denise suggested that her boss could have regular meetings with the CEO, explaining that this wasn't only for her boss's sake, but a strategic move to support all HR employees through partnership, instead of simply taking orders. Denise and other team members explained that meetings with the CEO would help the learning and HR teams work more proactively and have a bigger influence. This was exactly what the boss needed to hear. She quickly initiated meetings with the CEO, and positive results followed. Denise and her team led up by helping their boss learn to advocate in a new way and emboldening her to be more assertive for their sake.

Now ask yourself:
- Is your boss able to tell your team's story?
- Are they equipped and empowered to advocate for L&D in circles you are not a part of?
- Do they know when you need help removing a roadblock?
- Are they sometimes caught off guard with questions from others about L&D?
- How can you lead up to help them do all these things with greater impact?

HR and HR Business Partners

A strong partnership with HRBPs—or HR in general, depending on your company's structure—can provide a cheat code that helps L&D better understand the business as a whole and build trust quickly. Because an HRBP's role is to build relationships with leaders in their assigned area of the company—assisting with people management and employee relations challenges—most are in continuous communication with the area. As a result, they keep their fingers on the pulse of successes and challenges. A strong partnership with HRBPs allows L&D leaders to leverage a lot of knowledge without doing the legwork themselves. That's what makes HRBPs (or HR in general) a key stakeholder.

Kristine, the director of talent development for a large health solutions company, explained to me that the first thing she did in her role was build relationships with the HRBPs. "I knew that building trust needed to start with my own HR family," she said. "If you think about it, they're the bridge (to the rest of the company)."

Kristine knew that the HRBPs could reach more people and gather more information about successes and challenges within the company than her small team could gather alone. So, she worked to build a relationship that encouraged working together and keeping one another in the loop. After getting to know the HRBPs, Kristine kept them informed regarding talent development requests from leaders in their assigned areas.

Whenever a leader reached out to her with a request, Kristine's first question was, "Have you talked to your HRBP?" If they hadn't, she let them know that she would inform the HRBP about their conversation. Likewise, the HRBPs did the same when they talked with a leader who mentioned thoughts on potential talent development opportunities. The result of this strong partnership was deeper trust extending from leaders to HRBPs to talent development professionals.

Nate—the senior manager of talent management, design, and leadership at a large outdoor retailer—agrees with Kristine's approach. "I have worked with so many HRBPs over my career," Nate told me, "And I see the influence they have. If I can work with them, we get more done."

Kacie, the SVP and director of organization development for a small community bank, stresses that the process of working effectively with HR is continuously evolving. She meets regularly with the HR director, often to iron out who does what in real-time. They discuss what makes sense given their unique skills and expertise and create clarity through conversation. Working continuously to establish clear boundaries creates a stronger partnership and gives them the information they need to advocate for each other with other stakeholders throughout the organization.

HR and HRBPs can become extensions of your L&D team and you of theirs. Ask yourself:

- What is your current working relationship with HR or HRBPs?
- Do you have open communication about initiatives and challenges?
- Are you able to advocate for one another?

Executives and Senior Leaders

The people who are considered executives or senior leaders will vary based on your company structure, but they're all key stakeholders—primarily because they are responsible for two things that directly affect L&D's work: creating overarching company strategies and goals and deciding where to invest company time and resources.

Executives and senior leaders view projects from a greater distance than frontline managers and SMEs, but they are often called on to provide sponsorship or high-level oversight, especially for projects that directly affect significant company initiatives. As an L&D leader, you should understand this group's goals and maintain communication so you can reach them when needed. If your organization won't allow you to sit in meetings with executives and senior leaders or to receive communications about decisions, find out who in your circle—such as a top L&D or HR leader—does have access. Ensure you are sharing information with this person, and they are sharing with you.

Executives and senior leaders rely heavily on data and information from others when making their decisions. They need to understand the current challenges and successes that are either moving the company forward or holding it back. They take in all available information to make the best decisions possible. Your job is to make the executives' priorities *your* priorities and to provide the data and information that will help them make informed decisions.

One of my favorite experts on this topic is Liz Wiseman. Before she started researching and writing, Liz was well respected in her HR role at Oracle. One of her colleagues observed that she always got solid support from upper leadership for projects she was working on and asked Liz for advice. How could the colleague get executive buy-in for a project?

Liz said she didn't know how to do this, explaining that she had never really put anything important to her on the executives' agenda. Instead, Liz said that she had "made a habit of working on what was important to [her] stakeholders" (Wiseman 2021). In essence, Liz gained buy-in from senior leaders by aligning her projects with the overall company strategy. If you want to do the same, know your company's strategy and why it's important.

In addition to creating the company's strategic initiatives, executives and senior leaders decide where to allocate resources. I hate to break it to you, but

L&D isn't the only function in the company requesting resources at any given time. I once worked with a senior leader who wisely informed me that "there will always be more demands for resources than there are resources available to allocate."

I'm guessing you already have a list of ways to spend the company's money, and it's probably bigger than your current budget allows. Are you looking for money to purchase a new technology solution, hire subcontractors or vendors, provide professional development, or grow your team? So is everyone else. The resources available are always finite. To keep the organization in business, executives or senior leaders need to make smart decisions about resource distribution throughout the company—and that's where you come in.

Noah, the VP of talent development for a small energy company, explained it to me like this: "Any function—finance, IT, legal, and others—is coming to the executive team with investment opportunities. They say, 'I've got this opportunity, and I think that if we invest x here, we will get y in return.' Then, it's up to the executive team to decide where and how much they want to invest."

Asking for additional resources using data and perceived ROI while tying your ask to a strategic initiative is commonly called "making a business case," and it's vital for helping executives and senior leaders make successful decisions. Before you jump into developing a business case for a new initiative, ask yourself:

- How connected are you to your company's senior leaders or executives?
- Are you the one who communicates with them or are you just receiving the communication?
- Does the person who communicates and shares resource requests to this group understand L&D well enough to filter the best information as well as advocate for your work?
- Can you provide information to the senior leaders or executives that will help them make smart decisions about resource allocation?

Frontline and Middle Managers

Frontline employees are the people in your company who do the on-the-ground work, interacting with customers or clients directly. They turn leaders' visions into reality. Their supervisors, the organization's frontline or middle managers, have an up close and personal view of frontline employees' daily challenges. They see firsthand where breakdowns and disconnects occur. Because of this intimate and important knowledge, frontline and middle managers should be included on L&D's key stakeholder list.

Managers' plates tend to overflow quickly. They're making fast decisions while being hit with new challenges every day related to team member performance, customer satisfaction, technology, and more. They are responsible for ensuring their teams hit performance metrics and for working on large company initiatives. Their jobs are even more difficult if they are *working managers*, who are expected to lead a team while also completing frontline work themselves.

Frontline and middle managers have the potential to occupy an L&D sweet spot where you can have the biggest influence, or they can be your most significant detractors. Let's start with your L&D sweet spot.

Jason, the senior manager of L&D at a midsize solar energy company, found that working with middle managers was an ideal way for his team to quickly earn credibility for their work. He said a big part of working as an SBP is "finding the people leaders who are close to the front lines, the ones who are drowning and overwhelmed. Those are the ones who, if you can just take one thing off their plates, will remember that forever."

According to Jason, these leaders are valuable allies because they wield such credibility and influence. Often, he finds middle managers are drowning because "they're taking a lot on or people are giving them a lot of stuff because they're good at what they do, and people trust them."

After his team started partnering with these managers, Jason noticed his team's credibility was improving. The managers told others in the organization about L&D's work and how it was making an impact on the business. As a result, Jason's work and position as an SBP improved as well.

However, the influence of frontline and middle managers can also detract from L&D's work. If these managers send negative messages about training or L&D initiatives, their team members listen.

Sarah, the learning and organization development manager for a midsize retail company, explained that when managers tell their teams, "Sorry, you have to go do this crappy training," they have just created a feeling of dread among those employees. As a result, those employees are predisposed to hate the training experience and arrive with that attitude intact. Essentially, these managers have sabotaged their team's ability to learn.

Your relationship with key frontline and middle managers can make or break the success and influence of your work in L&D. Try to step into their shoes, and ask yourself:

- What challenges are the managers facing each day, and what pressures are they under?
- What data are they expected to provide?
- How are they held accountable?
- What successes do they celebrate?
- How can you partner to help them succeed?

These five groups of key stakeholders each play an important role in whether you will be able to work successfully as an SBP. They have the power to advance or block progress for the L&D function, so it's important to understand their value and who they are at your company. Take a few minutes to list the names of people in each group at your organization. If you don't know them, try to find out so you can take further steps to build your relationship (which we'll discuss in the rest of this chapter).

YOUR TURN

Define Your Key Stakeholders
Take a few minutes to identify the key stakeholders in each category:
- My L&D team includes:
- My boss is:
- My organization's HR leaders and HRBPs are:
- My organization's executives and senior leaders are:
- The frontline and middle managers that I am expected to work with include:

Define Stakeholders' Perceptions

If you know me, you know I love my colorful Converse sneakers. One day at an outlet mall, while in search of a new pair, I walked up to the large directory and looked for the most important information. Nope, it wasn't the store's location. First, I needed to find the big red circle indicating "you are here." We can't get where we are going if we don't know where we are starting.

If your goal is working as an SBP, and you have identified the key stakeholders who can help you realize that goal, you have already taken the first essential steps. But the path looks a little different for each key stakeholder. You will need to adjust accordingly based on where you are starting, and you will need something to help you find that big red "you are here" marker for each. Luckily, there is a tool that can help: the strategic business partner formula.

The Strategic Business Partner Formula

The SBP formula helps you identify each key stakeholder's current perception of your work and provide a clear direction for your next steps.

Creating this formula was a turning point in my work—suddenly, I could see why I wasn't gaining momentum with various stakeholders. The resulting aha moments cascaded one after another as I progressed more rapidly toward becoming an SBP. In addition to explaining why I wasn't progressing with specific stakeholders, the formula also changed the way I approached my work with them in a positive way.

The SBP formula includes two elements: respectful relationships and robust business knowledge. When you achieve both with each key stakeholder, you can become a true strategic business partner.

A Respectful Relationship

A respectful relationship is defined by how well you and the key stakeholder know each other. The relationship doesn't need to be deep and personal. You don't need to be their best friend, but you do need to respect each other's work. When questions come up regarding L&D, the stakeholder should think of you immediately. Likewise, when you have a question about their area of expertise, you should immediately reach out to them.

My favorite example of a respectful relationship was the one I had with Jolene, an HRBP whom I collaborated with regularly. She and I struggled to connect at first, in part because I picked up on something that felt like competition in our early conversations. She wasn't my favorite person in the company, and I know she didn't look forward to having me on her calendar either.

But, over time, we developed a powerful mutual respect. Instead of thinking about her as the competition, I reminded myself to assume positive intent and saw why Jolene was so good at her job. She began to respect my work as well. Our conversations were less contentious, and we became each other's go-to ally for HR and talent development challenges. We didn't go for drinks after hours or hang out at the park with our kids, but when it came to work, we were at the top of each other's lists.

Robust Business Knowledge

We've discussed the importance of understanding the basics of your business, but the SBP formula requires you to dig a little deeper to learn the specifics of the business that apply to each key stakeholder. When I talk about *robust business knowledge*, I mean that you need to understand—as much as you are able—what it's like to sit in a key stakeholder's seat each day. What are their biggest challenges, goals, and pressures? What key performance metrics measure their team's success? What are they doing to meet those metrics? You need to have a sense of the cadence of their work. When are they busiest? When do they have breathing room? What does the organization ask of them?

Most importantly, you should know the purpose of each key stakeholder's work and how they contribute to the overall goals and function of the company. You should be able to tell a pretty convincing version of their story, even if they aren't in the room to back you up.

For me, gaining robust business knowledge was the biggest game changer when I adopted the SBP formula. I knew how to build relationships and had solid knowledge of how the company functioned, its workflows, and financials. But I hadn't drilled down to understand each stakeholder's unique business needs. I hadn't studied their reports or asked business-related questions on the occasions when we met face-to-face or online. I almost always stuck to my script of L&D-related questions, which meant we stayed in an L&D-related

box. Is it any wonder they saw me as an order taker? I was the nice person who did learning stuff, not a business partner who did business stuff.

When trying to master the formula, remember that you may begin with a completely respectful relationship with one stakeholder but little robust business knowledge. In contrast, your standing with another stakeholder might be the opposite. To work as an SBP, you need to focus on the weakest element. How do you know your weaknesses? As we'll discuss in the next section, you can apply the formula to the SBP grid.

The Strategic Business Partner Grid

The SBP grid is where the real magic happens. When we use the SBP formula to build it, we combine elements in specific ways for each key stakeholder. The result is a visual representation of each key stakeholder's perception of your work, which you can then use to inform your actions. Let's try it.

Begin by drawing a grid with a vertical and horizontal axis (Figure 6-1). Label the vertical axis "Respectful Relationship" or just "Relationship." Label the horizontal axis "Robust Business Knowledge" or "Business Knowledge." Draw two perpendicular lines in the middle to form four quadrants. Where the axes come together in the lower-left corner indicates a low rating for each element. The further from the lower-left corner you travel on each axis, the stronger that element is in your formula.

Figure 6-1. Blank Strategic Business Partner Grid

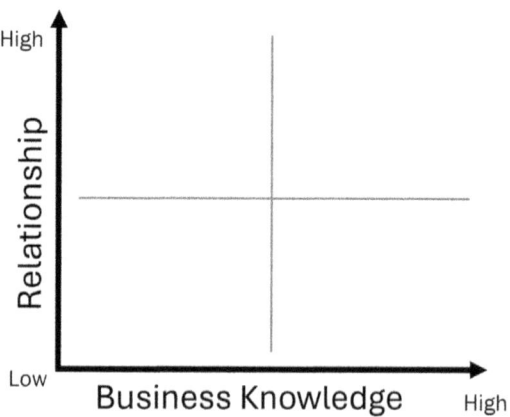

Next, think of your key stakeholders. These are the people you identified earlier in this chapter. Place each one on the grid based on your perception of the strength of your respectful relationship and your knowledge of their business area. I often find that it's easiest to start with frontline and middle managers. Be brutally honest—this grid is for your eyes only. Figure 6-2 shows an example of what adding stakeholders looks like.

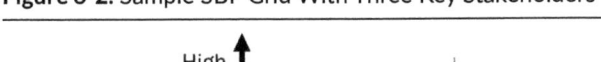

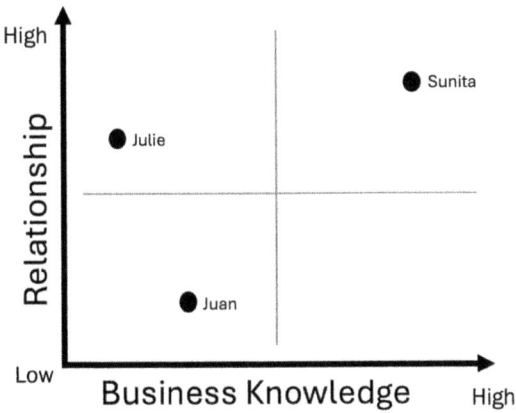

Once you've filled in this grid, you've got a visual depiction of your standing with each of your key stakeholders based on the SBP formula. If you are working as an SBP with a particular stakeholder, your respectful relationship and robust business knowledge are high, so that person will show up in the upper-right quadrant, like Sunita in Figure 6-2. If you lack a solid, respectful relationship and also lack knowledge of the stakeholder's business area, that person will appear in the lower-left quadrant, like Juan.

Most of us have key stakeholders in all four quadrants. Becoming an SBP isn't an all-or-nothing proposition; it's a process that progresses differently with each person. By identifying stakeholders with whom your standing is low, you can create a perfect starting point to begin moving the needle.

I have labeled the four quadrants in Figure 6-3, one for each type of learning leader that key stakeholders might perceive you to be based on your interactions. Are you an SBP (top right), instructor (bottom right), notetaker (bottom left), or friendly advocate (top left)? Let's consider what each label means and what they look like in real life.

Figure 6-3. SBP Grid With Quadrant Labels

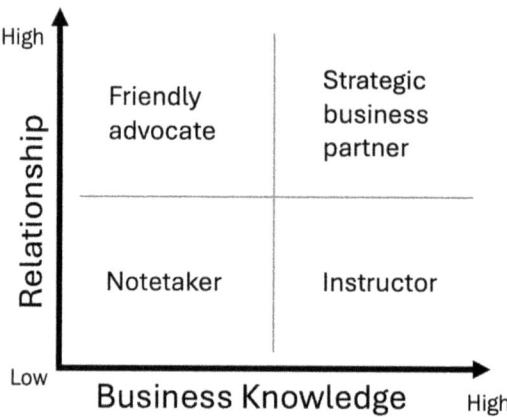

The Notetaker

If you placed a key stakeholder in the bottom-left quadrant, you have little knowledge of that stakeholder's business and you don't know each other well. For that stakeholder, you are nothing more than a *notetaker*. If you meet with them, you may take in information and write down the details of their order. You may ask good questions about learning objectives and success measures, but this won't be enough. The lack of a relationship with this person, combined with your lack of knowledge about their business, means you aren't poised to go deeper or push back on a request if you think it won't be received well.

I recall a moment after my company had been acquired when I left a meeting thinking, "I was nothing more than a notetaker for the past hour." My new boss had told me about a request to provide project management training for the finance team. I met with Ming, the finance VP who placed the request. I had never before met her and hadn't worked with her business unit yet. At the last minute, my boss joined our conversation and asked Ming to explain her request so I could understand the type of training we needed to create.

Ming's explanation was curt, and I sensed annoyance. She explained that she had participated in project management training at her previous company and wanted to provide the same thing in our organization. So, she needed the internal L&D team to create and deliver the whole training program.

I dove into my usual questions, with my boss listening to every word and jumping in to clarify or ask her own questions from time to time. Ming continued giving short responses, insisting that the training happen within the next couple months.

I didn't have a respectful relationship with Ming and had very little knowledge of her business, and she wasn't open to me finding out more about her or her work. I took notes and felt completely stuck. She was firmly located in the lower-left quadrant of my grid.

I wish our first meeting had played out differently. What if the expectation was for me to *learn about her business* instead of taking an order? What if I had known that my team might be working with this particular business unit earlier, and we had had time to meet and discuss a strategy before that crucial meeting? I knew I needed to build a relationship with Ming and establish more knowledge about her business to show up as a supportive SBP. Neither option was in play.

If you find yourself in the position of notetaker, as I did with Ming, your next steps need to be building a respectful relationship and increasing your robust business knowledge. If you have to begin by fulfilling the request, don't let the relationship end there.

The Instructor

If you have great knowledge of your stakeholder's business, but not much of a relationship with the person, you function as an instructor. You could (and maybe do) train others on business processes, technology, and workflows. Perhaps you even design training. Chances are, you know who the key stakeholder is, and they may know that you play a part in the training or learning function, but that's where your relationship ends. Your job is to deliver a simple training transaction, with the understanding that you know the business well. That's exactly what keeps you in an order-taking role.

When I was learning how to move away from the role of order taker toward becoming an SBP, I took on the challenge of building relationships and increasing my business knowledge with all our key stakeholders. Because our organization was growing rapidly, it soon became clear that I could not be the only person to perform this role. I started using my SBP formula and grid to coach and develop the skills of others on my team.

One of my team members, Bella, was stuck in the instructor quadrant. She had grown up in the company and worked in many roles before moving to the L&D team. She was a product expert who could recite everything about a particular product with ease, and she made it fun for others to learn. She excelled in onboarding and upskilling employees and became an effective facilitator. But, after she was promoted to a senior L&D team member, I asked her to go beyond instructor and take on an SBP role. Her struggle was real.

Although Bella could talk about products and business practices backward and forward, our key stakeholders knew her only as a trainer. She hadn't developed respected relationships with them and struggled to come out from behind her technical mask during meetings. So, I asked her to refrain from talking about training and the product she knew and loved. She looked as if I had presented her with the world's most complex and confusing puzzle. "But what will I talk to them about?" she asked. "I'm there to talk about training, right?"

I explained that her promotion meant that her job now included getting to know the stakeholders' interests and needs beyond technical training.

She frowned, "You know I'm not a warm and fuzzy person."

"Yes. I know that's not who you are," I chuckled. "But I'm not asking you to change that part of yourself. I'm asking you to change your conversation to expand the topics and show interest in their day-to-day work lives outside training."

We came up with a list of topics she could ask the stakeholders about, including what they liked most and least about their jobs, goals they were working on within their teams, how they thought those goals would lead to improvement, the biggest challenges and roadblocks they faced in meeting those goals, and recent successes.

Asking a key stakeholder to share more details about their daily work life and listening to the answers—even if you aren't the "warm and fuzzy" type—helps to improve a respectful relationship. Showing genuine interest, without pushing your agenda or topics (in Bella's case, training and product knowledge) is one of the fastest ways to improve a relationship and earn the respect needed to become an SBP.

The Friendly Advocate

If you have a great relationship with a stakeholder, but don't know much about the details of their business, you are a friendly advocate. You can say positive things about the stakeholder as a person and leader, but you don't know enough about their day-to-day business to create effective solutions or be taken seriously as a partner. They see you as a nice person who does training, not someone they can turn to for help with serious challenges.

This quadrant is where all of my aha moments began. I was meeting regularly with Sandy, a key stakeholder; we said hello in the halls and the breakroom, and she seemed to enjoy our conversations. But no matter what I did, I could tell she still saw me as an order taker. I couldn't move the needle.

The tipping point came when I began to ask Sandy more in-depth questions about her business. I asked to see the monthly performance reports she provided to the C-suite, which led to immediate confusion. I'm certain she was thinking: "Why would the training person want to see performance metrics? Well, I like her, and she seems interested. Fine. I'll give it a shot. I'm certain she won't read them anyway."

The next time I met with Sandy, I had read her reports thoroughly and had new questions. Once she understood I genuinely wanted to learn, she was delighted to share her struggles. That day, my standing with Sandy began to shift from order taker toward strategic business partner.

The Strategic Business Partner

If you have a solid respectful relationship with the stakeholder and a robust knowledge of their business, you are exactly where you need to be to work as an SBP. You will likely need to make a few tweaks along the way (as I'll discuss in the next few chapters), but you have a solid footing. You can push back on requests, ask more critical and in-depth questions, and engage in problem solving with the stakeholder without reproach. Chances are, the more you participate with them in this way, the more they will appreciate and expect your partnership.

The most solid SBP relationship I ever had was with Luis. Over the years, as we developed a respectful relationship and my robust knowledge of his business grew, my team evolved from an order-taking machine to a strategic business partnership in his eyes.

Meetings with Luis often turned into brainstorming and coaching sessions, and we'd leave energized and armed with the next steps. We talked about training and talent challenges. How could his team reduce their time doing administrative work so they could interact more with customers? How could we creatively help our customers gain more knowledge about our products and services without adding extra work to the team's plate? Luis welcomed the conversations that allowed us to partner to come up with solutions.

A Goal, Not a Reality (Yet)

Working with every key stakeholder within the SBP quadrant of the grid is always the goal, but I have yet to encounter any relationship that *starts* there. It's up to us to put in the work to move to that top-right quadrant. If you are in one of the other quadrants, pat yourself on the back for identifying your "you are here" marker.

> **YOUR TURN**
>
> **Use the Strategic Business Partner Grid**
> Return to the list of key stakeholders you created at the end of chapter 3. Place each one into an SBP grid based on your level of respectful relationship and knowledge of their business.

We can't earn trust without effort. It develops as we meet with and do our work with each stakeholder, not beforehand. The key is to use our initial work with someone as an opportunity to engage more deeply, moving toward the role of SBP through an intentional effort to improve areas that are lacking. The remainder of this chapter provides some suggestions for how to do this.

Improve Your Respectful Relationship

If your standing with a stakeholder landed you in the notetaker or instructor quadrants, your next step is to improve your relationship. I find the best way to do this is through a learning purpose meeting, but there are a few additional actions you can take to follow up and continue building the relationship, including holding regular touch-base meetings, following through on promises, and respecting the stakeholder's business goals and cadence.

The Learning Purpose Meeting

In a learning purpose meeting, the sole goal is to learn more about a person and their role in the organization. If you are new to your role, the company, or an area of the organization, it's easy to set this up. Play the "I'm new" card and ask for an introductory meeting to learn more. If the stakeholder is new to the organization, that's also an excellent opportunity. Ask about their philosophy and approach to work, setting the stage for further conversations as they get established.

If you have been working in the organization or with a stakeholder for a while, the meeting request may seem more difficult, but it can still be done. Ask for time on the stakeholder's calendar to step back and reframe your relationship so you can learn more about their work and become a better partner.

The learning purpose meeting should be short (30 minutes or less) if possible. If your company culture allows for a longer meeting, go for it! I have found that asking for 30 minutes is more acceptable and seems like less of an interruption in the day for stakeholders, but in some organizations, an hour to learn is the norm.

The key is to outline expectations up front. Stress that the meeting's purpose is for you to learn more about the stakeholder's role and their team's work so you can become a better partner in your role as an L&D leader. You can even provide a few questions in advance in case people like to think about and process their answers ahead of time.

Remember, this meeting is not about you. You can explain your role in the organization and share a version of your L&D purpose statement, but your goal is to be *interested*, not *interesting*. My favorite way to start is to say, "Thanks for meeting with me today. I'm interested in learning more about you, your team, and your role in the organization so I can do the best work possible to partner with you. In my role as [*insert your role*], my team and I focus on [*insert L&D purpose statement*]."

Then, I ask the stakeholder several questions to start learning. Here are some of my favorites:
- Tell me about your career up until this point. How did you end up in this role?
- What do you spend most of your time doing in this role?
- How many people are on your team?
- What are the different roles on the team?
- What do the people in these roles spend their time doing each day?
- What is your favorite part of this role?
- What do you find most challenging about this role?
- How can I (or my team) best partner with you and your team from here on out?

As you can see, none of these are hard-hitting or deep questions. The goal is not to solve problems or explore complex business challenges; it's to learn more about the person who is sitting in the stakeholder chair and to set the stage for future conversations when hard-hitting questions are more appropriate.

It's best to hold meetings with key stakeholders in person to form a stronger connection. The second best option is a virtual meeting with a camera on so you can use facial expressions to convey warmth and connection. If your goal is to know and be known in a respected relationship, sharing your face will get you further than your voice alone. If you absolutely cannot make faces a part of the meeting, then an old-fashioned audio phone call will do.

No matter the method, this meeting is designed to help you start to get to know your stakeholder better.

Hold Regular Touch-Base Meetings

If possible, ask each key stakeholder if you can set up a recurring touch-base meeting, beyond specific project meetings, to connect and continue to learn. The frequency can vary, and they should be only 15 to 30 minutes long. My touch-base meetings ranged from biweekly to quarterly, depending on the scope of work I was doing with a particular stakeholder and the time they had available. The purpose of these meetings is to touch base on goals and challenges. Again, try to see their faces, if possible.

Try adapting these topics to your organization and incorporating them into your touch-base meetings:

- **Status check for collaborative projects.** How are they going? What could be better? What is going well? Have you heard anything from others that I should know?
- **Performance metric trends.** Ask questions related to the data reports you are reading.
- **Updates or changes related to current challenges and goals.**
- **If you have time, ask another question;** for example, what has been the most fun or the most frustrating issue in your work recently?

Follow Through on Promises

Your goal is to create a strong, trusting relationship with each key stakeholder. One surefire way to quickly erode that trust is to fail to meet promised deadlines or complete promised work. If you say you'll do something, even something small like following up on a question or sending a meeting recap, be sure to do this by the deadline or earlier. Showing you can be counted on for small things opens the door to trust in larger initiatives and projects.

Respect the Stakeholder's Business Goals and Cadence

Show (don't just say) that you understand the stakeholder has other high-priority items on their plate. Ask about and make note of major goals, especially if they anticipate important deadlines or large amounts of work. Move touch-base meetings as needed and as requested. Keep the stakeholder's work cadence in mind when planning solutions. For example, don't recommend in-person training at the busiest time of year for the stakeholder and their team members.

> **YOUR TURN**
>
> **Create a Checklist for Improving Respectful Relationships**
> Your goal is to establish a relationship with each key stakeholder in which you respect each other's work and think of each other as a go-to supporter. Use these suggestions to guide you in starting and maintaining a relationship of mutual respect:

- **Set up a learning purpose meeting (20–30 minutes).** Focus on meeting and learning more about the stakeholder.
- **Set up recurring touch-base meetings (15–30 minutes).** Focus on increasing your business knowledge, staying up to date, and continuing to build your relationship. Listen actively and ask questions to help you understand.
- **Follow through on all promises, big and small (ongoing).** Respect the stakeholder's goals and business cadence. Move meetings to take urgent business needs into account.
- **Build your own checklist!** What additional questions would you like to ask your stakeholders to build your relationship with them?

Increase Your Robust Business Knowledge

Not knowing enough about the stakeholder's business is one of the biggest mistakes I see L&D professionals make. Without understanding the goals, daily work tasks, common challenges, and cadence of your stakeholders and their teams, it is almost impossible to create successful learning and performance solutions. Providing learning experiences that don't solve the stakeholder's problems wastes resources, erodes trust, and secures your place as an order taker rather than an SBP.

If the SBP grid revealed your standing with any stakeholder to be a note-taker or a friendly advocate, you'll need to begin working to increase your business knowledge. Learn the following essentials about each key stakeholder and their team:

- The role of the stakeholder's business unit within the overall business strategy.
- The stakeholder and their team's role in bringing in revenue and how much they bring in.
- The stakeholder's major expenses.
- The roles and responsibilities of individual team members within the stakeholder's business unit.
- The primary outcome the stakeholder is working toward each day.
- The cadence of the stakeholder's business, including the busiest and slowest times of the year and the type of work they do during each.

- The primary performance metrics that determine team members' success.
- The challenges the stakeholder and their team encounter most often and those they are currently facing.
- The goals and major initiatives the stakeholder and their team are working toward.

You will need several strategies to find all this information. Consider these options as a starting point:

- **Review the stakeholder's website or company intranet site.** An external-facing website will tell you what the stakeholder is communicating to customers, while the internal site will share information specific to team members and their work. It may even include goals, challenges, and organizational structure. And by reviewing this information online, you can learn more without having to set up a meeting.
- **Review relevant onboarding materials.** Find out what specific onboarding materials are provided to the stakeholder's new employees. Ask for access if possible and specify that you want to learn more about the stakeholder's business so you can provide even better solutions for their challenges.
- **Review business reports from key stakeholders.** Most business units and teams are responsible for reporting their progress regularly. Ask the stakeholder to include you in the distribution list or provide access to regular reporting. If you are initially denied, don't give up. Keep building your relationship and asking to learn more. Once you've deepened your trust, ask again. Be sure to share that you want to learn more about their business so you can partner in creating learning solutions that support their metrics and key results the company is asking of them. These reports can provide fantastic insight into the challenges a stakeholder is facing and their most important initiatives and outcomes.
- **Ask new questions as you learn more.** As you learn about the stakeholder's business through these materials, gather questions about items you don't understand or would like to learn more about. Then,

ask for more information at your next touch-base meeting with that stakeholder. This shows your interest in understanding and helps build your position as an invested partner. Stakeholders are more likely to trust L&D if they believe those professionals understand their business.

> **YOUR TURN**
>
> **Create a Robust Business Knowledge Checklist**
> Focus on learning about your stakeholder's business and their team's work. Revisit or clarify information in touch-base meetings. Use these topics as jumping-off points:
> - The role of this stakeholder's business unit within the overall business strategy
> - The role of the stakeholder and their team in bringing in revenue and how much they bring in
> - The stakeholder's major expenses
> - The roles and responsibilities of individual team members within the stakeholder's business unit
> - The primary outcome this stakeholder is working toward each day (for example, providing excellent customer service)
> - The cadence of the stakeholder's business including the busiest and slowest times of the year and the type of work done during each
> - The stakeholder's primary performance metrics (ask for access to any regular reporting)
> - The challenges the stakeholder and their team encounter most often and the challenges they are currently facing
> - The goals and major initiatives the stakeholder is working toward
> - Build your own checklist! What additional information would you like to access or know to better understand your stakeholder's business?

The SBP formula and corresponding grid are solid tools to assess your standing with each key stakeholder and point you in the right direction in terms of next steps. Determine if you need to improve your respectful relationship, increase your robust business knowledge, or both. Then, take the actions necessary to achieve those goals.

Summary

Five key stakeholder groups have the potential to advance or block L&D progress. These are the most critical groups that you must partner with if you want to move from order taker to SBP:

- **Your L&D team** must be on board with your goals and all rowing in the same direction. Use your internal L&D playbook and frequent communication to ensure everyone is working supportively together.
- **Your boss** needs to be able to advocate for L&D in circles where you do not sit. Lead up to help equip and empower this person.
- **HRBPs and HR** can help L&D quickly understand the business and build trust. A strong partnership allows both teams to serve as extensions of each other.
- **Executives and senior leaders** create strategic initiatives for the company and make informed decisions about where to allocate resources. L&D needs to know and align the initiatives and provide necessary data for decision making.
- **Frontline and middle managers** are close to daily frontline success and breakdowns. They often feel overwhelmed, so helping to solve their problems can be a way to gain credibility.

You can begin addressing what's holding you back from working as an SBP with your key stakeholders by applying the elements of the SBP formula to the SBP grid. With the information the grid reveals, you can identify your best next steps.

Becoming an SBP starts with a simple, two-element formula: respectful relationships + robust business knowledge. Place each key stakeholder on the SBP grid to assess which element needs your focus, and determine if you are currently a notetaker, instructor, friendly advocate, or strategic business partner in your relationship. Build a strategy in your work with each stakeholder to improve your respectful relationship, increase your robust business knowledge, or both.

PART 3

Daily Practice

CHAPTER 7
Partner With Your Key Stakeholders

If you've followed the guidance in the first two parts of this book, you have laid the foundation for your work as an SBP and are making progress toward many of your goals. You've embraced the business basics and created an internal and external L&D playbook. You've identified key stakeholders in your organization and examined their perceptions of your work. Now, it's time to build a sturdy, lasting structure on top of your foundation. In this chapter, we'll discuss how to navigate the daily demands of an SBP to form strong partnerships with stakeholders and create an environment in which you and your organization will thrive.

Eight Best Practices for Partnering With Stakeholders

In business, partners trust one another as equals, working to overcome challenges and achieve mutually beneficial outcomes. But partners inevitably have different personalities, approaches, and workloads. Partnering with your key stakeholders depends less on rigid rules and more on simple best practices for interaction. The eight best practices I recommend—which I've summarized in the checklist in the sidebar—can help ensure your stakeholder interactions are as productive and successful as possible, building essential trust in the process.

Best Practices for Partnering With Stakeholders
1. Rise above organizational politics.
2. Communicate continuously and consistently.
3. Lean into what's most important.
4. Trust your business partner's expertise.
5. Use facilitative leadership skills.
6. Tap into the naysayers.
7. Share your success.
8. Work with a partner mindset.

1. Rise Above Organizational Politics

Let's start with concept everyone loves to hate—organizational politics. In a 2023 study by Pepperdine University's Graziadio Business School, 59 percent of respondents reported a negative view of that topic. I used to be in that camp.

Early in my career, I was easily frustrated by the unwritten rules and relationships that seemed to run my workplace and sometimes derail progress. In my mind, the concept of *organizational politics* was impossible to nail down; it was a given that I was just supposed to accept. I eventually discovered that we don't have to simply accept the politics handed down to us or "play the game." We can do better than that.

When I began to look at organizational politics with more curiosity and explore the *whys*, I discovered two reasons politics exist. Together, these factors, which are unique in every company, determine organizational politics.

- Scarcity of resources paired with ambiguity results in competition and jockeying for power within an organization (University of Minnesota 2010).
- Humans who work together over time experience successes and failures and develop preferences about whom to trust and work with on various projects. We favor those who are easier to work with, support our fragile egos, and help us reach our goals.

As my career progressed, I discovered that the underlying problem wasn't organizational politics themselves. The projects I cared about were being derailed when politics were deployed strictly for personal gain. I also discovered that if I relied less on my emotions and ego and more on curiosity, I could escape most of the feelings of frustration and helplessness that resulted from the roadblocks created by organizational politics.

Your challenge as an L&D leader is to understand politics enough to rise above them while simultaneously navigating the system for the greater good of the company and its people. You can do this in several ways.

Set Aside Your Ego

This is perhaps the most critical change in mindset if you want to understand and navigate organizational politics. It means looking at the company's needs first and your own agenda second. Ask, "What is best for the company?" instead of "What is best for L&D?" to keep your ego in check.

Look at the View From 10,000 Feet

I had a mentor years ago who repeated the phrase, "Look at the view from 10,000 feet," like a broken record. He was a C-suite executive who didn't have time to focus on a single area to the exclusion of others, because if he did, the business would fail. He needed to pull back and see the big picture, and he wanted other leaders in his corner to see the world from a big-picture perspective too. He taught me to zoom out to see the company as a full ecosystem in which all parts, including L&D, needed to work together to achieve overall business goals. This higher-level viewpoint provides an important perspective on what is most important and ensures that organizational politics won't be used for personal gain, but to advance the company's goals.

You may sometimes need to behave like a detective when the politics of a situation seem especially ambiguous and need to be deciphered, but instead of zooming in with a magnifying glass, you should zoom out and look at the bigger picture. Sniff out more clarity by asking more questions, especially:

- What are the overall business goals in this situation?
- What will it take for everyone to meet the goals?

Then, use the answers you discover to inform your work.

Look at Problems From the Outside In

Looking at problems with an outsider's perspective is as valuable as looking at your organization from 10,000 feet. The best time to consider things as an outsider would is when you are new to the organization or have a new team member. Your (or your employees') fresh eyes haven't been clouded by years of living within the company bubble.

If you aren't new to your company, use your imagination, especially in challenging political situations. Imagine that you are a new employee. What do you notice? What makes sense? What doesn't?

The next time you are working with a new hire, take advantage of their new perspective. During their first few months, set up a schedule for regularly receiving feedback, asking what they are noticing and what is confusing. Another effective move is to work with an external coach or mentor who can ask you questions from a different perspective.

Find a Political Guide and Mentor (or Two or Three!)

Every company has people who are more politically savvy than others. They know the systems, unwritten rules, and the people who tend to make things happen. When starting work at a new company, be on the lookout for these people. If you're lucky, your manager will be one of them.

Over time, I recommend finding more than one political guide. Seek out people with unique perspectives or special knowledge about different areas of the company who can help you work through challenges. Consider some key questions:

- Who are your best political guides at the moment?
- How have you tapped into their expertise in the past? How might you do so in the future?

Identify Influencers and Champions

Influencers and champions are incredibly helpful when it comes to navigating organizational politics. *Influencers* are people everyone seems to listen to when they speak or whose names keep coming up in conversation because they are the go-to folks for key knowledge, processes, or projects. These are colleagues you want to know because they can be political guides and help you gain buy-in for your L&D projects.

Champions are people who believe in and understand L&D as a function. Often, they will seek you out before you can find them and, when you talk with them, the conversation will be easy and the collaboration even easier. Some champions will be in your corner from the beginning, and others will join you over time as you show your value.

Mechelle, the director of L&D for a small community bank, told me about an SVP who was a pleasure to work with from the beginning. This person honored the expertise that Mechelle and her team brought to the company, and he made her feel psychologically safe. If she didn't have an answer on a call, he never made her feel incompetent but would simply ask her to follow up. Mechelle didn't have to nurture the relationship much. In L&D, we sometimes say, "work with the willing," and this SVP was that willing supporter for her.

If you are lucky enough to find someone who is both an influencer and a champion, you've struck gold! These people can move initiatives forward quickly. No matter what, count every influencer and champion you meet as a key stakeholder. Put them on your SBP grid and make sure you understand them and their work. Build a respectful relationship and a robust knowledge of their business. Ask yourself:

- Who are the most valuable influencers in your organization? Pay special attention to those in areas where you frequently interact.
- Who are your current L&D champions?

If you're searching for more influencers, pay attention during meetings and to communications you receive. Which names are mentioned most frequently? Who is involved in decision making?

Work Within the System

Organizational politics operate according to unwritten rules. You will do better to follow the norms for communication and decision making rather than trying to change them. It may sound counterintuitive, but if you are going to rise above organizational politics, avoid expending emotion or ego trying to change these unwritten rules. If you don't agree with the rules, that's OK. Instead of struggling to change them, gently expand boundaries once you have earned the trust of others in the organization. To do that, ensure that you can answer two key questions:

- What is the process for decision making within the company?
- What are the unwritten rules around communication?

Always remember that you and everyone else in the organization are on same team, and work with that in mind.

2. Communicate Continuously and Consistently

Strong communication with stakeholders is the most important skill in your work as an SBP. Make all your communication continuous and consistent. *Continuous communication* means that you avoid long periods without any communication, and *consistent communication* means that you share the same types of messages repeatedly, in ways that make sense for your stakeholders. If you want to build strong, trusting partnerships, it is important to communicate with stakeholders so they understand what you do and how to work with you. Let's discus a few best practices for to stakeholder communication.

Adapt to Stakeholders' Communication Methods and Expectations

Communicate in ways that make sense to your stakeholders. I'm not telling you to adapt every message to each stakeholder, but you can adapt to the most common ways of presenting messages for various groups throughout your company.

For example, one executive may prefer communication focused on data points with charts and graphs attached. Your HRBPs may prefer emails or instant messages, while your own L&D team may prefer meetings with follow-up emails. A frontline manager might want frequent meetings and emails in the midst of a project and scaled-back communication as the project winds down.

The best practice is to determine what and how you will communicate based on what each stakeholder group prefers or needs and to establish a consistent cadence. Creating a repeatable system of communication not only helps keep you on track with your messaging, but it also trains your stakeholders on what they can expect. If you consistently send out a monthly report with some notes, for example, stakeholders will become accustomed to receiving this report and appreciate the information. Simply put, communicating according to stakeholder preferences and expectations is essential to building trust.

There are a couple ways to determine stakeholder preferences and expectations. The first is to simply ask them what they expect or prefer in terms of communication frequency and methods. I've often heard L&D leaders note they err on the side of too much communication, and that they assume stakeholders can just delete what they don't need. This may not be a good idea. Have you ever worked with someone who floods your inbox with a new message every hour? What's your impression of that person? Maybe you're grateful they are sending the information or maybe, like me, you find it annoying. A flood of communication can make you seem disorganized, and most stakeholders don't like an overflowing inbox.

On the other hand, many of us welcome a lot of communication when it's compiled carefully and sent regularly. We might not read the full email or click on all the links and attachments but we do appreciate the access to so much valuable information. It also allows us to return to it as needed, especially if it is laid out in an organized, easy-to-read fashion.

Another way to determine stakeholders' preferences is to figure out their expectations for communication with other partners or customers. If you can find out how team members are expected to communicate with customers, follow the same rules.

Finally, pay attention to how different stakeholders communicate with you. Do they send brief emails with minimal information or more lengthy, fully formatted messages with bullets and highlighted text? Do they randomly pop into your instant messages? Do they forward supplemental information with reports? Do they copy multiple people on emails or send them only to you? People generally communicate in the same way that they prefer others communicate with them.

Rowena reported to me for several years. She managed a group of facilitators who led onboarding and other training initiatives for a few areas of the company, including the customer service team, which lived by a few rules of communication. First, they responded to every customer question or request within 24 business hours. A response didn't need to be a resolution to a customer challenge or question, but it had to inform the customer that their question was received and that the team was working on it. This expectation was written down and the team's success in meeting it was measured. Team members' emails were long and in depth. They used bullets and highlights to call out important points, and often linked to or attached supporting documentation. Their goal was to be as clear and thorough as possible. They also followed up every meeting they organized by sending an email summarizing the main points and deliverables to all involved (within 24 business hours, of course).

When the customer service team's frontline managers reached out to Rowena with a question, instead of responding, she went to work to find the answer, which required reaching out to others and waiting for their responses. Once she had an answer in hand, Rowena sent an email of just a few sentences to relay the answer—her message had no bullets, highlights, or links to relevant documents. When Rowena organized meetings with customer service team managers, she took notes and captured deliverables, but they stayed with her. She didn't send out follow-up emails because she knew what needed to be done, and the plan had been discussed and agreed to during the meeting.

You can probably already see the mismatch in communication preferences and expectations. I got a call from the frontline managers' senior leader who told me that her team was frustrated with Rowena. From their perspective, she didn't appear to be taking their requests seriously. They didn't know if she was working on their issues, questions, or projects because they sometimes waited weeks for a response, and even then, the responses lacked depth and clarity.

When I discussed this situation with Rowena, it was clear she hadn't thought about the mismatch as problematic. She was working on stakeholder questions and tracking deliverables on her own—she was on it. But her key stakeholders didn't trust her because she didn't meet their expectations and preferences. It's hard to partner with someone who doesn't trust the work you do. I explained that in order to work as a partner, Rowena needed to adjust her communication style to fit more closely with their expectations and preferences and gain trust. She had to try to respond within 24 business hours and improve the details in her emails.

YOUR TURN

Learn to Partner Effectively

Think of each of your key stakeholders, and write a list or create a spreadsheet that answers each of these questions:
- What method of communication do they prefer and how often?
- How do they tend to communicate with you? Is it brief or thorough?

- Do they have expectations of their own team or other internal partners when it comes to communication? If yes, what are those expectations?
- What information is most important for each key stakeholder to know about L&D's work? What will help them to do their jobs better? How will you communicate this information to them on a regular basis, given their expectations and preferences?

Aim for Regular Face-to-Face Connections

In my experience, nothing can substitute for a regular, synchronous connection with each of my key stakeholders. In other words, you need a face-to-face meeting (which can be virtual or in person).

In a back-and-forth, real-time conversation, you can often learn much more about a stakeholder in a short period than you can through multiple written messages. You can immediately ask for clarification or dig in deeper with follow-up questions as needed—all of which helps build understanding and connection.

Showing your face in a meeting has a powerful psychological impact, demonstrating the importance of the meeting, building trust, and enhancing relationships more than either written words or audio alone (Grossman 2024). Simply put, we trust people whose faces we have seen. If your goal is to improve your respectful relationship and build trust that is worthy of an SBP, face-to-face meetings (in person or on video) are critical.

Another benefit of face-to-face meetings is that you can see the nonverbal expressions people share in any interaction. If you can see someone's face, you can read their expressions of confusion, distrust, or delight. You can tell if they are interested or distracted. Many L&D professionals tell me they got hooked on our profession by seeing light bulb moments in people's eyes when they learned something new. Those moments can happen with stakeholders too. It's just as thrilling to see a stakeholder light up when they understand how your partnership will move their initiatives forward or improve the performance of their team as it is to see a learner's face light up in a traditional classroom.

A face-to-face, synchronous connection is the ultimate form of communication, but it can be difficult to schedule with busy stakeholders. For example,

Joe, the director of L&D at a midsize automotive manufacturing company, noted how difficult it is for him to get time with any frontline or middle managers. Any success he has comes from ensuring meetings are quick and focused. He generally opens with something broad, like, "How's business going for you right now?" and then slips in one additional question about the business.

As a VP of learning, I attempted to schedule regular monthly or quarterly touch-base meetings with my key stakeholders and encouraged my team to do the same. My goals were to improve our respectful relationship and deepen my knowledge of the current state of their business. Unless we had a specific project to discuss or brainstorm, these meetings were generally no longer than 30 minutes, and the focus was almost entirely on the stakeholder. I spent a few minutes asking if they had any questions or feedback on learning initiatives for their team at the moment. Sometimes, I shared information about other initiatives my team was working on. Often, I sent reports in advance and then asked how L&D programs were influencing performance measures. But most of the time, I asked questions to help me learn more about their work and team.

Most stakeholders were willing to schedule a quarterly 30-minute meeting at minimum, but I experienced my share of last-minute cancellations or no-shows. I learned to respect each stakeholder's work cadence, and if a touch-base meeting was scheduled during a busy period, I would proactively ask if they'd like to reschedule it or communicate by email in lieu of a meeting. I found the best approach was to ensure each stakeholder found something valuable in our meetings, and that meant I had to understand their business challenges.

Let's return to Sandy's story from chapter 6. She was the stakeholder I just couldn't crack because she saw me as the "nice training lady." I was stuck squarely in friendly advocate territory with her until I asked to be copied on her team's performance reports. While I was a friendly advocate in her mind, Sandy frequently cancelled our monthly touch-base meetings. Why should we meet? She saw me as a "nice to have" contact, but not essential when her team was struggling.

Sandy stopped cancelling our meetings after I started reading and asking questions about her business reports. Once I understood her business challenges and started brainstorming with her about how partnering with the learning team could help solve them, she saw value in our regular conversations.

Sample Agenda for a Stakeholder Touch-Base Meeting

Building your business knowledge will also pay significant dividends to help you improve your communication with key stakeholders. Here's a sample agenda you may want to adapt for your own touch-base meetings.

Before the meeting:
- Review any reports, data, or current information related to the stakeholder's work or team. Prepare questions.
- Send the stakeholder reports or other key information about the L&D team's current initiatives, especially if it's related to their team or area.
- Along with the reports and information about L&D, send them questions or an agenda in advance.

During the meeting:
- Open with broad questions:
  » How is business going right now?
  » What is your team working on?
- Continue with any specific questions based on your preparation, as well as deeper dives on challenges and successes. For example:
  » I noticed in the report that you are working on the [*insert specific*] initiative, can you tell me more about that?
  » What is the biggest challenge for your team right now?
  » What has been your biggest recent success?
- Ask for feedback on related learning initiatives or projects and answer any questions on the information you sent prior to the meeting:
  » We're working on [*insert specific*] project with your team right now. Have you heard any feedback? Do you have any questions?
- Share information about any additional current initiatives and L&D team successes.
  » The learning team is also working on [*insert specific*] and [*insert specific*] projects right now, which are tied to [*insert specific*] company strategic goal.
  » We have been really pleased to see improvement with [*insert specific*] team in their performance, based on the implementation of [*insert specific*] learning program.

After the meeting
- Send a follow-up email detailing any agreed upon deliverables or action items.
- Attach or link to documents that you discussed or may be relevant for additional information.

Use Their Language, Not Yours

Language is important. You will gain much more buy-in if the way you communicate makes sense to your stakeholders. Don't expect them to know the language of L&D, and don't use L&D jargon to impress them. Your stakeholder doesn't care about pedagogy versus andragogy, the 70-20-10 framework, or the details of your LMS. They care about whether you can use your expertise to enhance performance and move initiatives forward. They care about what L&D means for them, their work, and their teams.

At Discovery Benefits, one of our major initiatives was to centralize our onboarding program, ensure there wasn't duplication, and make it more efficient and effective. The overall strategy looked the same for each area, even though much of the content was different. It included learning one topic or task at a time in a three-part approach:

1. An asynchronous online learning course, video, or content review
2. A live lab-style, problem-based learning course led by a facilitator
3. An on-the-job training component in which each new employee worked with a veteran team member to practice a skill in real time, with real customers

The new employee would then repeat this three-part cycle with their next task. We rolled out parts one and two first and shared the overall strategy with stakeholders, but then it was time to bring them into the fold a bit more intentionally. We needed to foster an even stronger partnership with them to identify and equip team members to serve as mentors to the new hires for the on-the-job training. We also needed them to sign off on the task checklists that would be essential to this on-the-job training completion.

In a touch-base meeting, I brought up the next portion of the strategy to Sunilee, the head of the customer service teams. "It's time to add in the last component of our onboarding overhaul, and we'll need to partner even more closely," I explained. "The final component is organizing and simplifying your on-the-job training."

Sunilee immediately shut me down. "What on-the-job training?" she asked. "We don't have time to do on-the-job training! Our plates are already full."

I left discouraged and confused because the customer service teams were already doing on-the-job training; they just called it "shadowing."

Then the aha happened—we weren't speaking the same language. Sunilee thought on-the-job training meant creating a brand-new training program. All we really wanted to do was better organize and structure the shadowing they were already doing to increase consistency and improve learning. In my next meeting with Sunilee, I brought up the same next step in our strategy but swapped out my language for hers: "It's time to add in the last component of our onboarding overhaul. Last time we met I mentioned on-the-job training. But, upon further reflection, that isn't really what we need. We don't need to create an on-the-job training program that is more work for your team. What we need to do is help you structure the shadowing you are already doing so it's more organized and creates more consistent learning as a result. It's all about structured shadowing."

Sunilee was delighted. She loved the idea of structured shadowing as much as she'd balked at the idea of on-the-job training. *Structured shadowing* isn't learning industry language, but who cares? I learned my lesson about the power of using the stakeholder's language to create buy-in.

Consider your own situation and answer these two questions:
- What language do your company's business teams use to describe learning?
- Does it make sense for you to use this same language?

Stick to Your Playbook

One of the foundational requirements of becoming an SBP is setting clear expectations for what it means to work with the L&D team. That is why we focused on creating an external L&D playbook with messaging about what you typically do, how you do it, and the different roles and responsibilities involved. Now, it's time for you to walk your talk.

Your external L&D playbook can serve as a great guide for communicating with stakeholders, especially when it comes to training them how to do business with L&D, but only if you use it consistently and repeatedly—and only if you're able to communicate your message effectively.

If done well, your playbook will allow for flexibility and creativity from project to project, but you'll still be consistent about the work gets done. Things like your intake process, project roles and responsibilities, and typical project timelines should remain the same.

You will need to share the same information multiple times, playing the role that author Patrick Lencioni (2012) refers to as the "chief reminding officer." These are leaders who make it their goal to remind people of key messaging as much as possible, but they do it patiently, without frustration, knowing that it will take many "reps" before the information makes it into long-term memory and becomes a habit. The CEO of Discovery Benefits used to say, "If they roll their eyes when you start to repeat your message, then you know you've shared it just about enough." Brilliant.

Now, revisit what you said in your external L&D playbook. Are you comfortable sharing this message? Does it still apply?

Ask for Feedback—But Only If You Plan to Use It

Feedback obtained from formal and informal methods is a great communication tool. It can help inform you about what's working and what isn't and expose gaps and inefficiencies you didn't think about. However, if you want true and honest feedback, you need to make sure people know you're really listening and are committed to using it.

SBPs highly value stakeholder feedback and take it seriously, addressing and implementing changes as needed. If you don't have a plan to use the feedback you receive, then don't ask for it. Most stakeholders need to be efficient, or they won't be able to accomplish even half of the things on their plates in a day. If they take time to provide quality feedback but don't see changes being made, they'll stop providing it because they'll think it's not worth their time.

Once you gather any feedback, use it to inform your practice, iterations, or change. Actions you take based on feedback should be communicated back to the person or people who provided it. Doing so is another step to build trust. Consider these questions about your feedback process:

- Where do you most need to ask for feedback right now?
- When you receive the feedback you request, what is your plan to use it? What is your plan to communicate its use?

Provide Clear and Simple Asks or Actions

Stakeholder communication should be as simple to follow as possible. What you ask should be clear, and you are more likely to get what you need if you request one thing at a time, gradually guiding the stakeholder down a path of singular actions. In other words, ditch your laundry lists!

Nate—the senior manager of talent management, design, and leadership at a large outdoor retailer—stresses the importance of following a one-thing-at-a-time approach because this allows the stakeholder to see progress. Tangible evidence of progress takes the pressure off and sends a subtle message that you've got things under control. You have a clear vision, and each step moves you closer to reaching it.

In every meeting or communication with a stakeholder, start by asking yourself what you need them to do. What's your main ask? Once you define your ask, call it out, put it on a slide, follow-up with additional information if needed, and provide a deadline if applicable. You are making clear what you need and by when, as well as setting expectations on how best to work together right now.

Over the years, I've learned to be very specific with the ask for each stakeholder in each communication. If my question is simply for informational purposes, I state that up front. I learned this lesson from the questions that bosses asked of me: "What do you want me to do with this information? Why did you share it with me?" or "If you share this with senior leaders (or I share it on your behalf), what do you need from them as a result?"

In addition to providing clarity and direction, a specific ask will help avoid stakeholder silence, which is a frustrating outcome. This is another lesson I learned the hard way. I had spent months putting together a carefully crafted learning strategy—I had done a full analysis of the need, clarified what parts training could address, and tapped into learning best practices to design the most effective program possible. My team was on board, my boss was on board, and it was time to present the new strategy to senior leaders and other key stakeholders.

The presentation went well. The senior leaders were engaged and asked good questions. Their last words were, "You put a lot of time into this. Thank you." That was it. The virtual meeting windows closed. But I didn't get what I needed from them: the green light to continue the project.

Looking back, I couldn't blame them. I didn't ask for their commitment to back the project and support the next steps. Buried in my own thoughts of perfecting the presentation, I assumed that they would either give a thumbs up or a thumbs down at the end. Instead, I experienced stakeholder silence, and it was my fault.

After that, I started to define my asks more clearly, ensuring that any presentation or communication outlined my specific need, instead of just clearing the way for a nice comment, at best.

> **YOUR TURN**
>
> **Practice Clear and Simple Asks**
> Think about the next meeting you will have or the next piece of communication you will send.
> - What is the one action (not the laundry list, just one) you need most from the stakeholders?
> - How can you place a specific and clear ask in that communication or meeting?
> - Is it appropriate to add a deadline? If yes, how will you do that?

Follow Through on Promises, Big and Small

Lack of follow through on promises is one of the main reasons trust erodes or is never built in the first place. Without trust, you will never work successfully as an SBP.

Following through on promises doesn't only apply to key project deadlines and major deliverables; it's just as important for all the small things, including communication. If you tell someone you will get back to them by Friday, get back to them by Friday. Even if you don't have an answer at that point, you should at least let them know you are still working on the issue and give an updated deadline. Use calendar reminders as memory aids.

Every little promise you keep adds up, like coins you put in a trust-building bank. If you build trust based on the small things, you are more likely to earn trust for the big things. Consider these questions related to the level of trust you have with your stakeholders:

- How well do you keep your promises? Even your small promises to follow up?
- Do you need to create a system to stay on top of your promises? If yes, do it today!

Stakeholder trust hinges on good communication, but that alone isn't enough to help you become an effective SBP. It's also important to understand others.

3. Lean Into What's Most Important

WIIFM—short for "What's in It for Me?"—has been used in sales and marketing circles for decades. Jane Friedman (2010), editor and publishing expert, called it "the most important marketing acronym." But it's taken L&D a while to catch on.

Sales and marketing professionals use WIIFM as a prompt to figure out what their potential customers think is most important. L&D needs to use WIIFM in a similar way. Usually, you can discern what's most important to stakeholders by learning the pressures they are under to succeed, the performance metrics they need to meet, and their sources of revenue. As you build your L&D strategy, you can share it with your stakeholders much like sales and marketing teams share ideas with potential customers—by focusing on what's in it for them and how your strategy will address their pain points. For stakeholders, the WIIFM will ultimately tie to overall company goals, and this common ground can become the foundation for your conversations.

YOUR TURN

Questions About Your Key Stakeholders

Think of the key stakeholders you placed on your SBP grid. Considering what you know about their pressures, challenges, and revenue sources, answer the following questions:
- What is most important to each stakeholder?
- How does it relate to or influence the company's overall strategic initiatives?
- What is currently blocking progress for each stakeholder? (These are their pain points.)
- How will the projects or initiatives you are currently working on address this stakeholder's pain points or remove their blockers?

4. Trust Their Expertise

One of my favorite quotes is from Mother Teresa: "You can do things I cannot. I can do things you cannot. Together we can do great things." The best, most successful partnerships and all great SBPs operate with a "together we can do great things" mindset.

You are an expert in all things L&D, but you are not an expert in your stakeholders' work. The good news is that you just need to trust them. Stand alongside them as a partner and master collaborator, eager to pair your expertise (what you can do) with their expertise (what you cannot do) to create an outcome neither of you could have created alone (do great things).

Like so much of working as an SBP, this requires setting your ego aside and entering conversations with confidence in your abilities and the humility to admit that you don't know it all. Recognize that the stakeholder knows more than you do about their area and then treat them as an equal who is doing their best to solve problems, just like you are.

It can be tempting to call out a stakeholder if you think you see a glaring gap or reason for their struggle. Take it from Joe—the director of L&D for a midsize automotive manufacturing company—who learned the hard way that this isn't the best course of action.

Joe was in his first L&D manager role, and he wanted the training function to be more performance focused. When he got a call from a manager saying, "My quality auditors aren't doing one of the reports they need to complete, and they need training," Joe was eager to determine whether training was really the solution to the problem.

He sat down with the manager and asked whether the quality auditors had ever completed the reports in the past. "Yes," she said. "They've all done them before. They just aren't doing them now."

Joe knew that if the auditors had done the reports before, they could do them again. The problem wasn't training. "It's not them," he explained to the manager. "It's you. You're not holding them accountable."

When the manager quickly ended the meeting, Joe realized his mistake. He hadn't trusted that the manager knew the team well. He hadn't even given her a chance to share her side of the story. He had to call her back, tail between his legs, with an apology. He told her that he made a mistake and asked if she would consider revisiting the conversation.

I find that the hardest time to trust the expertise of a stakeholder is when I don't appreciate their work style or genuinely don't relate to them on a personal level. I like to think that I work well with most people, but we all have colleagues who rub us the wrong way, and I'm no exception.

I've combatted my own frustrations in the past and built a path for trust by trying to figure out what each person is good at doing. The people who rub us the wrong way are in their role for a reason. An effective SBP tries to find that reason.

Simone was a challenging stakeholder for me. For years, our conversations didn't quite line up, and we were never on the same page. However, two things led me to see her genius. The first was a major company reorganization, ordered by a new chief operating officer. As leaders tried to make sense of the changes for their teams, I watched Simone passionately fight for her team and their customers. She was fiercely loyal and did her best to protect people. Loyalty and care were part of her genius.

I realized the second aspect of her genius when we were thrown onto a last-minute work team to solve an urgent customer education problem. We had to move fast, and I saw how brilliant Simone was at executing a plan and keeping everything moving.

Leadership leaks vertically. Simone and her team were focused first on caring for the customer and they combined that with a laser focus on the details of execution. After I better understood where her talents shone brightest, I developed a newfound respect for the way she did her work.

> **YOUR TURN**
>
> **Consider Your Stakeholders' Expertise**
> Would you say that you trust and honor your stakeholders' expertise? For example, do you ask questions that allow their expertise to shine? If you have a particularly difficult stakeholder, can you identify their genius? How can you partner with that person in a way that honors and taps into that genius?

5. Use Your Facilitative Leadership Skills

Facilitative leadership is a skill that many in L&D don't even realize is a skill because it often comes naturally. If you have ever worked as a true facilitator who draws knowledge out of others, as is done in many leadership and professional development courses, you have used facilitative leadership. The same skill translates to working effectively with stakeholders. It's part of the art of influence.

Unlike someone who walks into a room as an expert, a facilitative leader walks in with curiosity, leading with questions and patience. The questions provide the space for reflection and critical thinking. The patience allows both to happen without pressure.

Sometimes, to demonstrate this skill to learning leaders in conference sessions, I have them partner up and practice asking questions with two agendas in their head. First, I have them ask a simple question like, "What session have you found most valuable at the conference thus far?" I tell them to act impatient, like they don't really want to wait or listen for the answer. Then, I have them ask, "What has been your biggest takeaway from the conference thus far?" But this time, I tell them to do so with patience, showing they are willing to wait for the person to think and are OK with the silence that comes with it. They understand that patience is a gift to the other person, and give them time to process.

We debrief about how the two exchanges, modified by the question asker's attitude, felt different. The answers flood in. Many of the participants report feeling "safer" or "more thoughtful" in the second round. They talk about how the person's tone was calmer and more curious. Those asking the question report that the second round felt less stressful because they were more focused, calm, and genuinely curious. Asking a question with a modified mindset creates more space for answers.

Apply this technique with a stakeholder and watch similar results unfold, especially if you are helping someone see the potential implications for a decision or certain course of action.

Let's go back to Joe, the director of L&D at a midsize automotive manufacturing company. Despite his failed interaction with the quality manager, Joe has since developed his facilitative leadership skills to a high level and finds he leans on them, more often than not, in conversations with stakeholders.

He uses these skills as a strategy to co-create an idea with a stakeholder, instead of running in and announcing his ideas. Joe says that he stays curious and asks questions like, "What are the implications of this type of decision or this approach?" In response, stakeholders help create the outcome, which is often one that Joe already had in mind or some variation thereof. But because they helped to create it, the stakeholder is fully bought in.

Joe is quick to point out that as much as buy-in is part of his goal, he also wants to give the stakeholders the time and space needed to answer the questions for themselves. Often, what stakeholders—especially functional managers—share in these meetings is information they already have in their heads but don't have time in their daily work to stop and think about.

He finds this is typically the case when a manager requests training that Joe knows won't solve the problem. Now, instead of telling them training isn't the answer, he asks questions that help the requesters see the situation more clearly for themselves. His conversation provides the space for them to think critically.

> **YOUR TURN**
>
> **Apply Your Skills**
> Consider the most recent interactions you've had with key stakeholders.
> - Did you use facilitative leadership skills in conversation with them?
> - Did you start with curiosity and patience, allowing time and space to co-create a solution?
> - If so, how do you think the outcome benefitted? If not, what would you do differently?
>
> Now, consider the next conversation you intend to have with a stakeholder.
> - How will you ensure that you start with a curious and patient approach?
> - How will you ask questions in such a way that you provide time and space for critical thinking, while genuinely listening for the answers?

6. Tap Into the Naysayer Network

Every company has L&D naysayers—the people who seem to be against your every move. They are not willing to work with you as an SBP. They probably want to place you smack in the middle of order-taking territory and leave you there. However, these people can be an important part of your solutions, and they may even be influencers who can help you move a solution forward.

Elizabeth—the head of global learning and leadership development at a large, international manufacturing company—tries to strategically include those who are seen as naysayers when forming new programs and strategies. For example, when her team was working on their external L&D playbook, outlining how different groups throughout the company can partner with the learning team, she intentionally asked for feedback from naysayers.

She started by reaching out to those naysayers whom her team would need to partner with often in the future. Now, even if these people didn't provide feedback and remained in the naysayer camp, the learning team would be familiar with their objections.

Her ask was simple: "We're building a playbook of how teams can best work with learning and leadership development. Would you be willing to tell us whether what we come up with will work? We value your feedback."

Some of the naysayers were interested at first, and then their participation waned. Elizabeth followed up to make sure they weren't doing something behind the scenes and just hadn't communicated it yet, but also to give them an out. She let them know that if their priorities changed and they were no longer worried about the playbook, it was OK. They would have the chance to work together on a future project.

But some of the naysayers started to lean in and provide meaningful feedback, both formally and informally. Elizabeth ran into one of these naysayers in the company cafeteria. They said, "Hey, I've been meaning to reach out. I have some thoughts on how we might be able to revamp how we do our new-employee orientation. I wanted to run them by you."

This might seem like an inconsequential comment, but for Elizabeth, it was a significant step forward from order taker toward SBP. This naysayer now understood that they could work with Elizabeth and her team to brainstorm, instead of just making requests.

Mechelle, the director of L&D at a small community bank, successfully turned a naysayer into a partner by paying attention to that person's biggest needs. When Mechelle started at the bank, she continuously heard negative things about Sue. Others in the company didn't want to partner with Sue due to her sharp tongue and unpleasant attitude. But Mechelle believed in respect before rumors. So, she kept reaching out, inviting Sue to be a partner instead of running the other way.

In her first few meetings with Sue, Mechelle watched and listened. She was curious to find out why Sue had developed such a negative reputation. Then, Mechelle started to notice something. Sue started most calls skeptical and guarded, but if Mechelle followed up via email or communicated information in advance, Sue seemed lighter. She also noticed a common phrase in Sue's conversation: "I didn't know about that."

Mechelle put the pieces together and understood Sue's central issue: She didn't feel included. Everyone else was running from her, and no one was communicating with her. So, Mechelle started to do the opposite. At the beginning of every initiative or project, Mechelle called Sue to ask for her feedback. "Here's what I'm thinking, Sue. What are your thoughts?" Then, she included Sue throughout the project to review content.

Slowly, Sue's attitude toward the L&D team began to change. After working collaboratively on a particularly complex project, Sue spoke up with a rare compliment for Mechelle. "You know, when you first started this, I didn't think you would be able to do it," she admitted. "But you have made a believer out of me."

Mechelle converted this naysayer simply by paying attention to what was missing; in this case, it was inclusion and communication. Then, she doubled down to fill in the gaps.

> **YOUR TURN**
>
> **Analyze Your Network**
> Who are the biggest L&D naysayers in your company? Do you know how to provide what they need to feel more confident about L&D's work? How might you involve them in a current or future project to build trust?

7. Start With the Willing and Share Your Success

Your stakeholders won't all buy in or shift their thinking to begin working with you differently right away. It takes time, and some will be quicker to jump on board than others.

In the 1960s, Everett Rogers popularized an adoption curve related to innovation (Figure 7-1). The curve places adopters of innovations into categories based on when they are most likely to adopt something new. It's been adapted over time and applied to many different scenarios from technology to change management.

However, the basic idea is that there are a small number of innovators, who get on board right away, followed by early adopters. Then, the early and late majority emerge, which is where 68 percent of all people find themselves. Finally, there are the laggards, who will only accept a new idea once it becomes mainstream.

Figure 7-1. Rogers Adoption/Innovation Curve

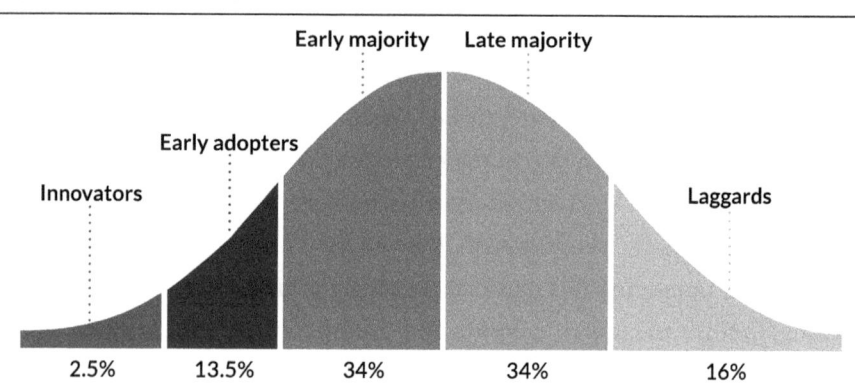

Source: Adapted from Rogers (2003).

You'll likely have stakeholders in almost every category on this curve. Yes, there will be those who are eager to work with you and try out the new ideas you suggest. They will easily accept your approach as it shifts from order taker to SBP. But even more people will be hesitant, like the early and late majority. Most won't be completely against something new, but they also won't be interested in the disruption that it may cause on their team if they don't have any proof it will work. Don't start here.

If possible, start your work with the willing—those who are in the early adopter category. I often refer to this as "going where the energy is." Someone or some group in your company will be more excited about trying new things than others.

At Discovery Benefits, this early adopter group was our contact center. Their large team was made up of lower-paid, entry-level employees. The work could be grueling, especially for those taking back-to-back calls from frustrated customers. As a result, turnover was high, and hiring was a constant.

This group's frontline and middle managers had seen it all. Given the number of curveballs they were thrown in a typical day, they pivoted expertly and exhibited a higher level of flexibility than other groups. They were continuously searching for ways to make their team's work easier and more efficient.

This team was the first to jump on board with an L&D team who wanted to brainstorm in partnership with them instead of simply receiving training requests. They were experts in their area, but also humble, admitting they rarely had all the answers or didn't have the time and space to figure them out. They relied on strong partnerships throughout the company.

I don't want to suggest that working with this group was a cake walk. They asked critical questions about our ideas, and we did the same with them. There were moments of disagreement and conflict, but we used those to produce good results. Ultimately, we were able to work with them in a way that was truly collaborative. By combining all our expertise, creativity, and critical questions, we came up with something together that we could not have created separately.

We started our move from order takers to SBPs by changing the way we approached onboarding with this group. Because they were hiring so frequently, we had a lot of opportunities to try something new, analyze what worked and what didn't, iterate, and try again. Along the way, we measured impact and started to see positive changes in new employees' confidence and competence.

Simultaneously, we were attempting to revamp onboarding in a similar way for other areas of the company, but it was more of a struggle. Other leaders weren't quite as willing to jump in and try new things. They weren't early adopters.

This is where we combined two approaches to eventually move forward. We brought up the idea of revamping onboarding, but in different ways with different leaders, often using WIIFM. We also practiced patience, waiting for them to understand enough to move forward.

It turned out that sharing our success was the ultimate strategy. I remember meeting with one particularly skeptical stakeholder. Sunita wasn't someone to quickly jump on board, but she also didn't want to get left too far behind; there was a competitiveness in her spirit. In our regular meetings, I would mention little slivers of the new vision for onboarding when it seemed appropriate. But she never bit.

One day, Sunita started sharing her frustrations about how the new employees on her team weren't ready to take on the work once they completed onboarding. I knew that her current style of onboarding was to share all the information a new employee would ever need to know in the first few weeks. There was little hands-on practice, and a lot of lecturing. I'd been sharing with her for months that breaking up the information into smaller chunks and adding in more practice could be an effective strategy, but she didn't want to change. Yet here she was, expressing frustrations about her current approach and providing me with the perfect opening.

I asked a few more questions about what she meant by "ready." What would it look like for a new employee to be ready? How would she know they were performing? After I had more info, I said, "Did you know the contact center was struggling with this same challenge? We've been working with them to revamp the way they do onboarding over the past several months. Just last week we gathered some data on how it's working. We found that new employees are now more confident and competent in their roles after onboarding, and their quality scores have shot up. It's been pretty cool to watch."

I could tell Sunita was listening, but she didn't respond. And so I said, "Well, our time is up, and I've got another meeting to get to."

The next time we met, Sunita again shared her frustrations with the new-employee onboarding process. But this time, she asked a question: "Last time we met, you told me about how the contact center had resolved some of their challenges by working with you to revamp their onboarding. I talked to a few of their leaders, and they confirmed it's working. Do you think your team could work with us to do the same?"

You know that feeling you have when there's a breakthrough? It's like the heavens open up in your head and angels start to sing. That was the feeling I had in that moment. Sunita was like the majority adopters in the Rogers Adoption Curve; she needed to know that new ideas were working before she would commit to trying them. But she also was competitive enough that she didn't want to be left behind. I was patient and shared the message a little at a time and then, finally, shared our success when she gave me an opening. Now, we had a green light to revamp onboarding with all the resources we needed.

There's one other note to this story, and that is about the leaders in the contact center. Due to the success that we had with them, they became some of our strongest champions in the company. Did you note that Sunita had reached out to them to confirm my story? I was actually hoping she would do that. Champions who tell your story, especially those who have experienced success in a new way of working, can be one of the best ways to gain buy in from other leaders.

We started with the contact center because they were willing. They were our early adopters. Then, we equipped them as champions by measuring performance both before and after the new onboarding process. Because they experienced the results and had the data, they were ready to tell the story on our behalf.

We weren't shy about telling the story of our success; I wasn't willing to let positive results be a background character. This was also intentional. When majority adopters get a whiff of success, they are more likely to get on board.

> **YOUR TURN**
>
> **Connect With the Willing**
> Consider a few questions as you make plans to connect:
> - Which of your stakeholders are your early adopters, or those who are willing to partner and try new things?
> - How can you equip them to tell your story and share your success?
> - How are you sharing success with those who are not early adopters so they are prepared to come on board?

8. Work With a Partnership Mindset

Your own mindset is one of the most powerful tools you have to move from order taker to SBP. It can't do all the work, but you also can't shift how the business works with you without shifting your own approach. Your mindset dictates how your responses, actions, and interactions play out daily.

The most important aspect of your mindset as an SBP is thinking of yourself as a partner, not a support function. As long as you approach every project with a supportive mindset, you will *remain* support and support alone. You will keep yourself in the order-taking box. To act like a partner, you need to think like a partner. The thinking comes before the action.

Unfortunately, those in a support function all too often assign themselves a status that is *less than*. When someone thinks of themselves as support instead of as a partner, they show up to meetings believing they're lower on the hierarchy and generally act as such. They work to please, not to partner. They are nice, but not effective, and they hold back the full power of their expertise.

A partner is different. A partner works *with, not for* their stakeholders. They approach all situations as an intellectual and creative equal, regardless of rank or title. A partner believes in their own expertise as much as they believe in the expertise of others. They show up ready to brainstorm, ask great questions, and work *together* to come up with a solution, not to be told what to do.

What would happen if you showed up to your next meeting with a stakeholder thinking of yourself as a partner instead of as support? For example:

- Would you act differently? How?
- What questions would you ask?
- How would you listen?
- How would you contribute to the conversation?
- How might you follow-up?

If you have been living in the pattern of an order taker for a long time, these habits and expectations won't change overnight, but you can start changing your mindset today. Show up as a partner. Then, pay attention and make note of what's different, what works, and how others respond. Repeat this approach with every stakeholder meeting and communication from here on out.

Partnering effectively with stakeholders is an art that taps into nontechnical but essential skills. Practicing them will help you hone and adapt your interactions with stakeholders in a way that will continuously move toward working as an SBP.

Partnering effectively with stakeholders is also an important part of creating an atmosphere where you work as an SBP. So is outlining your L&D strategy, which we'll discuss in the next chapter.

Summary

This chapter builds on the foundations built in part 2 by sharing best practices to partner effectively with stakeholders every day:

- **Navigate organizational politics** by setting aside your ego, taking a 10,000-foot view, looking at situations from the outside in, finding a political guide, surveying the landscape for influencers and champions, and working within the system as designed, not as you wish it were designed.
- **Communicate continuously and consistently** by adhering to your stakeholders' preferences and expectations, regularly holding synchronous meetings, using stakeholder language when possible, sticking to your playbook, using feedback, simplifying stakeholder asks, and following through on promises.
- **Lean into what's most important** by identifying and tapping into each stakeholder's WIIFM.
- **Trust stakeholders' expertise, treat them as equals, and recognize their genius.**
- **Use your facilitative leadership skills** to give stakeholders the space and time to think critically.
- **Tap into naysayers and turn them into allies** by asking for feedback and paying attention to what they might be missing in company partnerships.
- **Start with the willing and share your success.** Understand that not everyone will be on board with a new approach right away. Start with those who are willing to try something new and be patient with others. Share success to gain their buy-in.
- **Approach your work with a partnership mindset.** See yourself as a partner instead of support and watch your actions follow.

CHAPTER 8

Create Your Learning Strategy

What if you went on a road trip across the United States without a map? No GPS and no old-school paper map. The best you could do in terms of navigating from the West Coast to the East Coast would be to stop at small-town gas stations and ask for directions. "Turn right by the red barn," the cashier would say. "Pass six mailboxes until you get to the big, lonely tree, and then turn left." Oh, and one more caveat: You don't have much money and even less time.

What are the chances you would get where you want to go? What about efficiently and on time? Could you use your limited resources effectively?

I'm sure a few of you are adventurous enough to try something like this in a well-stocked RV or van, but for everyone else, this would be an exercise in frustration and a failure waiting to happen. I can picture myself out of money, out of gas, and out of luck beside that big, lonely tree.

If I'm being honest, this scenario isn't much different from the way we sometimes work as L&D leaders. We set out on the road to learning without a map, accompanied by unrealistic timelines and limited resources. Sometimes, we know our destination, but often we just keep driving full speed ahead, stopping at whatever landmarks catch our eye.

If you're going to become an SBP, you need to work *strategically*. A strategy is like a map that guides you, tells you what you should do along the way, and helps you reach your destination. It decreases the chances that you'll take costly detours or run out of gas.

In this chapter, I'll show you how to build a learning strategy using a series of questions. You may tackle them alone or with members of your L&D team. Find an approach that works for your unique situation and revisit the questions and this chapter whenever you need to revise your overall strategy. The best practice is to align the duration of your L&D strategy to your organization's business strategy. For example, if your company develops a five-year plan, the L&D strategy should also span five years. If your company doesn't have a written business strategy, try a three-year plan, which allows you to complete longer projects but won't require too many revisions along the way.

I suggest thinking of your L&D strategy in three phases:

1. Generate ideas.
2. Scrutinize your ideas.
3. Finalize your L&D strategy.

By following through on each of these phases to build an effective learning strategy, you will make a real difference in your organization and demonstrate your ability to work as an SBP.

Phase 1. Generate Ideas

Although phase 1 is about generating ideas, it doesn't start with brainstorming. That's because, as an SBP, the strategy isn't about you. An L&D strategy originates in business imperatives, not our L&D hopes and dreams. In other words, we start by looking at the bigger picture of the company, and then define the boundaries that we'll travel within by answering three questions:

1. What relevant information do you have about the business?
2. What is most important to the business?
3. How can L&D partner with the business to address what's most important?

1. What Information Do You Have?

You need to answer this question first to ensure that all relevant information is in one place. What key business data do you currently know or can find easily?

For this information dump, focus on these areas:
- Company goals or initiatives
- Core customer goals or initiatives (if applicable)
- Identified skills gaps
- Verified stakeholder feedback

Table 8-1 illustrates how you might gather all this information in a simple chart, but you can tailor it to fit your needs, as long as it is easy to read at a glance. Let's consider each item in the chart.

Table 8-1. What Information Do You Have?

Overall company goals or initiatives	• Company goal 1 • Company goal 2 • Company goal 3
Core customer goals or initiatives (if applicable)	• Customer goal 1 • Customer goal 2 • Customer goal 3
Identified skills gaps	• Skills gap 1 • Skills gap 2 • Skills gap 3
Verified stakeholder feedback	• Executives and senior leaders • Frontline and middle managers • HR and HRBPs • Your boss • L&D team • Other (overall employee feedback and other key areas of the company)

Company Goals and Initiatives

Executives usually set strategic goals or initiatives that define what the company wants to achieve or improve, as well as how it wants to outshine the competition. These are big goals. They need to be tackled cross-functionally, with participation and commitment from many teams or areas.

If you gathered the company's strategic goals and initiatives when building the foundation for your work as an SBP, you already have this information handy. If not, this is the time to compile it. Mature companies generally have systems in place for sharing company initiatives and goals via meetings, reports, or an intranet site. Start asking questions if you're unsure of where to find the latest information.

If your company is smaller or less mature and hasn't defined strategic goals, don't skip this section. If you can find a vision or mission statement, use that as a stand-in.

Core Customer Goals and Initiatives

Some L&D teams tie their work to a specific area, such as sales, IT, or customer service. Others work across the entire company to pursue leadership development, career development, and other goals. If you work with specific areas and their goals are not the same as or are more specific than the company's larger goals, include those in your chart.

Identified Skills Gaps

Sometimes, leaders are aware that certain employees lack the skills needed to perform successfully in their jobs or anticipate skills gaps in the future. As L&D leaders, our role is to improve and enhance the knowledge and skills of all employees within the company, so if you aren't already familiar with the skills gaps in your organization, it's crucial to identify them now.

Noah, the vice president of talent development at a small energy company, says that uncovering skills gaps is a "little bit of a puzzle that you have to put together." He has found that there usually isn't a single source of truth pointing to the gaps or telling L&D leaders which are most important. Noah likes to determine skills gaps in four ways:

1. He asks executives what they see as the most significant skills gaps, especially related to executing the overall company strategy.
2. He examines industry data from professional associations or governing bodies such as the US Department of Labor.
3. He analyzes internal company data on hiring and performance to discover what skills are and aren't available in the marketplace, and to find out where employee performance is falling flat.
4. He digs into historical data from similar companies to find out what their skills gaps were.

Try any or all of these approaches to fill in information about your company's skills gaps. If you have trouble finding the information, you may have to make some assumptions based on whatever data is available. Part of your learning strategy might be identifying and verifying skills gaps.

Verified Stakeholder Feedback

Stakeholder feedback comes in many forms, but for this purpose, you are looking for feedback that will inform your learning strategy. You need to know what is most important regarding learning initiatives for each key stakeholder group, including frontline and middle managers, executives and senior leaders, HR and HRBPs, your boss, and your team. Include additional notes on feedback from other groups as well, if it's helpful.

Avoid categorizing one group's feedback as more important than another's at this early stage. Your first goal is to gather all the information so you can see patterns and trends clearly.

Sometimes, all stakeholder groups will agree on what's most important. In that case, your learning strategy becomes obvious and getting buy-in is a piece of cake! However, you won't be able to see the full picture unless you gather as much information as possible. How do you do that? The most obvious approach is to simply ask for feedback using specific questions.

Brianna—the senior manager of L&D at a large, rapidly growing technology company—saw a need for leadership development. To narrow down what was most important, she interviewed each executive, asking what they wanted to see in a leadership program and what they thought employees needed most.

The information she gleaned from these interviews wasn't a surprise, but it confirmed that the L&D team's instincts were correct. Brianna and her team could use the information to prioritize their work based on the strongest trends in the executives' answers, and they could always say they were responding to their feedback: "We asked, and you answered." The interviews allowed the team to hone its strategy and get buy-in all at once.

Many L&D teams rely on feedback from an all-employee survey, combining survey information with interviews or focus groups to drill into specifics and determine what questions to ask in future surveys.

Julianne, the head of talent for a large global logistics company, did just that when she went on what she called a "roadshow" after receiving the results of the annual employee engagement survey. She visited multiple sites and ran focus groups to dive deeper into a few specific areas that directly related to talent, learning, and performance. Julianne found a few strong trends that could be used to inform her L&D strategy.

Denise, the training and development manager for a small healthcare technology company, also used the annual employee engagement survey as a starting point. The original survey asked employees to rank the importance of opportunities to upskill and develop, as well as their satisfaction level with the currently available opportunities. The results gave Denise clear data to indicate which development opportunities were important. She then worked with her manager to add more questions for the following year that were tailored specifically to training.

> **Verify Feedback With Data**
> If your stakeholder feedback comes from well-designed evaluation systems, like interviews or a survey, chances are the information is valid. However, if feedback comes from a single stakeholder or area, it's wise to verify it with additional data. Anecdotes will help you illustrate points but shouldn't be used as the only source of information when building your learning strategy.

At Discovery Benefits, we worked with one stakeholder group who came to us certain that L&D's onboarding process wasn't working. Two out of three new employees in their current onboarding class were struggling—they didn't seem to comprehend the information and couldn't put anything into practice.

Leadership from this area came in hot, saying, "You need to change your whole onboarding system. It doesn't work! Just look at these two new employees!"

Instead of panicking, we turned to the data we had collected in the past year measuring competence levels of all new employees during onboarding. Our numbers showed that 98 percent of new employees completed their onboarding with the ability to perform their main work tasks. The current class was an exception rather than the norm. Based on data, rather than emotions, we decided not to include reworking onboarding on our strategy list.

Ask Yourself: What's Missing?

Before moving on to the next question, pause to review all the information you have gathered. Is there anything important regarding talent development that isn't included? If so, add it to your list now.

Whether you take a direct approach to gathering feedback, start with an employee engagement survey, or a combination of both, aim to gather as much verified information as possible, instead of depending on your assumptions. If you don't have feedback from all five key stakeholder groups, can you allow additional time to attain it? If not, start with what you have and keep going! Getting started is more important than striving for perfection.

2. What Is Most Important to the Business?

It's now time to scan and analyze all the information you've gathered and develop a list of *commonalities* (anything that's included multiple times) and *criticalities* (anything that is crucial to the success of your organization).

Commonalities

Scan your information for common themes. Any data or observation that comes up multiple times across multiple categories should be noted. For example, is an overall company goal tied to a skills gap and mentioned by multiple stakeholders? Highlight or mark it with a symbol to set it apart.

Criticalities

Now, put your business leader hat squarely on your head. Set aside your ego and L&D expertise and look at the information you gathered. Based on what you know about the current state of the business, ask yourself these questions:

- What issues are most critical to move forward?
- Do you see problems that, without intervention, will result in a backward slide for the company? Could one of them lead to dangerous working conditions or legal action?
- Which goals and initiatives are so big they would require input from every corner of the company to achieve?
- Which challenges are so pervasive you can't ignore them?

If you are performing this analysis with your team or a group of stakeholders, consider asking everyone to vote on what they believe to be the most critical issues to address or to rank them using a scale of one to three, with three being the most critical.

Make sure to note supporting evidence for your decisions. Are there metrics indicating a backward slide? Has revenue fallen? If you have measures, then use them!

On your chart, indicate the most critical items with a symbol, such as a star or asterisk. Keep in mind that sometimes an issue is critical because no other critical objectives can be met until it's resolved. For example, you may need to shore up processes and procedures on the L&D team before you can tackle other challenges effectively.

Ask Yourself: What's Missing?

Once again, take a moment to step back and reflect. Is there information critical to the business that isn't included in your analysis? If you think something big is missing, add it to the list with the appropriate marker.

After you determine commonalities and criticalities, decide whether to ask for verification from others before continuing. This isn't the only point in the overall process when you can do this, but in some company cultures and political landscapes, the best move is validating that L&D is on the right path before diving deeper.

3. How Can L&D Partner to Address What's Most Important?

Now, it's time to develop a list of ways for L&D to partner with other areas of the organization to achieve goals and address skills gaps. For those of you who want to exercise your problem-solving muscles, this your moment.

Focus on the commonalities and criticalities—no need to waste time and energy on anything that didn't make the cut. At this point, if your chart or list is getting messy, put the commonalities and criticalities on a separate page, leaving space to record new ideas for each. Usually, criticalities are more important to address than commonalities, but this isn't always the case. Keep all the information you gathered to answer the first two questions in case you need to return to it later.

Start Brainstorming!

How could you and your L&D team partner with others in the organization to address these issues? Don't get mired in the details, and don't censor your ideas at this stage. There will be plenty of time to refine your thoughts in phase 2.

Rather than trying to list out specific learning or performance outcomes, jot down simple notes like:

- Add conflict management module to existing leadership development program.
- Create content management system that allows easy access during a team member's moment of need.
- Revamp onboarding to reduce costs and improve time to production.

After the Storm?

Depending on your situation, you may choose to complete your brainstorming session in a couple different ways. If you are working in a group, you may want to ask each member to take away the commonalities and criticalities and think of a few ideas on their own before coming back together to discuss. You could also ask team members to brainstorm during a meeting, using a virtual or physical whiteboard or sticky notes. Do whatever works best for you and your team. Of course, if you are an L&D team of one, you get to choose your own method.

When you are finished, you should have a solid list of ideas ready to scrutinize and carefully edit. They won't all make the cut, and that's OK.

Congratulations! You've completed phase 1.

Phase 2. Scrutinize Your Ideas

Now that you have a list, it's time to shorten it. Unless you are the rare L&D team with only one or two ideas that you can easily accomplish, you will have to pare your list down to a reasonable number you can pursue. Where will L&D make the biggest difference? Let's create two lists: one scrap list of ideas to discard and another that will become a draft road map to your learning strategy. We'll consider these four questions:

1. Which ideas align with company goals?
2. Which ideas will have the biggest impact?

3. Which ideas can realistically be accomplished?
4. Which ideas require more resources?

1. Which Ideas Align With Company Goals?

Simply put, scrap any ideas that don't align with company or core customer goals or L&D's purpose. This is also the time to consider any additional company drivers.

Revisit Your L&D Purpose Statement

Are there ideas on your list that don't make sense for your L&D team? For example, you might have included an idea about improving leadership development training, but your L&D team is focused only on technical training. If you pursued leadership development, you might step on another team's toes—put that idea on the scrap list.

Look at Other Company Drivers

What else—other than the official mission or vision statement—is important to your company when it comes to defining success? Think about defined leadership behaviors or specific values that everyone holds in high regard.

At Discovery Benefits, our work was guided by five values: leadership, open communication, continuous learning, integrity, and teamwork. The company gave out awards to employees who best demonstrated these values each year, and our L&D content and programs reflected them.

If you haven't already identified these values or leadership behaviors, do that now and determine whether any ideas on your current list run counter to those drivers. If the answer is yes, put them on the scrap list!

2. Which Ideas Will Have the Biggest Impact?

Eliminate ideas that you know will have little to no impact on the company as a whole. Then, consider the impact of each remaining idea on your whole organization. Using the lenses of scalability and difficulty should help.

Scalability

Remember that SBPs love to add value. One of the ways you can do this is to think about scale. Avoid one-and-done experiences because they reinforce the order-taking narrative, keeping your L&D team small and in an order-taker box. You want any programs L&D creates to grow across business units, last a long time, and expand with the company. One exception to this rule would be if you need a solution for a short-term, critical challenge.

Kalli, the talent and organization development manager for a midsize professional services firm, saw an opportunity to scale in the need for consistency. Several ideas on her list included requests for onboarding to meet the needs of her rapidly growing company. Many were targeted to specific office locations, and Kalli saw an opportunity to create consistency.

She proposed adding consistent onboarding programs focused on roles, rather than locations, to her strategy map. "Yes, we have people in different locations, but they are all doing very similar jobs," she explained to her stakeholders. "We want a consistent process for everyone. We don't train people separately simply because they sit in different places. We train them the same way whether they are in Warsaw, Denver, or Chicago."

As a value add, this new consistent onboarding process allowed Kalli and the L&D team to include company-wide components, including a focus on company culture. Because they thought about scale instead of individual requests, they were able to improve and enhance onboarding while decreasing the time it took to create and deliver the training—a win for both effectiveness and efficiency!

In a different situation, Brianna, the senior manager of L&D at a large technology company, added leadership and team development to her strategy but had limited capacity to handle new initiatives. Her solution was to create a repository of what she called "team tools," which encompassed various activities that managers outside the L&D group could use on their own or in collaboration with L&D.

Brianna told me that her team created about 30 team tools for this space. Then, if managers asked for help from L&D, they could customize a tool, depending on the group using it. Instead of reinventing or creating an entirely new piece of content with each request, they built a solid system that scaled easily and lowered demands on the team.

One of my biggest career failures occurred when I opted for a one-and-done solution instead of trying to create something that could scale. We had to train everyone on new software, and when our IT team recommended the process used by the software supplier, I was happy to let members of my team act as coordinators instead of creators for the training. The software company's trainer conducted a series of small-group, in-person classroom sessions prior to the launch.

This trainer was one of the best I've ever seen in terms of engaging participants, but things went south when people started to revisit the new software to get their work done. Our internal IT team started receiving so many service tickets, phone calls, and messages requesting assistance that they were completely overwhelmed. Employees had been trained, but the forgetting curve and lack of follow-up resources meant the training program was unsuccessful. It was almost as if we hadn't done it at all.

I learned my lesson. The next time the company needed another software rollout, my team focused on scaling it rather than creating one event. We developed videos, tip sheets, and job aids that walked employees through each major task. These training resources doubled as the assistance employees could use at any time.

As you look at the items remaining on your strategy list, ask whether each idea is a one-and-done solution or if it has the potential to scale over time. If it won't scale and isn't truly critical, add it to your scrap list.

Impact Versus Difficulty

If the potential impact of an idea is significant and undeniable but it is so difficult that it will take years and vast resources to achieve, will it be worth it? *Impact* refers to how big a difference a learning solution will make in the business. Ask yourself, will it:

- Save time and money?
- Reduce risk?
- Add revenue?
- Improve effectiveness and efficiency?
- Scale over time for a compounding effect?

If the answer to any of these questions is yes, approximate to what degree it is true (large, medium, or minimal).

Difficulty, on the other hand, refers to the level of complexity of a learning solution. Again, ask yourself a few questions:

- Will it take more hours, people, and collaboration?
- Will it require new systems that don't currently exist?
- Will the company need to orchestrate change management processes?
- Can the solution be accomplished quickly with minimal effort?

In Figure 8-1, I've combined the concepts of difficulty and impact into a simple tool to help you map ideas and determine whether they are worthwhile.

Figure 8-1. Difficulty Versus Impact Grid

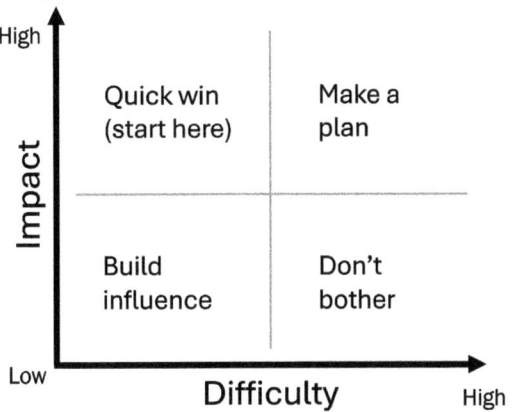

The vertical axis is labeled "impact," and the horizontal axis is "difficulty." Each axis illustrates a continuum from low to high. Take a look at the four quadrants, starting in the top-left corner. Let's review how to use each one in building your learning strategy.

Quick Win = Low Difficulty + High Impact

If an idea on your list can easily be completed with your current resources and capacity, it's a quick win and you should start there. It can demonstrate the value your team can bring or build momentum, motivation, and buy-in for a project.

One of my team's learning strategy ideas was to recreate training for some frequently used internal software. Stakeholder feedback told us that this software was causing errors and performance issues, but after some research, we discovered that the same task was tripping everyone up. So, we created a screen recording that showed how to complete the task and added it to the team's knowledge base. We spent only a couple of hours on this solution, but within a few days, more than 100 people had watched it and errors had decreased significantly. It was a quick win!

This quadrant could also be called the *no-brainer* category. Keep any idea that falls here on the list and add it to your strategy road map.

Make a Plan = High Difficulty + High Impact

Ideas in this quadrant will have a tremendous, positive impact on the business, but they won't be easy to accomplish. They tend to reduce expenses, increase revenue, increase efficiency, or improve performance. These ideas also have a ripple effect, affecting many people in an organization.

At Discovery Benefits, an important part of our learning strategy was providing robust resources that customer service team members could access in their moments of need. Essentially, this was a content management strategy we could pivot to become a training strategy that was focused less on memorization and more on practice using resources. Our resources improved the efficiency and effectiveness of onboarding and reduced calls to supervisors because agents could find answers to questions on their own.

When we thought of the idea, we knew it had the potential for high impact, but that it would be complicated to create and execute. We had to create a plan and work on it over several years, shifting training a little at a time until our entire library of resources was complete. But it was worth it once it was done.

If you have a project like this, you will need to create a detailed strategy road map. You'll also need patience because the project won't happen fast or without a few roadblocks and detours along the way.

Build Influence = Low Difficulty + Low Impact

The learning solutions in this quadrant won't be hard to complete, but you should think twice about initiating them because they won't have much impact. However, if a project has the potential to build influence for L&D or strengthen your relationship with an important stakeholder, it may still be worth adding to your strategy because it could pay off in the long run. Often, these projects allow you to take something off a key stakeholder's plate and win their gratitude. If you solve their problem, they may become an advocate for your L&D team and see you as a partner.

As part of the learning strategy for a major software implementation, I identified some parts that were not especially critical. Jackie, the director of purchasing, told us she would like assistance with training people across the company on how to use the software for purchases. She didn't want the L&D team to create the training program; she just wanted us to review it and help her improve it. Jackie was a stakeholder with influence and had many employees who might help us with future training initiatives, so we happily added a review of her training program to our strategy. We invested only a couple of hours, and the work had very little influence, but we won big because our efforts strengthened an important relationship and opened the door for more collaboration.

Not Worth It = High Difficulty + Low Impact

What should you do if an idea requires a lot of effort and has only minimal impact? Don't bother! This is a case when "the juice isn't worth the squeeze."

Years ago, I worked with a business unit that wanted my L&D team to create a full-scale, multilevel onboarding and upskilling program for one of their teams—a team of four people. The time and effort required would have been massive, and there was no guarantee it would be used by more than a few current employees and a new employee every three or four years. Plus, tech changes meant that anything we created would quickly be outdated. That idea went directly to the scrap list.

> **YOUR TURN**
>
> **Create and Use a Difficulty Versus Impact Grid**
> Draw a simple difficulty versus impact grid, and then use it to evaluate your remaining ideas by placing them into the quadrants. If any ideas are in the "not worth it" quadrant, move them to your scrap list.

3. Which Ideas Can Realistically Be Accomplished?

By this point, your scrap list should be growing, and your strategy list should be shrinking. It's time to eliminate unrealistic ideas and prepare to negotiate additional capacity and expertise as needed. The items that remain on your strategy list will have a big impact, but you need to get real about what your L&D team can accomplish. Do you have the capacity and expertise to tackle them all? If not, which ones should you pursue?

Determining your team's availability and ability to complete strategic projects isn't always easy. I've already covered how to track team member capacity and stressed the importance of incorporating data and personal situations, such as whether you have people away on parental leave. Team members' recurring work also limits your capacity to commit to projects in a new L&D strategy. You'll need to consider how many courses your team regularly facilitates, as well as the time involved in updating content, running reports, gathering data from the LMS, and maintaining relationships with stakeholders.

Calculating capacity isn't enough to determine whether pursuing an idea is realistic. You'll also need to determine whether your team already possesses the expertise to make the idea a reality or whether they can easily enhance their skills.

Finally, the biggest question of all is: Does the capacity and expertise of your L&D team match? Do the people with the necessary expertise have enough capacity to execute the ideas?

I have yet to encounter an L&D team, including my own, that's overflowing with time and resources. And most of the time, the team members with the most expertise already have a full workload of projects. If this is the case for your team, don't give up on an ambitious strategic plan. Instead, look at the situation with eyes that are critical, creative, and wide open. Those happen to be the eyes of a strategic business partner.

What Can the L&D Team Do?

Look at your list again. You're probably now focusing on all the things that you *cannot* do. Go a level deeper to think about how you can creatively reach your ideal destination or somewhere close.

Can You Increase Capacity?

Could you define your team's capacity differently, especially its capacity to participate in critical strategic projects? Answer these questions to get your creativity flowing:

- Is all your L&D's team's current work serving the company well?
- Is any work no longer relevant or effective?
- How can you make your current processes more efficient?
- Can you shift tasks to other team members or other teams to increase your capacity for more strategic work?
- Are you holding onto work that shouldn't be yours?
- Are there partners in the business who would benefit from sharing specific tasks, projects, or workloads?
- Is this idea critical enough and your capacity limited enough to consider adding additional temporary or permanent employees?

You may be able to use the issue of capacity as a negotiating tool with other teams in your organization. For example, if the customer service team started maintaining their own content, would that open up capacity for the L&D team to work on a more strategic project on their behalf? The more creatively you can think about your current capacity, the more likely you'll be able to keep some key strategic ideas off the scrap list.

Can You Increase Expertise?

When it comes to workloads and projects, sometimes capacity and expertise don't add up, and you have to make a choice. Consider your answers to these questions:

- Can a team member who has capacity but not expertise learn the skills needed to work on a project in a reasonable time?
- Can you pair up two team members and ask the one with more expertise to mentor the other? (This works best if you set clear expectations from the start and ask the more experienced team member to provide guidance, but not do the work. The advantage for the mentor is that they gain leadership experience.)

- Can you shift existing workloads to allow someone with more expertise to work on the critical project? A job shift has the potential to level up other team members' skills.
- Is the idea you want to include in your strategy important enough to consider adding additional employees permanently or temporarily?

Should You Scrap It or Negotiate?

With capacity and expertise in mind, look at your list again. What should you move to the scrap list? If you discover truly critical ideas that cannot happen without additional capacity or expertise, but you haven't landed on a creative solution, create a third list focused on *negotiables*.

At this point, you may be imagining a few scenarios: "We could accomplish x and y, but not z," or "We could accomplish z but nothing else." *Negotiables* are ideas that are not feasible within your current context or span of control. To come to a conclusion about the negotiables, you will need to reach out to others for validation and collaboration. But, before you do that, let's consider the final question in phase 2.

4. Which Ideas Require More Resources?

Look at your strategy list, including the negotiables, and determine what additional resources are required to make them a reality. Write them all down. Do you need additional software? Committed, collaborative time from other business units? More employees—permanent or temporary?

A Draft With Three Lists

Now that you've completed phase 2, your draft L&D strategy should consist of three lists:

1. **Strategy list.** These are the ideas you are adding to your overall L&D strategy. They align with company goals, initiatives, and drivers. They are common or critical and have a large impact. Your team has the capacity and expertise to work on them or can add enough capacity and expertise in an appropriate timeframe.
2. **Negotiables list.** These are the ideas you believe are critical or will have a large impact on the business, but that you can't pursue

without additional commitments or resources. Because these ideas are critical, you will involve others in decisions about whether to include them in your final L&D strategy.
   3. **Scrap list.** These are the ideas that didn't make the cut because they don't align, won't have enough impact, are too difficult, or won't scale, or because your team lacks capacity or expertise. Yes, your scrap list will include great and important ideas, so don't completely scrap your scrap list! Keep it for future reference because they may become relevant in the future. You can also use this list to show a stakeholder why their idea didn't make it into your strategy.

Armed with your three lists, you are ready to embark on the final phase of L&D strategy creation.

Phase 3. Finalize Your L&D Strategy

Your strategy lists are filled with ideas based on information from and about the business, and you've carefully scrutinized them to consider what is most achievable. There are only five steps left to complete your L&D strategy:
   1. Work through negotiables.
   2. Draft your final strategy.
   3. Acquire signoff.
   4. Share the strategy with stakeholders.
   5. Plan to operationalize.

Let's discuss each step in more detail.

1. Work Through Negotiables

It's time to move items from the negotiables list onto the strategy or scrap list based on feedback and commitments from others. The word *negotiation* scares many L&D leaders because they think of it in dramatic terms. Negotiation, for our purposes, isn't an all or nothing—it's a form of partnering to solve a problem.

The stakeholders you will be negotiating with probably understand challenges like lack of capacity and resources, especially if they sit in leadership roles. They may even be struggling with similar challenges.

The people you include in these conversations will depend on your negotiables list and your company's political landscape and organizational structure. You may need to have your boss present. Is it best to talk with senior leaders first or with frontline and middle managers first? If you aren't sure, ask!

Show up to these conversations with a spirit of curiosity and a willingness to understand and acknowledge the perspectives of others at the table. At the same time, set the scene by describing what led you to this point. Use these questions as a guide:

- Why do you believe this idea is potentially critical to the business?
- How does it align with business goals and initiatives?
- What measures support its importance or impact?
- Why didn't you move this item to your scrap list?
- What can you do to address this item given your team's existing capacity and expertise?
- What creative ideas have you come up with to remedy the situation, and what are their implications?
- What can't you do, given your team's existing capacity and expertise? In other words, exactly where and how do you need help?

Sample Conversation: Starting a Negotiation for Resources

Consider this imaginary conversation with a senior leader to help you start negotiating.

Jess: Thanks for meeting today. I'm working to finalize the L&D team's strategic plan for the next few years and could use your help. Based on the current company strategic initiatives, we have narrowed down our direction to the projects that seem to be the highest priority. That includes X and Y. Am I on the right track about what's most important?

Jill (senior leader): Yes. You are on the right track. Those areas are both really important to our future success and need to be addressed soon.

Jess: Great. I'm glad we're on the right track. I've also been looking at the current capacity and expertise of the L&D team, and I have concerns that, as we are currently staffed, we won't be able to achieve both goals.

I've looked at our current projects and we can open up capacity by sunsetting a few of the programs that are no longer performing. The data on these programs over the past few years indicates that participation is decreasing, despite the commitment hours from our team remaining the same. I think we can point employees who are still seeking development of these skills toward courses within our LinkedIn learning library instead.

That gives us a bit of time to work on X project. But we still lack the expertise to do it well. If this really is important, I've got a few ideas in mind, but they require additional resources.

Jill: OK, tell me about the options.

Jess: First, I've thought about hiring a new team member who is an expert in this area and can be fully dedicated to this work now and in the future. This option would mean we have a little longer ramp time to get someone up and running, but after that, we can move more quickly.

Second, I've considered hiring a consultant who could work part time to provide guidance and train a few team members in this area. It would require us to free up capacity for team members in the future but will also upskill our current team.

Finally, we could ask a couple L&D team members to create a piecemeal solution that would help, but wouldn't fully solve the issue. This would mean it would be addressed slowly, over time.

No matter which solution we choose, we will need to partner with subject matter experts across the company to ensure that the content is accurate. This means asking for time and commitment from your team members as well. Depending on how robust we need this solution to be, we may need to purchase additional software to operationalize it, adding to our costs.

We've agreed that this is an important initiative, what are your thoughts on these options?

The conversation would continue, with me asking Jill to help produce ideas or support existing ideas using her resources. If she is unable to help, I might note that we won't be able to do much other than piecemeal work and might question whether that is worth everyone's time. Ideally, we could come up with a creative solution that is realistic and maximizes impact. I would end the conversation by confirming the commitment Jill is willing to make, if any.

If stakeholders are willing and able to partner in a way that makes an idea realistic, move it from your negotiable list to your strategy list. If not, move it to your scrap list. Continue having these conversations until each item on the negotiables list have moved to one of the other lists.

2. Draft a "Final" L&D Strategy

Your final L&D strategy or road map is something you can present to stakeholders for approval. I often use quotation marks around the word *final* because, while I know I'll continue to revise the document, this version is one I'm ready to share. At this stage, your strategy list is probably complete, but it's worth taking a moment to ask two questions:

- Is this list realistic given the negotiated capacity, expertise, and resources?
- Can L&D do this?

If you answer yes to both questions, you're ready to draft your L&D strategy. If your company uses a particular format for its overarching strategic goals and initiatives, the best practice is for L&D to use the same one. Aim for SMART goals (specific, measurable, achievable, relevant, and time-bound).

3. Acquire Needed Signoffs

Who needs to see your strategy and validate that you are on the right track? Usually, it's your boss and possibly other senior leaders or executives, depending on your organization's political landscape.

Is there a time of year when strategic plans need to be completed for approval? Work within the existing company structure to the best of your ability to build credibility and elevate your status as an SBP.

If you aren't sure who needs to sign off or when to share your strategy, start by asking your boss. Be ready to explain why each item on your final strategy made the cut, and accept additional questions, thoughts, and feedback to iterate if needed.

4. Share With Key Stakeholders

Once your strategy is approved, you can start to share it more formally with key stakeholders. This will look different depending on your company's political and operational landscape. Consider all five of your key stakeholder groups—your L&D team, your boss, HR or HRBPs, executive or senior leaders, and frontline or middle managers. Determine the best way to share information with each group, especially if they weren't involved in the approval process. Follow the best practices in communicating, whether that means sharing ideas in a team meeting, in one-on-ones, or in an email with a link to a shared file of the full strategy. Consider the WIIFM question, and also ask yourself:

- What information would be most beneficial to share or highlight?
- How will you reinforce the information over time?
- Where should the L&D strategy live so stakeholders can access it over time?
- How will you document and communicate progress?

You want to be able to keep the document top of mind for easy reference and share it with others as needed.

5. Plan to Operationalize

You're almost done! You have a valuable road map to your destination; now, you just need to provide the L&D team and your stakeholders with a little more information so no one ends up sitting at a lonely tree by themselves. For each point of interest on your road map, answer these questions:

- What is the timeline for this item? Are there important benchmarks?
- Which L&D team members need to be involved?
- Which members of other teams need to be involved?
- What measures already exist that can go into a measurement plan?
- Do you need to add measurement components?
- How will people who need to access this solution learn about it?
- How will you market it or communicate it?

Tie your L&D projects to the cadence of the business, carefully involving others according to the timelines and working practices that are best for them. If needed, add benchmarks L&D team members can use for performance goals.

Finally, put on your SBP hat and determine if there are any additional ways to add value to the business, improve collaborative relationships, or increase visibility using the items in the plan.

Every strategy requires flexibility, and an L&D strategy is rarely final, so don't write it with a permanent marker. Be prepared to iterate, adapt, or pivot, should business needs change. (More on this in the next chapter.)

Summary

Create a realistic road map for L&D to maximize impact, based on the most critical business priorities. Align with company processes and best practices.

- Start by gathering information about and from the business including goals and initiatives, skills gaps, and verified stakeholder feedback.
- Identify the most common and critical items.
- Brainstorm how L&D can best partner to address these items.
- Scrutinize your ideas to ensure they are in alignment with the business, will maximize impact, and are realistic in terms of capacity and expertise. Determine if additional resources will be needed to make the ideas a reality.
- Sort the ideas into three lists (strategy, negotiables, and scrap).
- Hold conversations with stakeholders to describe challenges and ask for additional resources or solutions.
- Create a final strategy, gain approval, and share it with stakeholders.
- Operationalize the strategy with a plan.
- Be prepared to adjust and iterate the strategy based on company changes.

Tool 8-1. L&D Strategy Creation Checklist

Use this checklist to create your own L&D strategy.

Phase 1. Generate Ideas

Set your ego aside. Start with the business, not L&D.
- ❏ Gather relevant company information:
  - » Company goals and initiatives
  - » Core customer goals and initiatives
  - » Identified skills gaps
  - » Verified stakeholder feedback
  - » Ask yourself: What's missing?
- ❏ Determine what's most important to the business:
  - » Identify commonalities.
  - » Identify criticalities.
  - » Ask yourself: What's missing?
- ❏ Brainstorm how L&D could partner to address what's most important:
  - » Create and complete your idea list.

Phase 2. Scrutinize Your Ideas

Carefully sort ideas to create a strategy list, negotiable list, and scrap list.
- ❏ Ensure the ideas align with company goals, the L&D purpose statement, and any additional company drivers.
- ❏ Determine which ideas will have the biggest impact:
  - » Consider scalability.
  - » Consider impact versus difficulty (use the impact versus difficulty grid).
- ❏ Decide which ideas could realistically be accomplished by the L&D team:
  - » Can you increase capacity?
  - » Can you increase expertise?
  - » Should you scrap it or negotiate?
- ❏ Outline any additional resources you need.

Phase 3. Finalize Your L&D Strategy

Gain approval and plan to operationalize:
- ❏ Work through negotiables.
- ❏ Draft a "final" strategy.
- ❏ Acquire needed signoffs.
- ❏ Share it with key stakeholders.
- ❏ Plan to operationalize.

CHAPTER 9
Master the Strategic Yes and No

Congratulations on writing a realistic L&D strategy that will maximize your team's impact. Now your stakeholders will stop coming to you with other requests, right?

Wrong! A strategy isn't a stop sign. Working as an SBP doesn't mean you stop taking requests. It doesn't even mean you stop saying yes to requests. But it does mean your response will be more thoughtful and intentional. You can look at all requests through the lens of your L&D strategy and determine whether fulfilling them will support the strategy's success or help you and your team advance your work as SBPs. From this point forward, you will be able to reply to those who make requests with a *strategic yes*, avoiding any flavor-of-the-month and people-pleasing traps.

However, by necessity, responding to stakeholders with a strategic yes also requires something that may make you uncomfortable: deploying a thoughtful, strategic no. In this chapter, we discuss the responsibility of saying yes and no for the right reasons, as well as how to adapt your mindset and ask practical questions when deciding how to answer. We'll also examine when and how to dive deeper into the power of a strategic yes.

There Is a No Inside Every Yes

Because time and resources are finite, whenever you say yes to one thing, you have to say no to something else, even if you don't verbally acknowledge it.

I learned this lesson the hard way. Many years ago, I was saying yes to all requests for speaking engagements and volunteer commitments because I was flattered to be asked and believed in the related causes. With so much of my time taken up by speaking preparations and volunteer work, I was missing out on time with my young children, and my health began to suffer thanks to a lack of adequate sleep or exercise. Unintentionally, I had said no to my family and my health when I said yes to other things.

All the engagements I committed to were good. They helped others and improved the community, but at what cost? I had to reassess my values and learn to say no strategically and intentionally so I would have the energy to thrive in all areas of my life. I needed to say yes only to the things that mattered most to me professionally and personally.

As L&D leaders, when we say yes to requests that don't align with our strategies or that won't help us become SBPs, we lock ourselves solidly into the order-taker role because we no longer have time or resources for strategic work. This is the case even if the requests are good ideas! Fulfilling them will help someone. But again, the question is: At what cost?

You need to make each yes and no response strategic and intentional. This starts by shifting your mindset, engaging in intentional practice, and creating new habits. In the pages that follow, we'll first discuss the importance of our mindsets and then move on to practical ways to build the habit of saying yes and no strategically through intentional practice.

The Details Trap

When we understand that each response is a strategic move, we can usually overcome common mental roadblocks like pleasing people and avoiding conflict. The most difficult hurdle when sharing a strategic yes or no is often a workload that leaves us drowning in details. It's incredibly difficult to be strategic while also focusing on multiple things.

Recently, I was working on a project that included many highly detailed tasks related to coordinating the registration, attendance, make-up work, and overall learning for hundreds of people attending a customized series of live training sessions. The LMS was inefficient, and each task required several manual clicks and overnight processing. The work was tied to the major organizational initiative for which I had been hired. I didn't mind rolling up my sleeves to execute the details, but I wasn't prepared for what happened next.

Email requests arrived in my inbox at an impossible pace, and I had to do research to resolve them before completing the manual tasks in the LMS. I worked at top speed to assist everyone as quickly as possible, cranking out answers as fast as my fingers could type. In the midst of all that, one of the project's executive sponsors asked if I could come to a team meeting to do a quick presentation on the changes that the project would deliver. Without missing a beat, I said yes and moved on, glad to get the item out of my inbox.

My change management partner on the project was copied on my response, and she immediately reached out, asking, "Are you sure that's the right answer, Jess?"

My heart sank as I realized what she meant. Of course, it wasn't the right answer. Buried in the details, I had responded to a strategic question in the same way I was responding to task execution questions: "I've got this." I had turned off my strategic brain.

If I had done the presentation as requested, every team in the company would soon have been asking for the same thing, which would be impossible for me to do. A personalized presentation was not aligned to the L&D strategy and was not the best use of my time. The change management strategy anticipated other ways for leaders and their teams to get the same information and take ownership of it.

Naturally, I started kicking myself and squarely hitting my forehead with my palm. In any other situation, I would have asked those questions to ensure the strategy aligned. But I was so buried in the details that I'd provided a knee-jerk response just to get through my day.

Is this a familiar feeling for you? Do you often fail to think strategically, simply because you're trapped dealing with details and a heavy workload?

Mindset Shifts That Work

When the get-the-details-done villain takes over, you need good systems in place to reinforce a mindset shift in favor of the strategic yes and no. I recommend three effective and simple ways to shift your mindset:

- Set aside time to revisit your learning strategy outside your workflow.

- Create personal response rules.
- Block frequent time on your calendar for strategic thinking.

Set Aside Time to Revisit Your Learning Strategy

Schedule time outside your intense, deadline-driven daily workflows to focus on and realign your strategy. Use this space to keep your learning strategy top of mind, which will be especially valuable when new requests come your way. I recommend setting aside a minimum of two hours each quarter.

Create Personal Response Rules

Put rules in place or make promises to yourself about how and when you will respond to requests. For example, will you wait 24 hours? Consider crafting a standard immediate response that says something like, "Thank you. I appreciate you reaching out. I'll get back to you by [*insert date*] with an answer."

Perhaps you'd rather direct people back to your intake process or suggest a meeting to learn more. Ask yourself what would help you adhere to corporate expectations of turnaround times but also give you the space you need to ensure your response is strategic and intentional.

When I create a new rule for myself it tends to land on a brightly colored sticky note attached to my computer. Do whatever it takes to help you remember and adhere to your rules.

Block Regular Time on Your Calendar for Strategic Thinking

Like blocking time for certain projects, making regular calendar appointments to think strategically is worthwhile. If you have an hour set aside each day or every other day for strategic thinking and analysis, you can wait to respond to requests until after one of those blocks. That way, you'll be able to look at those requests while you're in a headspace that doesn't contain a flurry of detail-oriented activities.

Set a personal agenda for this time to review requests and ask yourself what response would be best aligned with your current L&D strategy, the overall business goals, and your movement toward working as an SBP. Determine your next move based on the answers to those questions. If you haven't received any requests, you can use this time to reflect on whether your work still aligns with your L&D strategy and is moving you toward SBP status.

What About Saying No?

Strategic business partners say no. In fact, they say no a lot. But they do so strategically to maximize their time and resources. The best SBPs are able to say no in a way that also honors and empowers the requester. We'll discuss that approach in the next section.

A Decision Tree for Consultation and Analysis

Sometimes you will know right away whether a request aligns with your strategy. But often the right answer isn't immediately obvious. How do you know if something qualifies as a strategic yes? And if you need to say no, what's the best way to do so?

I recommend a using a decision tree to explore each request and come to the best conclusion, whether that's a strategic yes or a well-thought-out strategic no. Take a look at Figure 9-1 for an overview of the process, and then we will go over each essential question individually.

Figure 9-1. The Four-Question Decision Tree

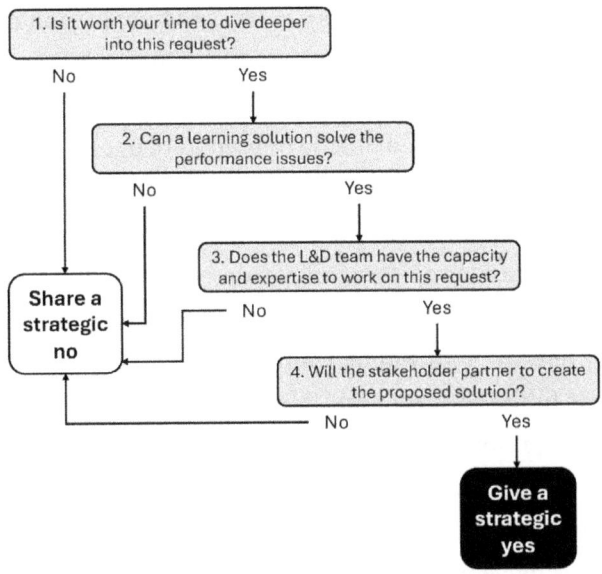

1. Is It Worth Your Time to Dive Deeper on the Request?

Generally, you will explore the question of whether a request is worth your time in an intake process and consultative conversation in which you are trying to answer other important questions, including:
- Does L&D already have something ready that can fulfill this request?
- Does this request tie into a larger strategic initiative?
- Is this request based on compliance or a current critical need?
- Is L&D currently working to build trust and influence with this stakeholder?
- Will fulfilling this request improve L&D's influence or visibility?
- Will fulfilling this request provide a solution that scales?
- Will fulfilling this request avoid future problems?

Because it's so important to determine whether spending time on a request is worthwhile, I've created a second-level decision tree just for that (Figure 9-2). Let's carefully examine these component questions.

Does L&D Already Have Something That Can Fulfill This Request?

Try not to feel discouraged or frustrated when you get requests for information, content, or learning solutions that already exist. Most people in your company are not aware of everything in the L&D library and only consider what they can find in a sudden moment of need. This tendency reminds me of one of my favorite quotes by Chinese philosopher Lao Tzu: "When the student is ready, the teacher appears." In other words, most of us can't truly learn something and make the information stick until we need to apply the concepts. We don't have room in our memory banks for irrelevant information.

When a stakeholder or company leader asks you for a program that already exists, it becomes an opportunity for you to share the resource at the moment they need it. This will be your easiest strategic no. You are saying, "No, we won't fulfill your request," but you are doing so by providing an alternate, existing resource—one that the requester can access immediately.

However, if something doesn't already exist to meet the requester's need, you will require additional information to determine whether to dive deeper. If that's the case, move on to the next question.

Figure 9-2. A Dive Deeper Decision Tree

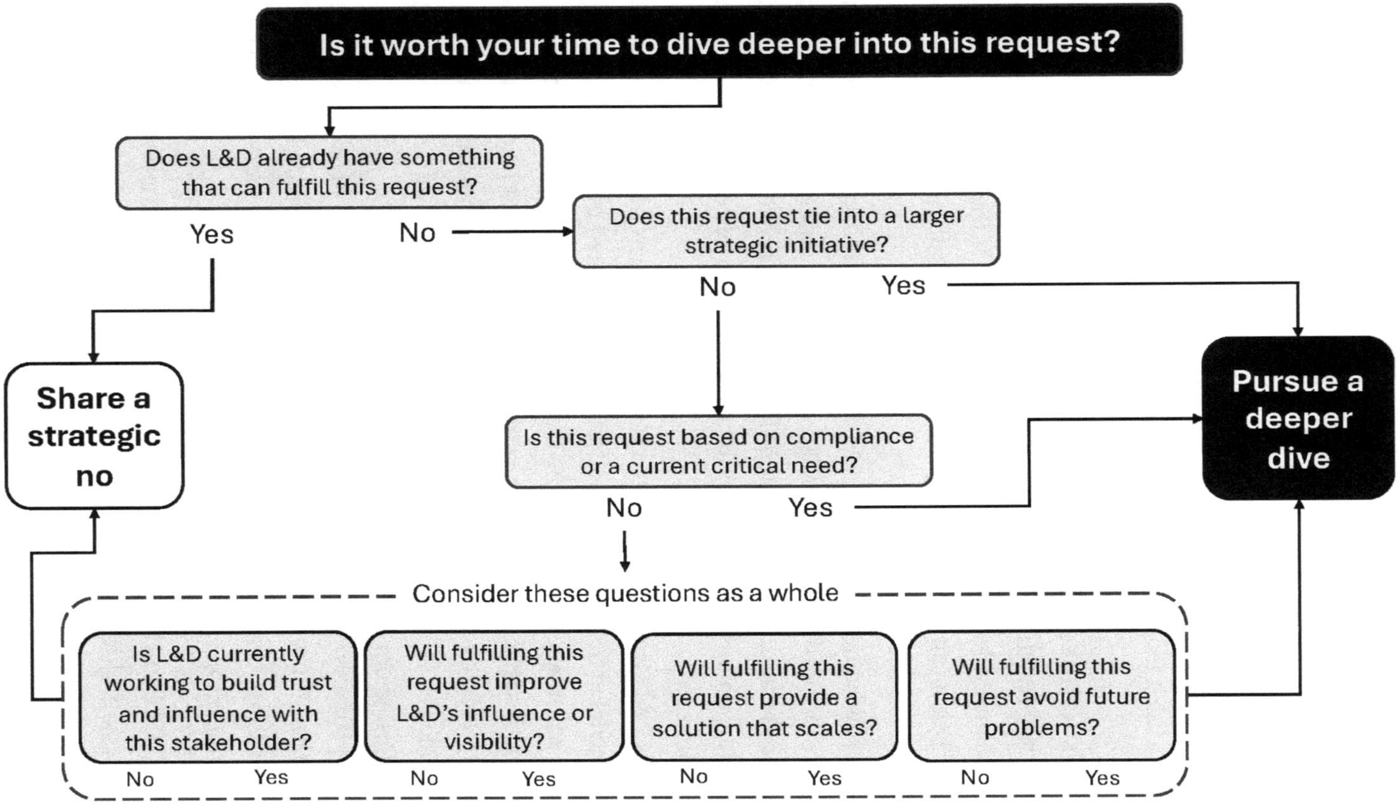

Is it worth your time to dive deeper into this request?

- Does L&D already have something that can fulfill this request?
  - Yes → **Share a strategic no**
  - No → Does this request tie into a larger strategic initiative?
    - Yes → **Pursue a deeper dive**
    - No → Is this request based on compliance or a current critical need?
      - Yes → **Pursue a deeper dive**
      - No → Consider these questions as a whole:
        - Is L&D currently working to build trust and influence with this stakeholder? (No / Yes)
        - Will fulfilling this request improve L&D's influence or visibility? (No / Yes)
        - Will fulfilling this request provide a solution that scales? (No / Yes)
        - Will fulfilling this request avoid future problems? (No / Yes)

If the answers collectively lean no → **Share a strategic no**
If the answers collectively lean yes → **Pursue a deeper dive**

Master the Strategic Yes and No | 221

Does This Request Tie Into a Larger Strategic Initiative?

When you created your L&D strategy, you looked at your organization's goals and initiatives, skills gaps, and verified stakeholder feedback. You determined how to best align your team's capacity and expertise to work on what was most critical, but maybe you missed something. If the request doesn't tie into a larger strategic initiative, it doesn't mean you will say no (yet). Instead, you'll need to ask a few additional questions.

Is This Request Based on Compliance or a Current Critical Need?

Compliance rules are often set by outside entities. If they're not followed, the organization can incur hefty fines, so L&D usually doesn't have the option of saying no to such requests.

Beyond compliance issues, you may discover unforeseen critical needs not initially included in strategic goals, but which now require a learning solution. One of the most consequential unforeseen critical needs of the COVID-19 pandemic on businesses was the increased number of requests for new learning solutions.

My L&D team partnered to create learning materials for our customers, who included both employers offering health-related benefits and employees taking advantage of them. As the US government changed its policies regarding health savings accounts in response to the crisis, we needed to quickly educate employers and help their employees understand the changes. We responded to this request based on a new critical need with a resounding yes and adjusted our L&D workloads accordingly.

If your answer to this question is also yes, you can dive deeper to determine the best way to partner with others on the project. However, if the answer is no, continue by asking these four qualifying questions and considering the answers as a whole.

Is L&D Currently Working to Build Trust and Influence With This Stakeholder?

Showing your value by fulfilling a stakeholder request, especially if you can exceed expectations, is a terrific way to build trust and influence with important people in the company. If this request will allow you to collaborate closely with a particular stakeholder or team with whom you need to build trust, it might be worth the time to dive deeper.

Will Fulfilling This Request Improve L&D's Influence or Visibility?
Some requests have a large enough scope that they allow the L&D team to gain greater visibility throughout the company or a specific area. If visibility is something your team needs, and this request provides that opportunity, it may be worth the time to dive deeper.

Will Fulfilling This Request Provide a Solution That Scales?
Sometimes creating a particular piece of content is just what the organization needs as a foundation for a scalable solution in the future. As learning leaders and SBPs, we should always be thinking about scale. If a request has the possibility to reach a broader audience or create efficiencies that can be used down the road, it may be worth your time to dive deeper.

Will Fulfilling This Request Avoid Future Problems?
Some requests seem innocent at first but eventually open up a can of worms that become difficult or impossible to contain. If you think that a request could create more problems later, it may not be worth pursuing. I wish I had asked this particular question when the executive sponsor I mentioned earlier requested a personalized presentation.

If you think that fulfilling the request could potentially create more problems in the future, you may need to abandon a deeper dive completely. However, gaining a partner or more visibility occasionally outweighs the potential for problems, which is why it's so important to consider all these questions together with your current situation and goals in mind.

What About Your Strategic No?
If you have determined that a request isn't worth a deeper dive, let the requester know your answer is no. There are ways to say no while respecting and empowering the requester. Two effective options are circling back and flipping the narrative.

Committing to circling back later is best if there is a possibility that you will pursue the request in the future. In that case, respond like this:

> Thank you for your request. It's a great idea, but right now our team is focused on projects that tie directly to the company's strategic initiatives. Because this request doesn't meet the criteria, we will need to hold off on pursuing it. Let's circle back in a few months.

Another option, and one of my favorites, is to flip the narrative of how L&D and stakeholders work together by offering to serve as a learning SME. That could sound something like this:

> Thanks for the request. It's a great idea, and I can see how it may be helpful for your team. Right now, we don't have the capacity to take it on, but if you want to get started, we can act as your subject matter experts for the learning portion. That means you would create the content, and we would review it and offer suggestions for improvement. How does that sound?

In this instance, you offer to guide the requester while they create the content. They may not have access to your e-learning tools, but they can create quick videos, job aids, and other forms of training to share in a team meeting. You and your team members simply serve as mentors or guides offering suggestions and support.

Both strategic no responses share the message that the L&D team is unable to take the project and run with it, but they also provide valid alternatives focused on what L&D *can* do.

A Note on Consultative Conversations

There is an art to talking with a stakeholder about whether you will dive deeper and pursue their request. You may lead the person to alternate resources, determine whether their request is tied to a larger strategic initiative, or take any number of other actions.

Travis—the senior VP of talent at a midsize insurance, financial services, and HR consulting company—shared one of the best approaches to consultative conversations I've ever heard. It's also one that is easy for anyone to follow. His team uses three words and one technique. Let's start with his three words:

- **Helpful.** Always be helpful to the requester, even if the L&D team can't pursue their project in the way they want. The focus should be on how you can help. What *can* you do?
- **Curious.** In conversations, the L&D team should be relentlessly curious to find the reason behind the request. Is it tied to a strategic initiative? What does the requester want to accomplish? What behaviors are they attempting to change? How do they know performance is lagging? Staying curious combats defensiveness and frustration, which can easily creep into the picture if the L&D team member is tired, talking with a stakeholder who has come back with the same request multiple times, or knows there is a simple solution that already exists. The L&D team member needs to swap frustration for curiosity to keep the conversation positive.
- **Strategic.** Think of the bigger picture and whether the request fits into it. Know what the L&D team and the company are trying to accomplish and whether this request aligns with it. Keep things like visibility, influence, and scale in mind if those are goals for L&D.

Now, for the simple technique, which Travis explained this way: "Be positive no matter the request or idea from the stakeholder." Acknowledge the request and agree that you want to help.

For example, try saying, "Thanks for bringing that up. I'd love to learn more," or "Thanks for bringing that up. Let's see how we might be able to help." You're not committing to any specific solution at this point, so you're just acknowledging the requester's point of view.

Travis says that by helping his team pair the desire to be helpful, curious, and strategic with positivity in their consultative conversations, team members can strengthen their relationships with stakeholders and get the information they need to make informed decisions about whether to proceed with requests. This approach is also respectful and empowers the requester, even when the answer is a strategic no.

If, after this initial round of questions you have answered yes and recognize the need to dive deeper, let the stakeholder or requester know. Indicate that you would like to learn more and that you have additional questions to determine the best way to help. Be careful not to commit to a learning solution yet; you are simply committing to *learning more*. It's time to consider the remaining questions in our decision tree (Figure 9-1).

2. Can a Learning Solution Solve the Performance Issue?

The next item to explore is whether a learning solution can truly alleviate the problem. This kind of analysis initially spurred my desire to work as an SBP instead of an order taker. When we try to fulfill orders without answering this question, even the most fantastic learning solutions won't solve the problem, and we end up wasting time and resources.

First, we need to do our due diligence to determine a problem's cause. Often, a stakeholder's request is tied to a symptom rather than a root problem, and addressing symptoms rarely solves problems. I like to use a short tale to illustrate this disconnect between symptoms and root problems:

> Once upon a time, in a small, peaceful town, children walked to and from school together each day. Regardless of where they started their walk, they eventually ended up on the same final path to arrive at the school. One evening, a rockslide roared down a nearby mountain, and boulders covered a portion of the path. The children now had to climb over and around the rocks, which had sharp edges that scraped their knees and elbows. After a few days, the school nurse began to run out of bandages and had to order more. The parents began to wonder why so many bandages were needed and why their children were in such a terrible, bruised, and bloody state when they got home each day. At a meeting to decide how they were going to help the school pay for all the extra supplies, a visitor spoke up: "Have you considered solving the problem of the rocks? Could you build an alternate path for the children or move the boulders out of the way?"

See where I'm going? The townspeople had become so focused on fixing a symptom—the skinned knees and elbows—that they had forgotten to look for a solution to the source of the problem: the rocks.

We all fall into this trap sometimes, including our stakeholders, who often come to L&D with requests for a bandage when they need to move a boulder.

Determine the Cause

When stakeholders request training, they are looking for something to improve the performance of their team or the company overall, but not all problems can be fixed with training. Our first task is to determine the cause of performance challenges. We can do this by sorting the challenges into categories of *performance influencers*—which can be anything that influences an employee's performance on the job.

They can either improve or inhibit performance. If we can first determine which performance influencer is negatively affecting performance in the situation described in a request, we can then determine whether training can correct it.

I've created a model to help you analyze performance influencers (Figure 9-3). It's a modification of Thomas Gilbert's (2007) Behavior Engineering Model.

Figure 9-3. Performance Influencers

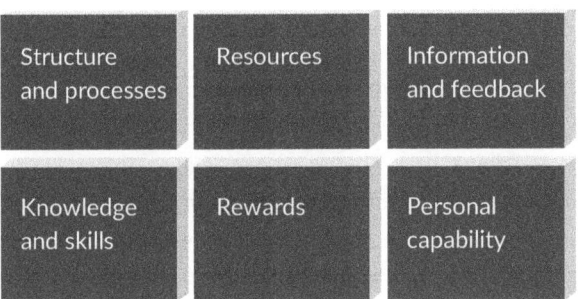

In the model, there are six defined performance influencers that can affect an employee's performance:
- **Structure and processes** are performance influencers related to how the team is structured and how the work gets done. This includes organizational or team structure, reporting relationships, processes and procedures, workflows, and decision-making authority.
- **Resources** include the tools, materials, technology, staffing, budget, and time needed to get a job done.

- **Information and feedback** covers an employee's access to the information needed to do their job, including reliable data, accurate reference materials, customer feedback, performance feedback, coaching, and clarity in role expectations.
- **Knowledge and skills** refers to whether an employee has the necessary knowledge and skills to do the job.
- **Rewards** are the drivers and motivators for performance, such as recognition, performance-based pay or incentives, bonuses, and benefits.
- **Personal capability** refers to the employee's physical and mental health, mental capability, social adeptness, and previous experience.

Now that you understand all six performance influencers, here's the kicker: Only one category—knowledge and skills—is improved by training. The rest require a different solution.

Training and learning solutions are designed to improve knowledge and skills but have no effect on the five other categories. Even if you provide the most awesome training course ever created, you cannot fix broken or clunky processes, make up for outdated technology, or align reward systems correctly.

When Training Won't Solve the Problem

The leaders of a team came to me requesting training on complex tasks because no one was doing them. They were just sitting in the queue and causing the team to miss turnaround time expectations and service level agreements. The leaders assumed team members weren't completing the complex tasks because they didn't know how and needed more training. It was time for me to ask more questions.

It didn't take long to discover that the team definitely knew how to do the complex tasks. The problem wasn't a lack of knowledge or skill; instead, it was the reward system. The hourly employees received bonuses based on the number of tasks they accurately completed in a day. More tasks completed and fewer mistakes meant more money in their pockets. The complex tasks took longer to complete and there was a greater chance of error. So, by taking on the complex tasks, the team members would make less money. They were incentivized to skip the complex tasks.

> I pointed out the problem to those who had requested the training. I asked them to adjust the bonus structure first, and said we could revisit the question of training after that if nothing changed.
>
> Of course, we never needed that follow-up conversation.

How Deep Should You Dive for an Answer?

Chances are good that the stakeholder who comes to L&D with a request thinks the problem is related to a lack of knowledge and skills in some way. But is it really? Or is the stakeholder focusing on the symptom of a larger problem or missing the underlying issue like my reward system example. You will need to do an analysis to confirm the reason behind the ask. But just how deep should you dive in analyzing the problem? You typically have three choices:

1. The yes is obvious! No analysis needed.
2. The answer may be more complex. It requires you to make an assumption and ask questions—in other words, a light analysis.
3. To get to the right answer, you will need a truly dive deep, which may include interviews, going to the gemba, and gathering data or documents—a full analysis.

Level 1. The Yes Is Obvious

You will rarely know immediately that a request requires a learning solution. Generally, this happens with a new challenge—something very few people at your company have experience doing—involving knowledge or skills that do not currently exist in the company. For example, this could include the rollout of a new product or the implementation of new software. Here are some things to ask:

- **Is this request for learning based on something new for employees at this company?** If the request is for something new and the need to learn is obvious, you will want to determine how much your team will be needed.

- **How many people will be affected?** A new software package that affects four people is different from one that affects hundreds or thousands. Your response should match those numbers.
- **Are there existing learning resources?** Your team may not have resources available, but that doesn't mean they don't exist. In the case of a new software rollout, for example, the software company may have learning resources and training materials that allow your team to step back and help coordinate training rather than create something new. If a new product is rolling out, find out whether the product team created any resources that you can use as a starting point.
- **How complex is the new item?** If a new software product is similar to another version or product, it might not require as much time to learn and, therefore, will need fewer new resources and programs. In the spirit of ensuring that performance influencers match the solution, ensure that it is completely obvious when relying on level 1.

Level 2: Make an Assumption and Ask Questions

If it isn't completely obvious that you need a learning solution, the next level of analysis requires you to make one simple assumption and then ask a lot of questions.

We're often told not to assume things. (Remember the adage: "When you assume, you make an ass of u and me"?) In this case, the assumption is critical to framing the rest of the analysis: Assume that neither you nor the requester *really* knows what the problem or solution is—yet. This lands you squarely in a mindset of curiosity where you can play detective and ask questions to determine the real problem. It also ensures that you don't jump to conclusions.

I often see L&D leaders ask questions that reinforce the assumption that the solution *must be* learning or training; for example, they might ask about learning outcomes, success measures, and what learning modality might work best for the audience. But, we can't ask these types of questions if we drop our assumptions about the problem and solution. The goal here is to determine whether a learning or training solution could solve the problem or solve part of the problem.

Now we can put the performance influencers and our questions together to determine if something other than a lack of knowledge or skills is inhibiting employees' performance. It's best to meet with the requester and anyone else who may have information related to the request if it's possible and appropriate.

Start your conversation by diving into the identified problem and asking more questions about where it's coming from. With your detective hat on, search for evidence of how the problem started. Your job is to facilitate a conversation that exposes any additional evidence the stakeholder might not have considered.

Keep these six performance influencers in mind. You don't need to share them with the stakeholder, but listen for indications that something other than a lack of knowledge or skills may be at play. If no further relevant information exists, you should move on to level 3. Try out these questions (with follow-ups, if needed) to spark conversation:

- What's the reason you are requesting training for this?
- What's not working that indicates training is needed?
- What evidence do you have that it isn't working?
- Have team members done this successfully in the past? If yes, what's changed?
- What does it look like to perform this skill well? How do you know when someone is performing it well?

Level 2 Analysis in Action
I sat down with Samira and Helene, managers of a large account management team, to discuss their request for a communication "boot camp." As they described it, account managers were having a hard time responding to customers' questions, concerns, and requests. Many weren't meeting the desired turnaround time for a response. In addition, some provided too much detail, and others not enough.

As a final blow, their team retention numbers were abysmal. Samira and Helene thought a series of training courses would help. They had already outlined more than 15 training topics that they needed my team to create and deliver. As they confidently handed over their list, I was both suspicious and extremely curious. I had never come across a team that solved a retention problem with only training, but I knew these managers were in pain, and I was committed to helping them figure out the best direction forward.

I started by asking questions about the challenges they brought forth regarding turnaround time and level of detail. "How do you know the team isn't meeting the turnaround time?" I asked. They easily answered this question because they had related reporting and measurement systems.

My next two questions about the details had them stumped: "How do you know team members aren't providing the right amount of detail?" and "What is the right amount of detail?"

Samira explained that seasoned team members were analyzing complex questions themselves instead of following the new process to pass them along to the customer analyst team to do the in-depth work. However, the words came out of Samira's mouth, Helene jumped in to contradict that thought. She said it was fine if an account manager, who knew how to find an answer, spent time doing the analysis instead of passing the question along.

I saw warning lights going off. The expectations of success from these two managers couldn't have been more different. If this was the issue (and I suspected that it was), the performance influencer was related to structure and processes, not knowledge and skills. A learning solution wouldn't clarify expectations, which had to be addressed first.

I gently pointed out this discrepancy, letting Samira and Helene know that my team wouldn't be able to provide training until there was a clear and consistent definition of the expectations for success. They understood and began to talk with leadership to reach a consensus. Once they aligned their expectations, their team's performance started to improve immediately. There was no longer a need to create a lengthy boot camp training program.

Often you can determine through a few performance-focused questions that training isn't the best solution, but this isn't always the case. Sometimes, the real reason for the training request isn't clear-cut. That's when you will need to employ level 3, gathering information for a full analysis.

Level 3. The Deepest Dive: Information Gathering and Comparative Analysis

This is the most in-depth analysis you can do and it will take time. For that reason, it's probably only warranted for requests that tie into the largest strategic initiatives or those in which the problem is quite unclear. On the other hand, if the effort involved in a full analysis doesn't seem worthwhile, it's probably time to respond with a strategic no or determine if your team can provide a minimal learning resource to gain some influence and visibility or create something that can scale. Remember, working as an SBP is all about what you *can* do, even within constraints.

The time a full analysis will take depends on the number of roles and teams that will be affected as you look more closely at each of them. It can take a few weeks or a few months, depending on the degree of complexity and depth required. A full analysis gathers information from three sources and then pulls them together to identify the gaps:

- Interviews with key and standard performers, as well as their managers
- Observation of the work being performed (the gemba)
- Review of current data and documents

You can gather all this information simultaneously, but depending on your company's needs, you may require information from only one or two sources. Let's discuss each in more detail.

Interviews With Key Performers, Standard Performers, and Managers

The first information source will be a series of interviews with the people who are doing the work and those who manage them. This includes a handful of key performers, a handful of standard performers, and their managers. If you are looking at a particular program, like onboarding, you may want to talk with people who recently completed that program to ask about their experience and whether it prepared them for their job.

Key performers are employees who are performing to the highest degree on the team. Somehow, they do more, and they do it better than others. Often, this is because they have figured out how to access different resources or created their own job aids and systems. Your task is to figure out what they do differently.

Standard performers are the steady people on the team. They are solidly average. They get their work done and do it well, but they aren't exceeding expectations. In most teams, this is the majority of employees.

Try to talk with a few key performers and a few standard performers within each role on the affected teams. Usually, three to five interviews within each group are plenty. Like most qualitative data gathering, you will know you have talked to enough people when you start to hear the same things repeatedly.

Notice that I don't include those who are low performers or struggling to do their job in this mix. On every team, there's probably someone who's barely hanging on. Chances are they are already on performance improvement plans or their managers are actively attempting to coach them out. It would be great to get them to the level of a standard performer, and we will include them in any initiative, but that's not worth your energy at this point. You want to look at the majority of the team for answers.

You can use the same questions for interviews with both the key and standard performers because your ultimate goal is to discover the differences between them. The questions you ask are about how these people do their work, and they should in some way relate to the different performance influencers. (I've shared a sample questionnaire in Tool 9-2 at the end of this chapter.)

There's no need to let people know they are key or standard performers. That won't help your interview. Instead, tell them that they have been selected as employees who can help you learn more about what it's like to do their job and leave it at that.

3 Tips for Interviewing Team Members
1. Choose Key Performers Based on Performance, Not Preference
Try to ensure that you choose key performers based on how they do their jobs, not based on manager preferences. There is usually more than one way to get to the same end goal, and sometimes less likable people are also more successful. If you want to determine what success looks like, you need to rely on real numbers.

I've fallen into the trap of choosing the wrong key performers myself. There was a facilitator on my team who everyone loved, including colleagues, those she trained, and the stakeholders she worked with regularly. This facilitator frequently brought up concerns about a high level of stress in our one-on-ones. But she could never quite put her finger on what was stressing her out, at least not with me. Eventually, her stress led her to seek a job outside the company and she left. Then, the fallout began.

As we started to train a new facilitator and fill in the gaps left by her absence, we discovered the reason for her stress. She said yes to everyone. Even when she shouldn't have. Even when it was for things we had agreed as a team that we wouldn't do. Even if it caused her more work, or it meant she needed to secretly work overtime to get it all done. She couldn't say no. Everyone loved her for it, but working this way wasn't sustainable.

Before discovering this, I would have said that she was one of the team's key performers, someone that we wanted to emulate. Once we found out the amount of unnecessary work she was doing behind the scenes to make everyone happy, I was glad we weren't trying to raise the performance level of the team based on her example. I would have had a team of stressed-out people pleasers who kept us in order-taking mode.

2. Ask Follow-Up Questions With Performance Influencers in Mind
By asking these questions, you will discover exactly how team members see their success or failure based on their expectations. You can then use this information in recommendations for a future performance management strategy.

On a recent project, I was conducting interviews with operations team members in a small construction company. When I asked how they knew they were successful, they didn't have much to say, other than they knew if someone told them they were.

I dug in to ask the question differently, "How do you know, at the end of the day, that you did a good job, even if no one tells you?" The answers became more concrete: "If I've answered all the questions that came my way that day," and "If I completed all the tasks on the task list."

Now I knew how the team was looking at their success in terms of their own expectations. Ultimately, we were able to use this information to make recommendations for a future performance management strategy.

3. Listen for Personal Resources
You will find that key performers often have access to additional resources or have created their own to help them do their jobs well. If team members talk about this, especially when they get stuck, ask them to share those resources and include them in your documents to review.

> I once interviewed a key performer who had designed a full spreadsheet listing key tasks that his new team members needed to learn in their first three months. But, no one else used it or had access to it. The project I was working on included items that needed to be learned when onboarding specific roles. Gaining access to this key performer's spreadsheet meant I didn't have to start from scratch. I simply modified and enhanced the spreadsheet as part of the overall onboarding strategy and resources. It was amazing!

Managers of key and standard performers are the third group you will want to interview to help you determine whether there are gaps in expectations of how job roles are done and what's most important between the two groups. For interviews with managers, I use a separate set of questions include follow-ups customized to each specific team and project. (I've shared an example questionnaire at the end of this chapter in Tool 9-3.)

Interviews provide quite a bit of information about performance, and you may be able to start identifying gaps and determining whether they are related to training or not. The next data source, the gemba, will provide information that you may never hear in an interview.

Observation of Work Being Performed (the Gemba)

It's one thing to hear someone tell you about their job and another to watch them do it. As discussed in chapter 4, in many companies, this observation is referred to as "going to the gemba," which means going to the place where the work is done. The gemba in each company will look different, but the value gained from spending time there is undeniable.

Colin, the learning and organization development manager for a midsize manufacturing company, recalled a project in which going to the gemba provided clarity that an interview would never have revealed. He had received a request to provide training to improve the skills of the company's press brake operators. The press brake machine bends metal into various configurations that can then be accurately included in the manufacturing process. Managers were finding that metal was being bent incorrectly, which meant that it needed to be rebent. This error resulted in multiple inefficiencies, including lost time and potentially unusable supplies.

Colin decided to go to the gemba and watch the press brake operators work. While looking at the computer directing the bend, he noticed operator adjustments that were intentional and based on a variety of factors affecting how the metal bends. Even humidity can make a difference. When the press brake operator realized they needed to adjust something, they keyed it into the computer, but that change wasn't saved or noted in the system. This meant that if another press brake operator wasn't paying attention, they might not notice the previous adjustment.

At the gemba, Colin interacted with press brake operators who had been doing the job for many years. He realized there was an error in process, not an error in knowledge or skill—the operators knew how to perform bends correctly. Now, Colin could share this information and have a different conversation with those who requested the training and ask them to standardize the process first.

When you go to the gemba and observe employees at work, you have an opportunity to discover additional information that might not be shared via a survey or an interview. Here are some questions to consider as you observe—and make sure to do so without judgment:

- Does the predetermined process match the reality of what is happening on the job? Is the process followed accurately? Does the employee follow an alternate process?
- Where do team members go when they are stuck or need to solve a problem? What resources are they consulting?
- Are there places where employees often get stuck, or are there things that cause them to frequently need to rework something?
- Are there things the employee does that seem to work well or guarantee success?

Remaining Neutral
Several years ago, I was approached by Aaron, the SVP of sales with a request for a communication boot camp to help the sales team reach their highest sales goal yet in the history of the company. This was a strategic initiative and thus, warranted a deeper dive to determine if training would really solve the

problem. The first two levels of analysis hadn't provided an obvious performance reason for the request so I dove into level 3.

While going to the gemba in this situation, I listened in as sellers conducted regular sales calls and presentations with customers. I was looking for whether they were following a process, listening for when people got stuck, observing where they went for additional information, noticing what seemed to work well, and taking furious notes. That was it.

After listening to Scott present to a potential client, I received an instant message almost immediately. It was Scott. "Thanks for listening to my presentation," it said. "I'm always looking for feedback on what I can do better. What suggestions do you have for me?"

While I admired Scott's request for feedback, I had absolutely none to give. At this point, I was strictly on a fact-finding mission. I hadn't drawn any conclusions about what was good and what wasn't. I was only listening to *how* he conducted the presentation, not whether he did a good job.

If you are observing for this purpose, it's important to remain completely neutral. You are simply gathering data and therefore shouldn't be able to provide feedback on whether the employee was doing a good job.

Current Company Data and Documents

Company data and documents that already exist are your third important source of information. Ideally, you'll be able to get your eyes on all of it. But depending on the amount of information available, this can get overwhelming.

First, request access to any data and documents that inform the work in question, especially those that could support each performance influencer. The documents I typically ask to see include:

- Process or procedure documentation
- Team intranet pages, knowledge bases, or shared folders
- Team organizational charts
- Existing team onboarding or other training documents
- Job descriptions

- Data that informs performance, including customer satisfaction scores, quality scores, performance rubrics, sales numbers, and year-end review documents
- Data or processes that are used to determine raises and bonuses

It's rare that all these things exist and can be easily accessed, so I simply try to get as much as I can. As I conduct interviews and observations, I'm also listening and watching for the unofficial data and documents that employees use and I ask for access to those as well.

I suggest you do a first pass through the documents and use them when observing the work—like following along using a process document. However, you'll use them most when doing a comparative analysis of all the information you've gathered.

A Comparative Analysis of Information Gathered

After gathering all this information, it's time to do a comparative analysis so you can draw conclusions about the gaps and whether challenges in the company relate to skills and knowledge and, therefore, can be solved with training or learning. You might say that this is where the magic happens!

I love how successes and gaps are revealed through the comparative analysis process, and it's always fascinating and often surprising to me. My process involves three steps.

First, I break down the interviews and observations into topics. Create a list of topics that emerged during analysis and separate the specifics related to each one by the audience—key performers, standard performers, and managers. Note how frequently each topic is mentioned. This will allow you to see what comes up most often and therefore emerges as a trend instead of an outlier. Compare topics between groups, looking for differences and similarities. Differences indicate gaps or opportunities for improvement, and similarities can indicate a common understanding or thinking.

Second, note where data and documents align and where they fall short. Does the performance data line up with a certain group? Does it line up with rewards and bonuses? Make note of whether the information in documents matches or doesn't match information shared in interviews or observed in visits.

Finally, sort the topics by performance influencers. Take all the topics you have identified as trends, plus your notes on gaps and opportunities, and sort them into the six performance influencer categories. Note the gaps and opportunities you've identified and determine which performance influencer they fall into.

Now, let's return to the information you've gathered through some of the questions in Figures 9-1 and 9-2. Do you see gaps in the skills and knowledge performance influencer category? If yes, a learning or training solution can be used to solve all or part of the problem. Pay attention to gaps in other performance influencer areas as well. This will be valuable information to share with the requester.

If you have determined that a learning solution might best address the issues, take some time to think about what you will recommend. Consider what you know about the stakeholder, their team, their goals, and the way the work gets done. Ideas don't need to be fully baked at this point, so just develop a few high-level recommendations that you can share with the requester.

If they dictated a particular solution in their original ask—like the communications boot camp from the Samira and Helene example—you don't have to comply. Remember, you are the learning expert and should make recommendations as such. You need to be prepared to explain why your recommendation deviates from the original ask.

The next big steps are all about preparing to present your findings to stakeholders. Before you share, however, consider the third major question in the four-question decision tree (Figure 9-1).

3. Does the L&D Team Have the Capacity and Expertise to Work on the Request?

If you've made it this far, you've determined that it was worth it to dive deeper and that a training solution will solve the problem or part of it. But you haven't yet determined whether the L&D team has the capacity and expertise needed to work on the request.

For help answering this question, refer to your internal L&D playbook and the process you used to determine capacity and expertise when designing your overall strategy in the previous chapter—the difficulty versus impact grid.

Follow the same process to determine the difficulty and impact of responding to the stakeholder's request. Is it worth it? Are there any quick wins? If it's worth it, do you have the capacity and expertise needed? If not, can you propose a creative solution? Are there any resources you need to request? If your team doesn't have the capacity or expertise, is there anything you can do?

Once you have determined capacity and written up a few recommendations or key questions, you can prepare your final presentation and work toward a final yes, which also means you can clearly share your strategic no.

4. Will the Stakeholder Partner to Create This Proposed Solution?

Finally, it's time to share your findings to determine whether training will solve the problem your stakeholder has presented. Depending on who this person is and the degree to which they see you as an SBP, sharing this information may invite various levels of skepticism or acceptance.

Share the information you gathered about gaps and proposed solutions in the way that will work best for your stakeholder. Perhaps you'll opt for a simple conversation with a written follow-up. Or maybe you'll include a few visuals. It's all up to your preferences and the preferences of your stakeholders.

You don't need to reveal your entire process unless you think that's helpful for the stakeholder to see. Be sensitive to who will be present, especially if you identified some gaps that team members would be uncomfortable hearing or a message that the leader may not want to spread far and wide.

For example, when completing a full analysis in response to the request for a communications boot camp for the sales team, the data I gathered revealed gaps related to an unclear team structure. This led to confusion among sellers about the scope of their responsibilities. The information also revealed a lack of consistent feedback from VPs. While these were both important callouts because they were strong trends, I didn't think the SVP of sales, who originally placed the training request, would want them shared broadly. So, I told him separately, confirmed the need to keep it confidential, and left him to determine what to do next.

My presentation for all the VPs included the other items I had uncovered. My analysis showed that the problem wasn't poor communication skills (the topic of the original request); instead, it was inconsistency and a lack of direction when it came to the sales process, especially using data to inform progress. Another problem area was building confidence in new products. Both key and standard performers were great communicators who loved their jobs, but they needed additional direction and feedback. Communication training wouldn't have gotten them to the next level—and wouldn't have solved the problem.

The walk through this analysis took time, but it also provided more insight and a solid plan of action for improvement. Additionally, it raised the L&D team's credibility and improved our status as SBPs.

When you present your findings to stakeholders, keep a few best practices in mind:

- **Present the facts as logical, not emotional.** They aren't based on your feelings, but on the data you found as you went through your process.
- **Focus on what you can do.** Try to provide a recommendation to address each gap you uncover and whether the learning team will do the work to make it happen. In the sales example, I recommended standardizing some processes but knew that was outside my control and, therefore, didn't commit to helping. Instead, I pointed out that this would help them reach their goal, using data to back up my statements.
- **Share what falls in the realm of the L&D team and explain how you can help.** In the sales example, I said we could partner to revamp the onboarding program and offered to advise them on creating a consistent process for learning about new products.
- **Make a clear ask at the end.** To avoid stakeholder silence, end your conversation with a recap of where the learning team can partner. If you need commitment from leaders to continue this project, ask for it directly. If you need additional resources, ask for those. If you need them to consider specific questions or help brainstorm additional options, ask for that. Never assume they know what you are asking for when you wrap up the conversation.

Once you have done the due diligence to determine whether the stakeholder's requested solution was worth a deeper dive and what aspects of the problem L&D can partner to address, you will be able to respond with a strategic yes. You will also be able to ask them to give you a strategic yes in return by committing to partner in creating the solution.

If the stakeholder is unwilling to partner with you, then it's time to respond with a strategic no.

How to Communicate Your Strategic No

In most cases (other than one in which the stakeholder is simply unwilling to partner with you), a strategic no isn't a direct pushback, but a redirect. In all three deeper dive levels, instead of telling the stakeholder "No, we can't do that" and walking away, you can suggest alternative resources, brainstorm together, or share where learning could be most helpful and make other recommendations where it could not. The pushback is centered on what you could do to be most effective, given the data and resources available.

Focusing on what you *can* do, even if it is simply suggesting another place to look or another option to try is a form of saying no strategically. It honors the requester by listening to their concerns and taking them seriously, and it empowers them to take the action that will most benefit their team. It shows that you are their partner and are on their side. You want their team to improve and their problems to be solved, even if training isn't the answer.

Interestingly enough, when I have followed this process to share what I've learned, I've often built more credibility and stronger partnerships by responding with a strategic no by creating requested training, and I'm not alone.

Laurel, the senior director of learning experience for a global multinational technology company, feels the same. When customer satisfaction scores were dropping and the number of customer terminations were rising, Laurel and her team were pulled into the business transformation office with a request for training. It was both an overall strategic initiative and a critical issue, so they knew it was worth their time to dive deeper. As they started having conversations with stakeholders and SMEs, Laurel realized that while everyone knew the symptom was customer dissatisfaction, no one knew the cause. She could sense the frustration in the room. So, Laurel offered to run a level 3 analysis.

After a series of interviews, she uncovered a list of problems that training couldn't solve. There were issues with teams documenting critical information, misunderstandings of what needed to be documented, fields in the software that were needed but weren't required (which resulted in inaccurate reporting), sales leaders who were holding their teams to different standards, and more.

Laurel brought her findings back to the VP of business transformation, who had originally requested training. As she shared the results, the VP became increasingly grateful. They had no idea any of the problems Laurel shared existed. Because she didn't uncover anything that could be solved by training, Laurel didn't offer to create anything. She just made suggestions around fixing items in the software, making fields required, rewriting questions for clarity, and helping leaders get on the same page about standardization for performance across teams. Then, she walked away.

Over the next couple years, that VP came back to Laurel and her team a few more times, asking, "Can you guys do that thing again? That thing where you ask questions and then tell us what's going on?"

Even without creating a training solution, Laurel solidified her credibility as an SBP with this stakeholder.

Summary

An L&D strategy will help you prioritize work, but it won't stop requests from coming. To remain strategic, you will need to say both yes and no carefully and thoughtfully. Remember these tips:

- Shift your mindset so you won't say yes to everything.
- Create a system to strategically respond to requests, especially when you are buried in the details.
- Determine whether it is worth taking time to dive deeper on a request based on several questions.
- If a deeper dive is needed, aim to determine the cause of the problem to ensure that a learning or training solution can solve it.
- If learning can solve the problem, determine whether the L&D team has the capacity and expertise needed to create a solution.
- Confirm the commitment of stakeholders to partner in solutions.

Tool 9-1. A Review of the Strategic Yes and No

The next time you receive a request that isn't part of your L&D strategy, work toward four yeses using this progression of questions. If you can't attain these four, it's time for a strategic no.

Yes #1. Is It Worth Your Time to Dive Deeper Into This Request?
- Does L&D already have something that can fulfill this request?
- Does this request tie into a larger strategic initiative?
- Is this request based on compliance or a current critical need?
- Will this request help L&D build influence or visibility, provide a product that will scale later, or help you avoid future problems?

Yes #2. Can a Learning Solution Solve the Performance Issue?
- Determine the cause of the problem with one of three levels of analysis:
  » Level 1 (easy): It's obvious.
  » Level 2 (light analysis): One assumption with lots of questions
  » Level 3 (full analysis): Interviews, the gemba, and data and documents

Yes #3. Does the L&D Team Have the Capacity and Expertise to Work on This Request?
- Use the difficulty versus impact grid.
- Ask what you and your team can do.

Yes #4. Will the Stakeholder Partner to Create the Proposed Solution?
- Share the results of your deep dive and the reality of your capacity and expertise with the stakeholder.
- Ask the stakeholder directly for a commitment to partner.

Tool 9-2. Sample Questionnaire for Key and Standard Performers

Here is the set of general questions I tend to use for these analysis projects. I suggest modifying or customizing them depending on the performer's role and the company. You can also add more specific questions, but the overarching themes generally stay the same. Ensure those you're interviewing touch on all six performance influencers but avoid asking them to do so directly.

I recommend sending your questions in advance of the interview with the caveat that preparation isn't required. Some people prefer to see and think through questions beforehand, and the interview will be better if they have the chance to do so. Note that I've also included each question's related performance influencers and purpose for your information.

When did you start in this role? What was your background at that time?
- *Question purpose:* Provides a big-picture view of who is in this role and what their background is.
- *Related performance influencer:* Personal capability—previous experience

Give me a general overview of a typical day in your role. How do you start, how do you end, and what happens in between?
- *Question purpose:* To learn what it is like to do their job each day
- *Related performance influencers:* Structure and processes, skills and knowledge, resources, and information and feedback

What are the most important tasks you need to do each day or regularly in your job?
- *Question purpose:* Learning what takes up the most time in the role as well as what they deem most important
- *Related performance influencers:* Structure and processes, resources, information and feedback, and skills and knowledge

Where do you go if you get stuck or need additional information while working?
- *Question purpose:* Insight into key resources that they regularly use
- *Related performance influencers:* Resources and information and feedback

What gets in your way and stops you from doing your best work?
- *Question purpose:* To identify barriers and blockers
- *Related performance influencers:* All six

How do you know whether you are doing a good job and succeeding in your role?
- *Question purpose:* To determine if performance metrics are used and what success looks like in the role
- *Related performance influencers:* Rewards and information and feedback

Tool 9-3. Sample Questionnaire for Managers

Several questions for managers are similar to those for key and standard performers, but with a twist based on their perspective. Managers oversee the work of performers, rather than complete it themselves, so keep this in mind when you ask them questions. However, you'll still touch on all six performance influencers.

Like the interview for key and standard performers, I recommend sending the questions in advance to provide an opportunity for managers to prepare, should they desire to do so.

Which roles report to you?
- *Question purpose:* To understand team structure
- *Related performance influencer:* Structure and processes

When you consider the roles that report to you, what are the most important things they need to do on a regular basis? (Modify this question if you're only seeking to learn about one of the roles that reports to this manager.)
- *Question purpose:* To uncover what the manager sees as most important for the role
- *Related performance influencers:* Structure and processes, resources, information and feedback, and skills and knowledge

How do you know if your team members are successful?
- *Question purpose:* To determine how success is measured
- *Related performance influencers:* Rewards and information and feedback

What indicators tell you a team member is not successful?
- *Question purpose:* To uncover evidence of what isn't working
- *Related performance influencers:* Potentially all six

Where do you see team members getting stuck in their role most often? What happens when they get stuck?
- *Question purpose:* To determine areas that might be blocking performance as well as potential resources
- *Related performance influencers:* Potentially all six

When you hire someone for this role, what are the non-negotiable skills, experiences, and qualifications they must have?
- *Question purpose:* To determine the expectations of what someone should already know when they start the role
- *Related performance influencer:* Personal capability

CHAPTER 10
Measure to Make Decisions

Let's play a game. I'll give you two scenarios, and you consider which is more realistic.

Imagine some executives in a heated discussion about the best use of company resources. The current economy isn't helping the bottom line, and a tough decision needs to be made. The company's leadership development program comes up. The executives know employees enjoy participating, but the program isn't free. It pulls employees out of production for multiple hours, requires a program manager or facilitator, and relies on a purchased curriculum. The execs ask for details about program results.

In the first scenario, the VP of learning and leadership development pipes up, explaining that "the program is very well run and highly interactive. I can't say enough good things about the program manager. You're right that people enjoy participating. It boosts morale. We've heard managers say that the employees who participate are better at their jobs afterward. The program covers key leadership skills like communication, coaching, and giving feedback. It makes our leaders who they are. I can pull some direct quotes if that would be helpful."

In the second scenario, on the other hand, the VP of learning and leadership development says, "I've got some information about program results that we can add to the mix." Then, she shares these key statistics:

- Over the past two years, 200 people participated in the leadership development program.
- The current program cost is approximately $800 per participant, including time out of production, curriculum cost, and the program manager's salary.
- Of the 200 employees who participated, 75 percent were promoted to leadership roles within three months of completion, saving the company a minimum of $900,000 on recruiting, hiring, and onboarding costs.
- Those who participated in the program have, on average, a 20 percent higher retention rate on their teams than the rest of the company.
- Data from employee engagement surveys shows that team members who report to program participants report higher job satisfaction, better support from their leaders, and a better understanding of how to be successful in their roles.
- A postprogram survey that asked the participants' managers to report changes in behavior found an average of 50 percent improvement in coaching skills, communication skills, and the ability to provide clear feedback.

After sharing the key points, the VP said, "Let's put those numbers next to the other programs we are talking about to see where we get the biggest bang for our buck. We can also calculate potential longer-term impacts if that's helpful."

Based on your experiences, which of these scenarios do you think is more realistic? If you were one of the executives in the meeting, which scenario would provide the most helpful information for making the best decision for the business? Now consider which scenario would help the VP of learning and leadership development demonstrate she is a credible strategic business partner.

In the second scenario, the VP shared specific data about the program's impact, noting that this information could be "added to the mix" to determine what's best for the company's bottom line. She also exhibited an SBP's best practices by setting her ego aside and focusing on the business. She demonstrated savvy leadership by providing clear, factual data to inform the decision, without an expectation that it would be in her favor. Without desperation or panic, she behaved as a business leader first and an L&D leader second.

You may have seen something like the first scenario play out in your organization. Can you see why the second scenario is better? The VP in the first scenario was knowledgeable about the program and thought it was well run, but their report lacked concrete information that other leaders could use to make important budgetary decisions for the company. Her anecdotal evidence indicated that the leadership program was "nice to have" and "well-liked," but didn't provide any data. She approached the meeting as a learning leader—not as an equal business partner faced with a difficult decision.

If you intend to work as an SBP, you will need an effective measurement practice, which can set you apart, enhance your credibility, and demonstrate that your L&D team understands and behaves like the rest of the business. So, that's what we'll cover in this chapter.

The Real Reason We Measure

Most of us didn't go into the L&D profession because we love data and numbers, so we often consider measurement a necessary evil to prove our worth rather than a helpful tool in our everyday work. Because L&D is typically seen as a cost center that's not obviously tied to revenue, we tend to feel expendable. After all, we aren't selling things or servicing customers. But the urge to prove our worth with numbers is all wrong. "Prove it" energy usually produces more panic than productivity and can come across as emotional or desperate, depending on the situation. The first step to creating an effective measurement plan is to start thinking differently about its purpose: We need to measure what we do so we can make informed business decisions. Period.

My own experience as an L&D leader tells the story of this shift in thinking. For a long time, I was stuck believing I needed to focus on measurement because if I didn't, I might lose people or resources. The pressure to measure was stressful, and I felt overwhelmed by a task I didn't think I was good at. I often felt like my team was thinking, "Please, tell them what we do is valuable so we can keep our jobs!" whereas I was thinking, "I have no idea how to do that." At times, I felt paralyzed.

When I shifted my mindset and started to think of measurement through the lens of a business leader, realizing the data was for making informed business decisions, the stress began to melt away. I moved from thinking about measurement with my emotions to engaging the logical part of my brain. Instead of asking, "What data do I need to prove that my team is worth the expense?" I started asking, "What data do I need to make decisions about how best to serve the business, run my team, and do our best work?"

I began to see measurement as a way to collect, manage, and monitor data to reveal what was working and what wasn't, whether iterations were needed, and whether my team was spending time and resources in the right places, meeting our stakeholders' needs, or needed to make specific changes. I could act strategically and proactively in partnership with other business leaders. I could look for data that exposed gaps and challenges in which we knew a learning solution could make an impact. We could go to different business areas with recommendations before they came to us, or use data to inform our L&D strategy's next iteration.

Viewing measurement through this lens allowed my team to take "proving our worth" off the table. Ironically, once we focused on data when making decisions, proving our worth was no longer necessary—it was obvious.

Now it's your turn to shift your own mindset and get to work. As an SBP, you need an overall plan for measurement within L&D as well as one for every individual project or program. In short, you need a plan that allows you to make informed business decisions.

Your L&D Measurement Plan

The first time I created an overall L&D measurement plan, I intentionally listed it as one of my performance goals for the year. I needed accountability for what felt like a momentous task. My team already had a few rudimentary metrics in place, but nothing close to an overall plan that we were managing, monitoring, and communicating regularly with stakeholders. Like many L&D teams, we ran several programs for multiple business units and continuously created content aimed at a variety of audiences throughout the company. There was a lot we could measure.

As I sat staring at that goal, the months started to tick by. To say I was overwhelmed is an understatement. I had no idea how to get everything organized into an easy-to-follow, repeatable plan. I wasn't making much progress until I discovered three essential categories of measurement for L&D: efficiency, effectiveness, and outcomes. I found them in a book called *Measurement Demystified* by David Vance and Peggy Parskey. These categories—which align to parts of the familiar Kirkpatrick Four Levels of Evaluation and Phillips ROI Methodology—gave me a way to sort my team's existing data and determine where we had gaps in our plan.

Efficiency Measures

Efficiency measures, sometimes called *activity measures*, answer questions like how many, how much, and how often. Most L&D teams collect efficiency measures, even if they aren't regularly reporting them. They include the number of people who have participated in a training program, enrolled in a online course, or clicked on a learning article. They may also include metrics related to team efficiency, such as how many hours team members spent facilitating, how many new learning courses or videos were completed each quarter, and how much it costs to create a new course or train a new employee.

Effectiveness Measures

Effectiveness measures are focused primarily on the Kirkpatrick and Phillips Levels 2 and 3—learning and behavior change. They tell you whether L&D solutions are helping people learn new knowledge or change their behavior.

Often, effectiveness measures are tied to performance metrics that you don't own but need to monitor based on the problems you're attempting to solve. For example, if you're trying to improve quality scores for contact center agents, you'd monitor the quality scores (the performance metric) both before and after participation in the learning experience you design. The owner of these metrics is the contact center, so you'd need to collaborate with the key stakeholders in that area to access the information.

Effectiveness measures can also be gathered through surveys or evaluations related to the programs we administer. These should be designed to ask specifically about whether participants learned the information (acquired new knowledge) and whether their behavior changed as a result. Without related performance metrics, we can ask participants to self-report, or we can send the survey to the participants' managers to report on whether they have observed learning and the application of new skills and knowledge. If the learning team is administering the surveys and evaluations, they own and monitor the data, sharing results with stakeholders.

Outcome Measures

Outcome measures (which are tied to Kirkpatrick Level 4 and Phillips Levels 4 and 5) show an impact on overall business goals and initiatives. This is where most L&D professionals get stuck. But as Vance and Parskey (2021) note, we don't need outcome measures for everything we do, and trying to find them for every project creates unnecessary work and, subsequently, unnecessary stress.

Outcome measures should focus on the biggest and most important initiatives—the ones that align with the company's overall strategy. These are also likely the goals in your L&D strategy. On the other hand, your daily tasks (such as coordinating LMS training) don't need outcome measures attached to them unless improving those items is part of a larger company strategy.

For example, let's say that one of your company initiatives is to improve the efficiency of processes and reduce expenses. Your L&D team aligns with this initiative by setting a goal to reduce onboarding expenses. Because this goal is tied to a larger strategic initiative, it is worthy of the time and effort needed to measure the outcome. Your team puts measurements in place to determine current expenses, and then, after working toward the goal, shows the decrease in expenses as a result. You can report this decrease as part of your team's contribution to the overall company initiative. Outcome measure complete.

Start With a Measurement Audit

The first step in creating an L&D measurement plan is to understand what currently exists. Note what you are already measuring or data you are already monitoring and sort it into efficiency, effectiveness, and outcome measures. In essence, you are conducting a type of measurement audit. As you comb through what already exists, find answers to these questions:

- What are you already measuring? What category does it fit into (efficiency, effectiveness, or outcome)?

- What performance measures (not owned by L&D) are affected by the work you and your team complete?
- Which of your projects tie to your company's overall strategic initiatives? Do you have measures in place to determine impact?
- How frequently are you gathering data from each of these measures?

I find it helpful to list all this information in a simple template like the one in Table 10-1, which includes the name of the measure, the corresponding L&D project or program, the category, the owner of the measurement, and the frequency with which it is administered.

Table 10-1. Measurement Audit Template

Measure	Project or Program	Category	Owner	Frequency
Number of participants	Leadership program	Efficiency	Jess	Upon program completion

Once you have a list of measures that are sorted by category, step back and look at the overall picture you have created. Ask a few more questions to determine whether additional measures are needed to fill in the gaps or if you are using all the data you are currently gathering:

- Do you have measures in all three categories? Which category or categories are lacking? What might you need to populate them?
- Do you have outcome measures tied to each of those projects? Do they align with the company's overall strategic goals?
- Does every measure help you to make informed business decisions? (If not, you might be able to stop gathering that data. Don't spend time measuring for the sake of measurement.)
- Do you have systems or processes in place to regularly gather and analyze the measures you need?

Measurement for What?

A word of caution: Just because you *can* gather the data, doesn't mean you *should*. Early in my career, I had an excellent measurement mentor named Elaine, who had spent decades conducting assessments in several organizations. I loved meeting with her because she thought in both analytical and relational terms.

We often met at a coffee shop so I could get her feedback on a recent version of one of my surveys, measurement strategies, or an attempt at assessment.

One of Elaine's most common questions was, "What will you do with that data?" She wanted me to think about why I would include a question in a survey or attempt to gather data if I didn't have a plan to use the results. That would be a waste of everyone's time.

To this day, I still hear Elaine's voice in my head with every attempt at measurement. "What will I do with this data?" This is especially relevant when designing surveys and evaluations. If the information isn't helpful in determining whether you're hitting your targets and making informed business decisions, it isn't worth the time and effort to gather it.

After the Audit

After completing an audit, you should have the information needed to create a basic measurement strategy with items in all three categories. You may even be able to reduce some of your existing measures.

Years ago, when I completed my initial audit to develop a measurement strategy, I was pleasantly surprised. I discovered that my team had access to and was gathering more data than I had thought. The problem was that we weren't organizing or analyzing it.

I also discovered we were great at efficiency measures and could eliminate a few because they didn't help us make business decisions. We were only marginally OK at effectiveness measures, especially tying them back to performance data, so we needed to partner better with our stakeholders.

When I began thinking about outcome measures, I was initially overwhelmed. But then, I reframed my thinking. If I tied outcome measures only to strategic initiatives, that would lead to the simplification and clarity I needed. Thanks to my new focus on the three categories of measurement, I was able to create a robust measurement strategy that was realistic, even within our small team.

Measurement for Each Learning Project

As you develop your measurement plan for each learning project, it will be important to include all the key concepts for your overall measurement strategy on a smaller scale. Keep in mind that measurement's purpose is to help you make informed business decisions, using efficiency and effectiveness measures as well as outcome measures, if needed. And don't forget my mentor Elaine's advice: Do something with the data you gather.

Now, let's discuss a couple best practices that you can rely on to guide you:
1. Measure first, design second.
2. Focus on performance.

Measure First, Design Second

Measure first, design second means that you should always start by identifying what you'll measure before you design the solution. In some ways, this seems counterintuitive. How can we measure something before we have created it?

But the real question should be: How can we create something that results in a change or solves a problem without first knowing what needs to change or what problem needs solving?

In the spirit of using measurement to make informed business decisions, how will we know if a change occurred or a problem was solved if we don't have any way of measuring it? We may have feelings or anecdotal evidence that tells us things are different, but do we really know where we *started*?

The need to define a starting point is why we can and must measure first. Nine times out of 10, we are not measuring what we create; we are measuring the *impact* of what we create on already existing metrics indicating current performance. Often, L&D doesn't own these metrics, so we need to partner with others to understand and monitor them.

Before taking on a new project, Travis—the SVP of talent at a midsize insurance, financial services, and HR consulting company—asks anyone requesting help from L&D about business impact and measurement. For example, leaders from the sales team came to Travis with a list of classes they needed his team to create. After digging deeper, Travis learned that the outcome they wanted was for every salesperson to start working from a written business plan. The document would articulate the salesperson's goals and specific activities to complete to achieve those goals, and it would be followed closely and adjusted monthly in conversations between the salesperson and their manager. Travis then asked why this business plan was the ultimate desired outcome.

"We know that when a salesperson follows a written business plan, they are more successful," explained one of the sales leaders. "We have stats that show someone following a business plan generates three times the average revenue of someone who doesn't follow one."

Travis now had a new direction for the request: helping members of the sales team create written business plans. He also had measures (in the form of three-to-one revenue targets) against which he could monitor the outcome of any initiative. These measures were determined from the beginning, giving direction to the initiative.

A Hard Lesson Learned

When we try to figure out how to measure impact after a program has been rolled out or a project is complete, we make our work much more difficult than it needs to be. Yes, this is another lesson I learned the hard way.

I was in a program manager role, designing and implementing a large-scale leadership development program across my company. I had inherited the content but was working steadily to improve it. I knew I had made the program more efficient and had received feedback from participants that they enjoyed the experience and were learning new skills. This feedback came from informal comments as well as a short postprogram survey. That was the full extent of measurement in the program I inherited, but I wasn't worried. I was having fun in the role and, anecdotally, I knew the program was helping people succeed.

Then a senior leader asked for metrics to show participants' changes in behavior, and my brain went blank. These behavior change metrics didn't exist.

At the time, I knew about Level 3 and 4 metrics and had previously run programs that already had them in place. My new program was running well without them, which led me to attack my work in a way that I now see was backward. I focused on improving the program first—before considering measurement. (After all, that was more fun.)

After the request for metrics arrived, I had to reverse course quickly and try to figure out what evidence of program success might exist. I also suspected the question about metrics probably stemmed from other questions about the leadership program's value. Was it worth the time and expense or just a "nice to have" extra? Instead of focusing on making informed business decisions, I found myself feeling like I was on defense—that without the right metrics, my job might be in jeopardy. I was in "proving my worth" territory.

After multiple weeks of scrambling, including talking to stakeholders, analyzing mind-bending measurement struggles, and dealing with stress, I secured data showing that program participants were more likely to be promoted into positions with additional responsibility. Given the company's need to build a leadership pipeline, it was decent data. But I had gathered it too late, and it had taken way too much time and effort to uncover. I learned my lesson. If I had asked questions about business goals and which aspects of participant performance were expected to change up front when I inherited the program, I would have avoided a lot of stress and headaches later on. By waiting, I made the entire process much harder than it needed to be.

I never made that mistake again. I learned to start with questions about performance and dig into any existing data that would support a training request, identify changes that occurred afterward, and indicate if iterations were needed. I now understand that only after measurement is defined, should I start on the design.

With this simple flip to defining measurement first, the task becomes much easier. I no longer have go back to find or create the right measurement puzzle piece after the fact. Instead, it's my new starting point for driving a design process positioned for impact.

Find Your Measures as a Partner

Almost all the solutions we create as SBPs should be designed to improve the performance of people in our companies. But in L&D, we do not own performance data or assessments. We should not be monitoring whether a machine operator has completed their work accurately, a salesperson has met their revenue target, a contact center agent has met or exceeded their quality scores, or a leader is ready for promotion. We don't define what success looks like in any of those roles. Yet, because these measures determine performance levels and effectiveness in a variety of roles, they will also determine whether our learning or training solutions improve performance. Luckily, we don't need to create or monitor these numbers; we just need to *partner* with the people who do.

As part of your partnerships, you'll need to find out what performance measures exist in your company, and which ones need to improve because of your work. This is sometimes easier said than done.

If you're meeting regularly with stakeholders, determining how they measure performance should be covered in your conversations and part of your robust business knowledge. You might try proactively suggesting learning or training solutions by saying, "I see the quality scores are dipping around empathy. Let's explore how we might partner to change that."

Questions about metrics can also fast-track the start of a project with a stakeholder. For example, you could say, "I know you measure quality scores regularly with this team. Is that what you are hoping to improve as a result of this project?"

However, until you have established a trusting relationship, you will need to rely on a few detective skills to find existing metrics and determine how a learning solution might affect them. I like to ask these seven questions when I put on my detective hat:

1. How do you currently measure your team members' performance?
2. How do you know that someone on your team is doing a good job?
3. What metrics or evidence supports that? (Ask this question if the answers to the first two questions are vague.)
4. What metrics do you use to determine raises and promotions?
5. Regarding the project we are discussing, how will team member performance change as a result?
6. What evidence do you have that this behavior is *not* currently happening?
7. Regarding the project we are discussing, what metrics will tell you if it has helped team members' performance?

Note: Sometimes, it's necessary to ask the same question in a few different ways to help stakeholders understand what you are looking for. Also, you may not need to ask all these questions to determine the performance measures in play for a project—or you may need to ask more, especially if the requester isn't used to tying learning solutions to performance impact.

It's also possible that you'll ask all these questions and still won't come up with any concrete performance measures. Depending on the maturity of a company, the measures you want may not exist.

What If Performance Measures Don't Exist?

If you want to measure impact on performance, you need to show the difference between where someone started before the learning experience and where they ended afterward. Ideally, you'll be able to illustrate this with existing performance metrics.

But what if there isn't a starting point? How can you demonstrate movement if you don't know where participants are starting? It's like asking how we know how far we've traveled if we don't know our origin point.

If you're facing this scenario, you are not alone. In my experience, a lack of existing metrics is common, especially in smaller or less mature companies. The business pain or performance issue that needs solving is felt but not measured.

A lack of existing metrics doesn't mean that we give up trying to measure impact altogether. Instead, we pivot our approach from uncovering existing data points to partnering with a stakeholder to create them. There are two strategies that I have found helpful, depending on the situation:

- Partner with the stakeholder to determine the current performance benchmark before you begin.
- Gather data while creating and delivering the learning experience.

Partner to Determine the Current Performance Benchmark

Using this approach, you'll work alongside the stakeholder to create a current performance benchmark that you can use to compare performance changes after implementing the learning solution. For example, a stakeholder group came to my team requesting a new onboarding curriculum that would help new employees learn the basics of their roles. They said that their managers were spending too much time training new employees and it was taking new employees too long to learn their key tasks. Further, even after training, these new employees lacked key knowledge and confidence in their roles.

So, we asked them how much time supervisors were currently spending on training, how long it took for new employees to learn key tasks, and if there was any data on items new employees were not learning as well as their reported confidence. Note that all we did was ask for data on their current state based on the reasons they told us they needed an onboarding overhaul.

Our questions were met with blank stares. This business unit had never measured any of the things they wanted to change; instead, they just believed things weren't working. Benchmarks didn't exist—just feelings of stress and overwhelm. So, instead of starting to talk about design, we partnered with the stakeholders to determine current measures. We guided them on how to use calendar reports and questionnaires to gather data (in estimation) about the current time supervisors spent training. Similarly, we helped them start a process for reporting how soon new employees began contributing to workloads after their start date. Finally, we provided a copy of a post-onboarding effectiveness survey and asked the stakeholders to send it out to employees who started on their teams in the past four months to gauge current onboarding effectiveness, including both knowledge and confidence scores.

It took time to gather the data up front, but once we had it, we were better able to focus our design efforts. Note that this process also served as a light needs analysis. Had the data disproven the business unit's hypotheses—if managers weren't actually spending a lot of time onboarding, employees were contributing immediately, and effectiveness measures were high—we would have dug deeper into a root cause analysis to determine the reasons for their issues.

After we created and implemented the new onboarding program, we were able to compare the data on time the managers spent onboarding, time to contribution, and onboarding effectiveness and show movement (impact) based on our previously gathered benchmarks. We decreased the time a manager spent onboarding employees by 70 percent and decreased the new employees' time to contribution by 70 percent. We were also able to show improvement in effectiveness and confidence based on the new survey results. As a bonus, because we could easily match time to money, we were able to show savings of more than $800,000 in the first six months after implementing the new onboarding program.

Without finding the data first, we would never have been able to show those results. Yes, we could have created the program without data, but we would not have been able to determine whether it was helpful or just nice to have. Instead, we had impressive outcomes based on real metrics illustrating L&D's impact on business processes.

Gather Data While Creating and Delivering

Sometimes, we can't get a benchmark ahead of time; for example, if the stakeholder is unable to gather the information or the need is so urgent that the time to establish a benchmark simply doesn't exist. This was the case when Rory came to my team requesting assistance in creating a more efficient way to educate new customers. An unexpectedly large sale meant he had to quickly educate more customers than usual, and he worried the current process wouldn't work without overtaxing his team. But clear metrics didn't exist regarding the time or touches needed to complete the education process.

My team knew that if we could show efficiencies gained in this process for the business unit, it would help make future business decisions about the work they could take on (which is the main reason we measure). It might even make a case for software to automate some of the workload.

There wasn't enough time to determine the current metrics before beginning the project (the sale had happened and the customers would arrive soon), so we immediately dove into design. However, we made sure to set up points to measure the new education process along the way. We captured the number of customers using and accessing our solution. Rory's team also started capturing the amount of time spent working with other customers who were not using our solution.

Upon completing the project, we were able to compare our data and estimate that the automated system provided the equivalent of one full-time employee's worth of work per 200 customers. Now, we had the measurement to show that efficiencies were gained and were able to calculate an equivalent for cost savings that we (and the business unit) could use to make a case for future enhancements.

If you have determined that a learning solution could solve the problem at hand, that it will meet an urgent need, or that it aligns with an overall strategic initiative, and measures don't exist, it's still better to create them along with the project than to go back and create them afterward.

The Importance of a Measurement System

Measurement and all the data gathered as a result won't do any good if it isn't used to make informed business decisions. And it won't be used for that purpose if there isn't a regular system in place to monitor the data, analyze it, and communicate findings.

When I performed the measurement audit for my team, I was surprised by the amount of data we were gathering. I thought we had very little measurement in place because we lacked a system to monitor, analyze, and communicate the measures. In some cases, data gathering was inconsistent, and in others, we gathered tons of data but never reviewed it. Because we weren't reviewing it, we also weren't summarizing or sharing the results with stakeholders.

The data we gathered was going into a lovely dark box that we would get to *someday*. Because we hadn't put a system or process in place to do anything with it, someday was code for, "We will get to this after all the other priorities are complete." Can you guess how that worked out? We might as well have said, "We aren't going to do anything besides gather data."

The magic of measurement doesn't happen in the gathering; it happens in the rest of the process—the one we didn't have—to regularly monitor, analyze, and communicate results.

This issue reminds me of my dad, who has always loved numbers and patterns and was a math professor. For a long time (despite my genes), I was confident that I hated math because understanding numbers was harder for me than understanding words. When I went to college, I opened the course catalog and searched for all the majors that wouldn't require any additional math courses.

But I did love logic puzzles, and I also loved stories. I especially loved when logical stories could help people see things in a different way. That's what measurement is and that's what measurement does! Logical data is formulated in such a way that it tells a story about the current state. That story can then be used to help others understand reality through a different lens because it solidifies the evidence in a way that is more difficult to argue. It confirms or disproves anecdotes and emotions.

Once I figured out that measurement wasn't just about the numbers, but about stories, I fell in love. My dad loves numbers for the sake of numbers (counting sheep wakes him up instead of relaxing him), but I love numbers and data for the story that they tell.

However, that story doesn't emerge just by gathering the data. We must do something with it to both recognize and tell the story. Without a system or process to do so, the likelihood of transforming numbers into a story is slim.

Your measurement plan also needs a measurement system. It should be made up of three different processes—gathering data, reviewing and analyzing data, and communicating findings—and you should conduct all of them consistently (Figure 10-1).

Figure 10-1. Measurement Consistency Cycle

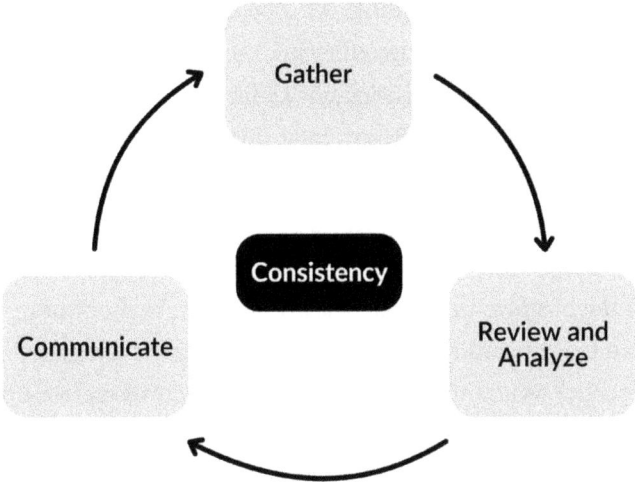

Gather Data

First, you'll need to be sure there is a consistent process in place to conduct any measurement activities and gather the resulting data. This process should find data in two locations:

- Data owned by L&D
- Data owned by stakeholders and business units

If L&D owns the measurement activity, regularly administering that activity and collecting the resulting data should be easy, as long as it is done consistently. The timing of administration and collection can depend on related programs or projects, reporting expectations, or both.

When L&D doesn't own the measurement activity (like performance metrics), it is necessary to obtain consistent access by partnering with the stakeholders or business units who own that data.

One of my L&D team's main responsibilities was to onboard all roles within the company. The extent of my team's involvement varied. For key business units—such as the contact center, operations, and client account management—we were involved with onboarding until the new employee could perform the most common tasks associated with their role, allowing them to contribute to regular production. For others—like marketing, sales, and HR—my team was involved only to introduce the basics of the company, including products offered, customer life cycle, and commonly used software.

Because we owned onboarding, we also owned much of the measurement surrounding it. This included efficiency measures like the number of new employees per business unit. It also included effectiveness measures from assessments during onboarding designed to indicate readiness (whether they know the information), as well as the responses to a self-assessment survey that was administered after onboarding was completed and included questions focused on learning and application.

Some of the business units had measures in place to monitor performance and progress after onboarding. This was the case with the contact center, which monitored quality assurance (QA) scores. These scores were owned by the contact center, but we partnered to receive access to them on a quarterly basis. That way, we could see further evidence of a new hire's ability to perform the role after onboarding was complete.

The key to gathering this data was to do it consistently to maintain accuracy. For example, we wouldn't have wanted to administer the post-onboarding survey at 61 days for some new employees and 91 days for others. The data wouldn't be comparable. Because our average onboarding program took five to six weeks, we chose to administer the survey 61 days post hire for everyone, which was enough time for new employees to get through the onboarding process and start applying their skills regularly on the job. We had a specific team member administer the survey, which was added to their calendar as a routine task.

This is an example of a measure that is gathered consistently based on the program. The measures we gathered from readiness assessments were also driven by the program because the assessments were administered at specific points throughout the onboarding program.

But when it came to overall efficiency measures and our partnership with the contact center, the frequency was strictly related to our need to share findings. Just like all other business units, the L&D team was expected to contribute a quarterly business report (QBR), which included key measures. That meant we needed to have our efficiency and performance effectiveness measures ready to report each quarter. So, we set up a system to gather this data and have it ready quarterly, adhering to common reporting practices.

I recommend ensuring the frequency with which you gather data makes sense for the program or project, as well as common reporting practices. Frequency needs to be logical as much as it needs to be consistent. Assign specific team members to gather data as part of their regular workflow. And make data gathering a repeatable process, according to the necessary frequency.

Review and Analyze Data

It's one thing to gather all the data, but another to interpret it. Without taking time to review and analyze what you see, all you have are numbers. You miss the most important part of measurement: the story it is telling. This will identify trends, successes, gaps, and areas of opportunity, as well as allow you to make informed business decisions. When you review and analyze the data, you reveal the story. So, after gathering the data, the next part of your measurement system is to review and analyze it to look for patterns and trends.

When conducting my own measurement audit surrounding my team's onboarding program, I realized part of our problem was that we were gathering information but not reviewing or analyzing it. So, we started to look back at our data to do that. Much of it revealed that our onboarding program was effective. Employees were learning new information and applying it. That was until I started to review data from the contact center—that's when I found a gaping hole. In the post-onboarding surveys we administered, we asked two open-ended questions. One asked what the most helpful part of onboarding program was and the other asked what we should be covering in more depth. As I started to look back on months and months of survey responses, the answers to what needed to be covered in more depth were almost all the same: There was one product that nearly everyone said they didn't understand after onboarding.

Believe me when I tell you this wasn't just a gap—it was a chasm. The data trend told us that onboarding was failing the contact center, the new employees, and likely the customers when it came to this product. The embarrassing part was it had been there for months. We could have easily identified the trend. We had the data; we just hadn't taken the time to review and analyze it.

Once we finally reviewed and analyzed the data, we uncovered the story. It told us we needed to make a business decision to redesign the way we covered that product during onboarding. Without the review, we wouldn't have had the story. Without the story, we wouldn't have known how to increase our impact.

Just as gathering data needs to be a consistent process, so does reviewing and analyzing it to identify trends and stories. Without consistent review and analysis, we might as well not gather data at all.

Communicate Findings

Your next step is to share your findings with each appropriate audience. Who needs to know what?

Communicating findings is based entirely on the stakeholder's WIIFM. Every stakeholder won't want to know about all the information you found. For example, the customer service leader probably doesn't care about whether your L&D team is working efficiently. Just like we don't want to provide stakeholders with laundry lists of to-do items, we also don't want to overwhelm them with our data. But we do want them to know about what's relevant and important to them.

The best way to communicate is in a snapshot—something that is easy to read and understand. This can be in a dashboard, scorecard, or report (bonus points if you can create an appropriate visual using a graph or chart). Challenge yourself to provide a minimal amount of information in a format that your stakeholders can view and understand in two minutes or less.

Let's return to the five key stakeholder groups we identified in chapter 7. Each one likely needs different information.

1. Your L&D Team

Each member of your team—including each key stakeholder—needs information about efficiency and effectiveness, especially if it relates to the projects or programs they own. They also need information about their efficiency and effectiveness when it comes to performance goals.

If your team is going to make informed business decisions about what to keep, what to toss, and where to iterate, they need access to data and trends supporting those decisions. Consider creating a team scorecard or report that can be shared with your L&D stakeholders. Distribute it in L&D team meetings, in shared files, and in one-on-ones. If the L&D team is more mature, team members may review the data and share findings with you. Regardless, make the communication of all your findings clear and consistent.

2. Your Boss

Your boss needs to know how the team is performing and the impact that L&D is having on the greater organization. They need to be able to tell L&D's story in circles where you do not sit so it spreads throughout the company. They also need to remain in the loop and not be caught off guard if someone asks about L&D results. Your boss may also be a brainstorming partner for you if data reveals a challenging situation.

My previous boss was the person who reported key data points and trends, like progress and impact, at upper-level leadership meetings. She needed to have and understand our data to do that, and I needed to make sure she had what she needed before those meetings.

If your boss is aware of the trends, challenges, and opportunities presented by your L&D data, you will be able to move farther faster. They will likely get on board with ideas sooner because they also have the supporting data to advocate for L&D projects and initiatives, including the resources you need.

The bottom line is this: Set up a way to consistently share information with your boss, whether that's via regular reports, one-on-one meetings, or simply letting them know where they can find your reports and emphasizing a few highlights. Be aware of and adapt to how they prefer to receive information.

3. HR and HR Business Partners

Think about how you can communicate the L&D data that will be helpful to HR. This will vary from organization to organization. Perhaps the HR team would benefit from seeing a broad picture of which L&D initiatives are succeeding and which are exposing possible employee issues. Do only HR leaders need to see L&D data? Do HRBPs need to see data related to the L&D initiatives within their assigned business units? Talk with HR leaders to ask what data would be most helpful to inform their work. Share information consistently in a way that works best for them.

4. Executive and Senior Leadership

Executive and senior leaders use a different lens to view the company as a whole. They are usually most concerned about high-level data, especially data related to progress on strategic initiatives. This group likely receives noncritical information on a regular basis in predetermined reports and presentations like QBRs. If that's the case, communication with this group should be aligned with their review process. This would be an opportunity for L&D to act like every other part of the company in terms of reporting its most important metrics and trends.

In some companies, executive leaders reserve time once a year for deeper dives. If that's the case at your company, provide more details during this period and keep other reporting at a high or general level. Most importantly, find out how your executive and senior leaders want to receive information and align everything to their standards.

5. Frontline and Middle Managers

The biggest concerns for frontline and middle managers include their people's performance related to key goals and revenue targets; so, when communicating measures with this group, focus on these areas. This may include a specific project or initiative you are currently partnering on or regular reporting on items related to their team.

For example, when my team worked to overhaul onboarding for a specific part of our company as part of an initiative to improve efficiency across the company, we regularly communicated progress and outcomes to that area's leaders. Onboarding was part of our regular responsibilities, so we sliced the survey data by business unit and provided frontline and middle managers with information related only to their business units. Naturally, the contact center didn't care as much about onboarding success in the operations team as they did in their own area, so why burden them with extra information?

Measurement is something that *all* L&D team members need to understand to continue their work as SBPs as they advance in the profession. You can bring them into the fold, using techniques we'll outline in the next chapter.

> **YOUR TURN**
>
> **Consistent Measurement Processes**
> Take a moment to look at your processes surrounding measurement and determine if changes are needed.
> - Do you have a consistent process in place to gather necessary data both from the L&D team and your partners? Does this process align with the required reporting frequency?
> - Do you have consistent processes in place to review and analyze the data you gather, looking for trends, successes, gaps, and areas of opportunity? What story is your data telling?
> - Do you have consistent processes for communicating the results of your measurement in a way that is meaningful for each stakeholder group?

Summary

The purpose of measurement is to make informed business decisions, not to prove your worth, so you'll need to create a balanced plan that covers three categories: efficiency, effectiveness, and outcomes. As an SBP, your challenge is to step away from "prove it" mode and put together a measurement plan designed to provide the necessary information to make informed business decisions. Remember these tips:
- Start by performing a measurement audit to determine what measures currently exist.
- Gather only the data you will use; everything else is a waste of time.
- Start every learning project by defining the measurement that will indicate changes in performance—don't wait!

- If you can't find the right measures up front, partner to create benchmarks or build new measures and the learning solution simultaneously.
- Work with stakeholders for each project to define and use performance measures. Set up a system to consistently gather data, analyze it, and communicate what you find.

CHAPTER 11
Develop a Team of SBPs

Your journey to work as an SBP can start with you, but it can't end there. If it does, no real change will happen. You might get to a point where you are a great partner with the business, but if no one else on your team has these skills, what happens when you leave? This work cannot depend on one or two individuals, no matter how awesome they are. To move more L&D leaders away from roles as order takers to SBPs, the profession itself must change. We can start with a few trailblazers but eventually, working as an SBP needs to spread to many more. Our solutions must scale.

To begin changing our profession, our team members must shift from order takers to strategic partners. They need to practice the same skills you do, to varying degrees, depending on their roles. As a learning leader, it is your responsibility to develop these skills in others—in this chapter, I'll talk about how to do that.

Share Your Vision
As with any change management practice, the people you want to be part of your strategic partnership need to know where you are headed, why you are going there, and what will happen if you don't do things differently. Be ready to share the vision of working as an SBP with others.

The Power of Repetition
Explain why your new vision is important, repeatedly—and I mean repeatedly. To make a difference, it needs to stay top of mind.

When you first share your vision with your team, you can expect strong reactions. Some people will be excited and energized, and others will be skeptical. But soon enough, everyone will become lost in their daily tasks and their interest in the vision will diminish—especially if the vision doesn't immediately and concretely affect the team.

Moving people from working as order takers to working as SBPs happens slowly, a little bit at a time. Often, the incremental changes aren't visible to others. As the L&D leader, your job is to talk about the vision so much that it becomes a little annoying and is therefore impossible for others to ignore or forget.

When I began sharing my vision for moving toward strategic partnership, several members of my team jumped on board right away. They were eager to have a bigger impact. However, three team members were not interested at all. They saw no need to change and were determined not to.

We began to implement some innovative ideas that were part of my vision—including concepts like, "Training can't solve every problem," and "We need to conduct consultative conversations instead of simply saying yes to requests." The three team members who resisted the new vision listened in meetings but refused to do things differently. Their manager repeatedly shared the vision, reviewing what everyone needed to do differently and stressing why the whole team needed to change.

Reluctantly, one of the three began to work differently. We soon discovered that his resistance stemmed from a fear of losing parts of the role that he loved most—interacting with people and telling stories. We helped him see that although some parts of the job might look different, his skills would still be valued. As he started to change, we rewarded his efforts, but the other two team members dug in their heels. Eventually, as the rest of the team moved forward, those two ended up leaving the company.

Be prepared to coach team members as they try to understand and adopt new ways of working. In some cases, this may mean coaching people who seem unwilling to take on alternate roles. But in other cases, it may simply mean making space for them to ask questions and giving them time to evolve in their understanding. At the same time, tap into those who are most excited to get started. Engaging them right away can spread positivity and build momentum. Whatever you do, keep sharing the vision.

Names Mean a Lot

One way to start signaling that your team needs to work differently is to look at any unintentional messages you may be sending. What is your team's name? What are team members' current titles? Do they reflect your vision for working as an SBP? If not, consider changing your team's name and titles to reflect your vision.

My team changed its name from the *training team* to the *learning experience team*. Our vision told us that we would be doing more than training; we'd be helping create diverse learning experiences to achieve business and performance goals. That meant facilitating access to a variety of content and company resources in addition to in-person and remote training. The new name signaled that our expertise was in *learning*. If we had remained the training team, everyone would have assumed that was all we did. Now, we were able to lay the groundwork for doing things differently.

In alignment with this new vision, we also changed some titles from *trainer* to *learning experience facilitator*—signaling our shift to facilitating learning. Our facilitators would now lead classroom experiences by asking questions, introducing activities, helping participants as they practiced skills, and encouraging them to use resources instead of standing at the front of the room telling them what they needed to know. This new approach for the organization was reinforced by the department and role changes. Consider your team's name and individual titles. Ask yourself:

- Does your vision of L&D as an SBP match your team's name?
- Do your team members' titles reinforce their work as order takers, or do they reflect their potential as SBPs?

If you wanted to change your team's name or titles, how would you do it?

Your L&D Hiring Profile

The people you hire will have a significant impact on your ability to work as a strategic business partner. Most leaders inherit team members with specific skill sets, but most teams also have turnover. Your challenge as an L&D leader is to develop new skills in current team members but also to revise your hiring profile to attract new hires with skills aligned to your future vision.

Julianne, the head of talent at a large global logistics company, knew that her team members would soon be experiencing change and growth—including the need to work as SBPs. As she hired new people, she looked for candidates who welcomed change and growth. She started asking new questions in the interview process:

- How were they engaging with the L&D community outside their workplaces?
- How were they keeping up with trends in learning?
- How were they developing themselves in new directions?

When I was hiring for my L&D team while transitioning to working as an SBP, I started to look more skeptically at candidates' motivations for applying to entry-level team positions. A lot of people work in L&D because they want to be the smartest people in the room, bestowing knowledge on others. But this isn't the way to approach work as an SBP. I wanted people who were motivated to look for creative solutions, work collaboratively, and think outside the traditional L&D box. I had to modify my hiring profiles accordingly.

Kalli, the talent and organization development manager at a midsize professional services company, revised her entire hiring process to focus more on partnership from the start. By involving key stakeholders when interviewing candidates, she discovered that this sped up new team members' success because, before they even started, they had buy-in from those key stakeholders.

For Kalli, this strategy worked, but it can backfire if the stakeholders aren't on board to work as partners. If you follow Kalli's model, make sure to clearly define who will make the hiring decision, and if it's you, let the stakeholders know you are looking for their input and will hire someone based on a combination of their feedback and the candidate's L&D experience. Be clear about the skills needed to be successful in the role, and ask for stakeholders' thoughts on that topic, too.

Although Julianne, Kalli, and I each took a different approach, we all found new team members who would help everyone on our teams work toward becoming strategic partners.

> **YOUR TURN**
>
> **Hiring SBPs**
> Try to articulate your vision of how an L&D team works most effectively as an SBP. When hiring new team members, consider:
> - What skills would make a new team member most successful?
> - Would it be helpful to include someone else, like a key stakeholder, in the hiring process?
> - Which stakeholders would you choose and why?

A Solid L&D Foundation Is a Necessity

Anyone in L&D who wants to work as an SBP needs to understand the foundations of learning and development. Basic L&D knowledge and skills—including learning outcomes, instructional design, assessment, effective learning techniques and modalities, and program or project management are non-negotiable.

Diversity in expertise is part of what makes any business effective. Survey other leaders in your organization. Very few started as generic leaders with overarching knowledge. Most first built expertise in a specific area like operations, marketing, sales, finance, customer service, manufacturing, or IT, and then perhaps moved into another area as they moved up the ladder. All leaders who work as strategic partners collaboratively share their expertise to make the best business decisions and lead as effectively as possible.

If you want to build an L&D team that approaches its work as a strategic partner, the best approach is to ensure team members start with a solid expertise in learning. If those skills are lacking, you will need to develop them in all your team members.

When Trainers Aren't Trainers

I began leading the learning team at Discovery Benefits during a period of centralization and growth. Hiring was at an all-time high, but employee training and development remained organic and inconsistent. As new employees were hired, they were told to sit with Megan, Jiang, Eduardo, and others who knew their roles and did them well. Training happened side-by-side, one person at a time.

Pretty soon, the volume of new employees overwhelmed Megan, Jiang, Eduardo, and everyone else. It's no surprise that when each department requested their budget for the next year, they all added more trainers. As the CFO tallied the numbers, he found requests for no fewer than 43 new trainers across the company—all slotted to do side-by-side training day in and day out. The CFO promptly said no, adding, "Until you can prove to me that there is no duplication in training happening across the company and that the way we are training people is the most efficient option, you will not be granted any additional headcount dollars for trainers."

That's when we began to centralize training to get a handle on what was happening from business unit to business unit, decrease duplication, and increase efficiency. I led the charge and my L&D team immediately inherited 27 new trainers. Only they weren't trainers in the way that L&D defines trainers (or facilitators). They were SMEs who liked helping people. On a scale of one to 10, their knowledge of the roles they were training people to occupy rated a 10, but their understanding of basic L&D skills rated zero.

I knew we had to bump up that zero to at least a six to be successful in any of our future endeavors, so that became my priority. This may be your priority, too. Before you can deeply develop your team's skills as SBPs, they need foundational L&D skills.

Combining Strategic Partner Skills and L&D Skills

Some SBP skills can be developed while you are filling gaps in L&D skills. For example, your team members can learn more about the details of the business and develop respected relationships with key stakeholders. Sharing your vision of the future is still essential to help team members understand where they are headed, but overall, the focus should be on developing L&D basics first.

If your team members already have a solid understanding of L&D skills and principles, you can move them further along the path toward strategic partnership. To get started, ask them to use the assessment tool at the end of chapter 3 to get a baseline understanding of their strengths and gaps. Then, create a plan to reinforce their strengths and develop important skills and knowledge within the gaps.

Seven Ideas for Leveling Up Your L&D Team

When it comes to developing a team of L&D professionals, I recommend seven field-tested best practices that are easy to deploy:

1. Maximize memberships in professional associations.
2. Enable networking.
3. Encourage relevant content discussions.
4. Nurture reflective practice.
5. Provide coaching and mentoring.
6. Establish accountability through goals.
7. Support recognition and rewards.

1. Maximize Memberships in Professional Associations

One of the reasons professional associations like the Association for Talent Development (ATD) exist is so those within the profession can grow and develop. Most associations offer multiple opportunities in the form of workshops or certifications, networking events, conferences, and digital content (such as blogs, magazines, online courses, and webinars). The cost to join is usually reasonable, with additional costs associated with some events and certifications.

Professional associations are a great resource for developing a team, especially if you can point people to specific events and content that relate to relevant skills. Many L&D leaders take this one step further and ask those who attend association events to come back and share their takeaways with the rest of the team.

One of the most powerful outcomes of exposing your team members to other professionals through associations is the magic that happens when they hear something that you have been telling them dozens of times and it finally clicks. A new voice can lend credibility or understanding to the information.

Jen, the director of HR for a small software company, was building out a new L&D team. She continuously shared her vision about how they could favorably affect the business. To help her team better understand the L&D industry, Jen took them to a local conference organized by a professional association. She wanted them to hear that this vision wasn't just hers and to see that others were also working in this way. It worked! Jen's team members returned from the conference more motivated and committed to the new direction. They heard the same message differently because it came from other voices.

Laurel, the senior director of learning experience at a global multinational technology company, needed to make a case for her team to participate in formal learning opportunities outside the company. "Who else is going to develop the learning team?" she asked. "We have to go outside and get training somewhere else because we can't learn the things we need to learn internally."

In short, remaining insulated and relying only on ourselves can limit professional growth.

2. Enable Networking

Networking is a multifaceted super tool if used well. Interacting with other people in your industry who work beyond the confines of your company has enormous benefits. You can use networking to ask questions and discover new answers regarding current challenges, and it can also help you find potential mentors and brainstorming partners.

We tend to underestimate the power of learning from other people, but when we do learn something this way, we rarely forget it. Encourage your team to build an enriching network of other L&D professionals outside your company. Suggest that they ask questions and share what they learn.

3. Encourage Relevant Content Discussions

Provide space for targeted discussions on specific topics using content that already exists. Books, articles, and podcasts are examples of content that can be consumed individually and then discussed by a group.

Book discussions were one of my go-to strategies to develop managers who reported to me. I would choose a book related to a topic or skill I wanted them to develop, and we would meet for regular discussions and conversations as a practical way to improve skills and build stronger relationships among the team. This, in turn, helped them better understand one another and encouraged collaboration.

When I took over as the leader of the learning team at Discovery Benefits (with 27 new team members and two managers), I knew that we wouldn't be successful in working toward the long-term goal of becoming SBPs until our leadership team could align on how we led the team. I couldn't think of a better way to do this than by using meaningful leadership books to learn together and discuss our management challenges.

However, I ran into a small obstacle: The two managers on my team didn't like to read and had never participated in a book discussion before. As the new boss, I had some leverage, so I invited them to a weekly meeting at a local coffee shop to discuss one of my favorite leadership books. Later, they told me that the only reason they said yes was because they didn't know me well enough to say no. My strategy worked!

I didn't prepare long lists of questions for the discussions. Instead, I simply asked the managers to highlight their biggest takeaways and note any questions that arose as they read the book. We discussed how to apply concepts from the book to our current challenges, helping one another make sense of difficult scenarios. We celebrated progress. They both came up with new ideas to strengthen our leadership as a team, and we learned a lot about one another. The growth, development, and connection that happened for all of us through those discussions was powerful.

After several months of meeting, one of the managers said, "I'm OK reading these books, even though I wouldn't consider myself a reader. But I enjoy the discussions more. That's when the learning happens."

Yep. She nailed it.

We kept up the book club for five years. When the COVID-19 pandemic began, we moved from our coffee shop to an online meeting space, but we kept the discussions going and gradually brought in additional team members. I believe this book discussion was one of the reasons the managers on my team became stellar leaders.

I've heard of other L&D leaders who use articles or podcasts as topics for similar discussions and learning together. I encourage you to experiment and try whatever makes sense to collectively grow your skills and strengthen your team relationships.

4. Nurture Reflective Practice

Regular reflection is one of the most powerful learning tools. Education theorist David A. Kolb argued that reflection allows us to start making sense of our experiences and truly learn from them (Institute for Experiential Learning n.d.). To date, I haven't quite figured out why L&D practitioners don't use it more often to encourage growth and development in their teams.

I once worked for John, the president of a growing insurance and finance company. Everyone at the company seemed to respect and admire John, and he was known as a strong leader who took care of people. He was quiet and unassuming without flash or any obvious charisma. I was curious about what made John so well-respected and influential. What made him such a good leader?

When I had the opportunity to sit down for a conversation with John, I asked him about his typical day. He responded with the usual—attending meetings, reading reports, and communicating with the board. It didn't sound like anything out of the ordinary.

Then he told me what he did at the end of the day. "You know, when I get in my truck at the end of the day and start my drive home, I do what everyone else does. I think about what happened that day, focusing on what went well and what didn't. Then, I plan what I'm going to do differently as a result."

That was it! John engaged in reflection every day with a focus on learning and continuous improvement. This daily reflective practice allowed him to lead with intention. He saw each day as an opportunity to do his job better based on his experiences from the day before. I also knew that, despite what John thought, everyone does not do this at the end of the day.

I was moved to action. From that day onward, I have written regularly in what I call my "TILT journal"—which stands for "things I learned today." It isn't formal, and it's just for me. Sometimes, my journal entries are complete thoughts, but other times, they're just made up of a few words and bullet points or a drawing. They're always focused on what I learned from my daily experiences.

I'm convinced that my regular reflective practice has set me apart in my work and career. My quiet moments spent "TILTing" often result in a new perspective, a potential solution to a problem, or the spark I need to develop a creative approach to a challenge. I encourage the teams I work with to create a TILT journal too—and to ask themselves a few questions:

- What am I learning?
- What is making me uncomfortable now? What might be the reason for this?

- What isn't quite adding up right at work? Why?
- What energized or inspired me today?

As a leader, I hope you are taking time to reflect on your days with curiosity. Encourage your team to begin TILT journals, and use them to review what's working and attempt new ways to tackle challenges. Ask them to reflect on the same topics regularly and then bring their questions and ideas forward as a result.

One of the managers who reported to me asked her team to close out their Friday each week by emailing her one thing they had learned that week and one thing that they had found challenging. She often followed up in regular one-on-one conversations to find out more. The team produced great ideas about working through problems, improving work processes, and building a sense of teamwork as a result.

Never underestimate the power of regular reflection as a tool to develop people, including yourself. Begin encouraging reflective practices in your team. Ask specific questions or leave it open ended, but be sure to provide a framework to help them start building the habit.

> **YOUR TURN**
>
> **TILT**
> Start your own TILT journal today. Use it to reflect on what you are learning through your own daily life.

5. Provide Coaching and Mentoring

Coaching and mentoring are particularly effective when you're helping your team members become SBPs. Coaching allows you to assist them with acquiring new skills at the moment they need them, instead of asking them to ingest information and then try to apply it weeks or months later.

Allowing someone to see a skill in action before handing over the reins a little at a time can be extremely effective. Coaching and mentoring are especially valuable when it comes to learning skills like consultative conversations or working with stakeholders to determine whether training is the answer.

Rose, the director of training and development at a midsize environmental services company, lives by the mantra, "No one starts alone"—especially when it comes to stakeholder conversations. To ease the stress of tackling a new skill and provide guidance, an L&D supervisor can bring a team member with them to observe several times. That supervisor conducts the conversation and then debriefs with the team member afterward. After several rounds of this process, the supervisor can start letting go so the team members can eventually have those conversations alone.

Nate, the senior manager of talent management design and leadership at a large outdoor retailer, intentionally pairs up experienced L&D team members with those who are less experienced to serve as coaches and mentors. He still provides coaching too, but because development doesn't fall solely on his shoulders, more experienced team members are able to grow by developing others as well.

Consider your current situation. What opportunities do you have to coach team members regarding specific skills like consultative conversations? How can you provide guidance or modeling and then gradually back away? Do you have experienced team members who can serve as coaches or mentors for others?

6. Establish Accountability Through Goals

Most people want to be successful and will do what they need to do to achieve top performance if they know what that entails. One of the best ways to motivate someone to learn and practice a new skill is to use your company's performance management system and write it into their goals. This is important for strategic initiatives, but also as you develop your team.

Goals vary from person to person, depending on their level of L&D knowledge and readiness to work as an SBP. If the goal is clear, and the team member knows how to achieve it, they will either work toward the goal or not. If they don't pursue the goal, it may be time for you to take the opportunity to have a different type of conversation about whether they are on board or want to continue working on your team.

Earlier, I shared that I inherited a team of SMEs with the challenge of turning them into L&D professionals working toward a new vision. One of the things I put in place was the task of creating goals that would allow them to slowly practice increasingly complex skills over two years. Here's how it worked: Each SME trainer had a portfolio of classes they were responsible for facilitating. To move them from SME trainer to learning experience facilitator, each person's stated goals in the first year were to:

- Write learning objectives for each course that you own.
- Rework classes to include an activity that engages learners every six minutes.
- Include either an informal or formal assessment activity in every class.

Then, in their second year, each person's goals were revised to include:

- Receive and incorporate monthly performance feedback from a manager regarding their facilitation, based on the facilitator performance rubric.
- Receive and incorporate quarterly facilitator feedback from a peer, based on the facilitator performance rubric.
- Provide feedback to two other facilitators monthly, based on the facilitator performance rubric.

The first year, our goal was to rework existing training programs and design new ones to be more learner-centric and less trainer-centric. In other words, we wanted them to stop throwing bullet points on a slide and reading them aloud without interaction.

We didn't just toss out these goals and then let the team fend for themselves. In the first year, we supported the goals by holding team workshops to write learning objectives and provide training on assessment. We reviewed ideas for activities in team meetings, allowing time for covering the concepts as well as time for practice and review. Participants continued to solidify their knowledge while working toward the goal.

Managers held regular goal check-ins and monitored progress. These goals could be measured without the team members being present because the managers only had to look at their training materials.

The second year was all about reinforcement and coaching. In addition to the first-year goals and workshops, we provided learning opportunities focused on effective facilitation. We created a rubric that could be used to measure facilitation skills; it also contained check boxes from the first year's goals to ensure there were learning objectives, interaction every six minutes, and some type of assessment. Managers and peers observed the facilitators, and facilitators observed one another, providing feedback for improvement.

It's important to note that these goals were for facilitators only. Other members of the team, like instructional designers, had different goals related to building their L&D skills in their defined areas.

I'm convinced that without these goals to hold them accountable, the facilitators would not have achieved the necessary skills. Of course, some were more willing to learn and change than others. The way we facilitated classes also wouldn't have changed without the goals, which was an important part of our strategic initiative to reduce duplication and increase effectiveness.

7. Support Recognition and Rewards

Recognition and rewards are part of employee development because what gets rewarded gets repeated. In other words, don't keep recognizing and rewarding behaviors that you do not want to continue.

Recognition and rewards are often tied to team and organizational goals, so the strategy of tying the acquisition of specific skills to annual goals can also be tied to rewards. This is especially true when goals can be tied to performance reviews, raises, and bonuses. But this isn't the only way you can or should recognize and reward team members. Some of the best approaches don't cost anything except a few moments of your time. Let's discuss some of my favorite recognition tips.

Give Specific Positive Feedback

When you catch someone practicing one of the skills you want to see more of, write a note or give verbal feedback reinforcing that behavior. Be as specific as possible so the person knows exactly which behavior to repeat.

Acknowledge Specific Actions

Instead of just saying someone did a good job, say, "Good job asking thoughtful questions in the stakeholder meeting today. I especially liked how you helped the stakeholder define their performance goals." You'll reinforce that asking thoughtful questions and getting to performance goals are things that you want to see. It's also important to provide feedback, if necessary, but never underestimate the power of calling out the positive actions.

Offer Sideways Compliments

If you get a compliment about a team member from someone else regarding a skill that you would like them to continue using, be sure to pass it along. For example, say, "Sandra told me today that she found the questions you asked in your last meeting really helpful. She said they helped everyone better clarify what was needed." It's powerful to know that others, outside your boss and peers, recognize your hard work.

Share and Celebrate Successes as a Team

As the team achieves successes related to learning and working as SBPs, be sure to celebrate them. Put it on your team meeting agenda or ask other managers to share the success in their team meetings. Send out a message to the full team with a note of congratulations. Continue to reinforce the skills that you are working to develop.

Ask Those Who Are Excelling to Share Their Top Tips

If someone on the team has mastered some of the skills you are working to develop, ask them to share how they did it or ask them to share their tips with others. Not only will this help the rest of the team develop, but it recognizes the person who is excelling.

Developing Others' SBP Skills Through Partnership Areas

The ideas we've discussed to develop team members have been fairly generic so far because the same principles you use to develop L&D skills in your team can be applied to developing skills to work as an SBP. But one less common structural component can help solidify the team's work as SBPs: By assigning team members to specific areas as learning partners, you, as the L&D leader, can take a broader view. This model is similar to that of an HRBP. You won't be solely responsible for building respected relationships or increasing your robust business knowledge with every key stakeholder in the company. Instead, that load will be split up across your team.

Laurel, the senior director of learning experience at a global multinational technology company, stumbled upon the concept of partnership areas because of funding restrictions, which she now sees as a happy accident. Laurel had been given the go-ahead to hire three additional team members with the caveat that they could only support the small business sales team because that team was funding the roles. Laurel was happy to have the new team members, but unsure of how this specificity would affect their overall work.

After the new team members were hired and acclimated, Laurel started to notice some unanticipated positive benefits. The learning experience team members who were only supporting small business sales were able to build strong relationships with their stakeholders. They learned about this business area in depth with a laser focus. The small business team began inviting the learning experience team members into key meetings, and then, organically, both teams began co-planning their work, building road maps together.

Potentially the biggest benefit of all was that surprise requests for training from the small business group disappeared. The learning experience team and small business sales team truly became partners, working in lockstep to address talent challenges in the short and long term.

All these benefits weren't lost on Laurel, and she put together a new plan for further partnerships. She assigned every learning experience team member to a specific area and stakeholders throughout the company, with the power to work as partners.

The way you divide up partnership duties may vary based on your team and company structure. Joe, the director of L&D at a midsize automotive manufacturing company, assigned partner areas to his L&D team based on their previous experience. One of his team members had been a supervisor at the company's largest plant. Now in the L&D department, that team member focuses on building relationships with plant supervisors, managers, and team leaders. Another team member had more interest in the technical side of the company and therefore easily partners with maintenance and engineering managers. The learning team regularly connects to compare notes about what they are hearing from the different areas they partner with most often.

When my team members had the L&D basics down and were ready to start exploring work as partners versus order takers, I assigned different areas based on expertise and role level. Those who had embraced the new way of working, were meeting their goals, and were on board with the vision were promoted to senior roles, including senior learning experience facilitator and senior learning experience designer.

I then assigned each senior team member an area of the company based on their expertise. In some ways, this was easy. Senior facilitators working in the contact center were assigned to the contact center, just as the senior facilitators for operations were assigned to operations. Senior designers ended up with partner assignments in areas not covered by facilitators, like marketing, sales, and IT. The degree to which each team member partnered with other areas depended on the work involved, but all were improving their consultative skills and gaining robust business knowledge. They often worked with frontline managers and key influencers on their assigned teams.

The managers on my team had already been working to build partnerships, but at this point, they shifted their focus to those at a similar level—middle managers or the people to whom the frontline managers and key influencers reported. I kept my focus on partnering with those at a VP level and above across the company.

No matter what methods you choose to develop your team, start with where they currently are in terms of their knowledge and expertise. Then, work to gradually expand their skills so they can become strategic partners to the degree that it makes sense for each team member.

Summary

You can expand your work as an SBP by developing your L&D team members' skills. One way to do this is to share your vision of how to work as an SBP, including the reasons you are moving away from order taking and what will happen if this change doesn't occur. Some approaches to building a team that supports strategic partnership include:

- Change your team's name and titles to signal a new approach.
- Revise your hiring profile to attract people with skills that align with your vision.
- Ensure all team members understand foundational L&D skills, like learning outcomes, instructional design, assessment, effective learning techniques and modalities, and program or project management.

- Use professional associations, networking, relevant content discussions, regular reflective practice (such as TILT journaling), coaching and mentoring, accountability through goals, and recognition and rewards for team member development.
- Try a learning partner model in which each team member partners with a specific area in the organization or a key stakeholder, increasing their robust business knowledge and improving their respective relationships.

CHAPTER 12
Find the Opportunity in Every Order

I started this book by talking about the need for L&D leaders to move from order takers to strategic business partners and then shared best practices and practical tools to get you there. I acknowledge that this transformation won't happen overnight. It's more of an evolution than a revolution.

If you have gotten this far and feel discouraged because of the circumstances in which you are working, this chapter is for you. Many of you are probably saying to yourselves, "This all sounds great, but it won't work in my company." Or "I can't imagine a day when I can wake up and say, 'I'm an order taker no more!'"

I've been there. The good news is that working as an order taker and working as an SBP are points on a continuum—they're not mutually exclusive (Figure 12-1). Most L&D leaders work somewhere in the middle a majority of the time and move along the continuum daily based on changing factors in their organizations.

Figure 12-1. Strategic Business Partner Continuum

Strategic initiatives change. Critical issues arise. New key stakeholders who aren't used to working with L&D as a strategic business partner come onto the scene. Most of us will work as order takers and SBPs simultaneously to varying degrees from day to day and moment to moment.

My goal is to help you position yourself closer to the SBP end of the continuum. You can achieve this by implementing the strategies in this book, a few at a time, and using them regularly in your work. As a reminder, those strategies are:

- Approach your work with a new mindset.
- Understand the business.
- Get your own house in order by developing internal and external L&D playbooks.
- Identify and partner effectively with key stakeholders.
- Create an aligned L&D strategy.
- Say yes and no strategically.
- Measure the impact of your work.
- Develop a strong and effective team.

Yes, it's a lot to do! And even if you implement all these concepts, you will sometimes have to work like an order taker to fulfill a training request. Being an SBP is never all or nothing.

This brings me to the final strategy I'll share in this book: What to do when you must take an order. This is a vital part of the change process when moving from transactional order taker toward SBP. Think of it this way: *If you have an order, you have an opportunity.*

We can't expect people to buy into our vision and start working differently overnight. We need to create change slowly, starting with our stakeholders' current understanding of L&D. Often, this change process starts with taking the order. It's what we do *with* that order that moves us down the continuum toward SBP.

When to Take the Order

Let's start with when to take the order. In every company, no matter the circumstances, sometimes taking the order is the best option. You might decide that it's not worth the conflict to push back or go through the steps to determine if training is the right solution because any resistance would create more headaches for you and your team.

In these instances, taking the order can be an effective move because it allows you to lay the groundwork for more strategic work later on. Let's consider some common situations when it's usually best to start by taking the order. The opportunity lies in *how* you fulfill the request.

A Compliance or Regulatory Request

Governing bodies and legal entities often dictate that a company must provide training to be compliant. In these cases, people with more power than you are making decisions about whether to conduct training, what needs to be covered in the training program, and even how long it needs to be. This kind of order is often written into legal contracts, which means your ability to push back is nonexistent.

You may not be thrilled about the need to create dictated compliance training. You may believe it will be ineffective and won't help people learn. You may be annoyed that this keeps you from doing other, more effective work. But before expressing those thoughts, stop to consider the senior leaders' point of view: The training needs to be done to ensure the company is compliant. Companies not in compliance with regulations risk financial penalties, reputational damage, security breaches, and loss of productivity. In extreme cases, lack of compliance can lead to business closure.

It's likely that senior leaders' hands are tied. In these situations, you will be most useful to the company if you help it meet expectations and comply with regulations. In other words: Take the order.

An Unforeseen Critical Business Need

Even the best-laid plans go awry. We all spend time creating lovely strategic road maps based on overall initiatives and then may need to reroute them from time to time as a result of unexpected, unplanned situations. Ideally, you will be able to reroute in partnership with key stakeholders, but sometimes a critical need creates an obvious gap that must be filled by training.

If the business need is indeed critical, you won't have time to do a deep analysis or proceed methodically. However, helping to address the gap quickly will be in your L&D team's best interest.

An Opportunity to Build a Needed Relationship With a Stakeholder

When a new stakeholder arrives on the scene, they probably won't understand how to work with your L&D team as SBPs. Instead, they'll likely be mired in the legacy mindset of L&D as order takers. They may also be in a position where you are unable to push back on their requests. But you don't have to. Take the order so you can start building a respected relationship, add value, and lay the foundation to work with them more strategically in the future.

An Opportunity to Build Trust

You may receive a request from a stakeholder who doesn't know you or your team and also doesn't trust your abilities. They may even look at you with suspicion—through a narrowed side-eye.

One way to earn a stakeholder's trust is to demonstrate the great work you and your team can do. Take this order to show that you are easy to work with, deliver on your promises, and do high-quality work. This approach will start building the trust you need for a more strategic partnership.

An Opportunity for More L&D Visibility

If lack of visibility across the organization is part of the reason you and your team are not yet working as SBPs, it's worth taking a request that provides this opportunity. Producing a high-quality solution that will be used by many employees across the company can do wonders to highlight the value you and your L&D team bring to the business.

A Political Necessity

As much as we all dislike organizational politics, they exist in every company. You may not want to play political games, but you will always need to work within a political framework to create any type of change. If someone with a lot of political power—such as your new boss or a C-Suite executive—requests a training solution, it may be in your best interest to comply.

Take and deliver on orders from those with significant power to learn more about navigating company politics in the future, including the circumstances when you can push back successfully.

All six of these instances are opportunities to shift perceptions when taking an order if you *work differently* within the ask. L&D leaders who are content to remain order takers will take and deliver on an order exactly as directed. But if you are a leader working toward becoming an SBP, you will lean into your expertise in learning, think creatively, and work differently—going beyond traditional confines. You will add value that the stakeholder didn't know they could ask for and move further across the SBP continuum.

Become a Strategic Business Partner Within an Order

So, you had to take an order. You didn't have the opportunity to decline, push back, or even ask additional questions to determine if training would solve the problem. It's time to figure out how to leverage the order into an opportunity.

Remember the adage, "Dress for the job you want, not the job you have"? When applied to fashion, the advice is outdated in many industries, but the underlying concept is gold. We can translate it for L&D as, "Work as if you have already achieved the status of SBP, not as if you are still stuck in order-taker mode."

The opportunity within any order you take is your chance to work as an SBP would. Ask yourself how an SBP would approach this situation differently than an order taker. What questions should you ask? What insights can you offer for greater impact? How can you add value as a learning SME and business partner? In short, what can you do differently and creatively within the confines of fulfilling the order, laying a foundation for the future?

Based on conversations with learning leaders who have done the work as well as my own experiences, I suggest four ways to take advantage of an order:

1. Add unexpected value.
2. Work backward.
3. Add measurement.
4. Share a new vision.

1. Add Unexpected Value

Exceed expectations. Surprise and delight your key stakeholders by adding components to requested training initiative that make a bigger difference than anticipated. Add unexpected value to everything you deliver.

Sarah was working as the learning and organization development manager for a midsize retail company that had recently undergone an acquisition. When a request to transition required safety training into the new LMS came across her desk, she saw a huge opportunity. She knew that if she could shift the training from serving as a check-the-box experience in the LMS to one that changed behavior, she could "blow everyone's mind." So, she set out to revamp the safety training with that goal.

The program she inherited was a series of 20-minute videos that appeared to be vintage 1980s productions, followed by a quiz on paper. Managers had to grade the quiz by hand and then submit it before employees could get credit. Employees had to watch the videos every year to remain compliant.

Sarah pitched a value-added solution in which she would produce shorter, more enjoyable videos designed to improve safety metrics and eliminate the need for managers to grade a quiz. She also proposed that instead of mandating that employees watch the videos consecutively, the company should share them periodically to align with the time of year when the video's featured type of accident was most likely to happen.

Sarah then requested a new budget based on the fact that her new safety training would reduce the amount of time each employee needed to be pulled off the floor to participate. The math was simple. She added up the time saved overall because of shortened videos and multiplied it by the average hourly pay rate. The budget's approval became a no-brainer.

Next, Sarah worked with the company's safety team and operations leaders. Instead of focusing on learning objectives, she took a performance-based approach and asked about the accidents that regularly happened on the job. When and where did they occur? Why did they happen? What was at risk when they did?

After Sarah created videos based on real-life events and rolled them out according to the new cadence, the company saved production time, safety incidents began to decrease, and employees' attitudes toward the training improved. Safety became a year-round conversation rather than a one-time event. People took note. Company leaders noticed the reduced safety incident numbers and production savings. Sarah's credibility as a partner who could deliver shot upward.

In another case of adding value to an order, Renata, the director of training and development at a midsize outdoor services company, told me that she regularly uses the "respond and then expand" strategy to add value within a request. For example, a common request her team used to receive was to "Load this PDF into the LMS and then ask employees to acknowledge they received and read it."

Usually, a request like this was tied to a compliance need based on new state legislation. The employee acknowledgment avoided a company fine for noncompliance. But, of course, a PDF isn't training. Employees would acknowledge they had received the document (and some might even read it), but that was unlikely to lead to long-term knowledge or behavior change. Renata's team couldn't deny or push back on the compliance request, but they could add value in the long run.

Her team responded first by agreeing to do exactly what had been requested: uploading the PDF into the LMS and requiring employees to acknowledge they had read it. Simultaneously, however, they also brainstormed how to design a new deliverable that would improve the user experience, increase retention of the new information, and increase the chances employees would apply it to their jobs. What started as a simple PDF was soon built into the L&D team's overall learning strategy.

As L&D leaders, we need to remember that stakeholders requesting training don't have the same expertise and creativity around learning as you and your team. It's your responsibility to ask yourself how you can add unexpected value in a way that increases impact.

2. Work Backward

Many of the processes outlined in this book assume you are starting at the beginning—performing a deep dive on whether training is the best solution before agreeing to design the training program, for example. But this isn't reality in all instances.

When you have to take the order, chances are you won't be able to proceed according to an ideal plan, but you and your team can still provide added value by working backward. For instance, you can put the pieces in place to do a root cause analysis after the fact.

Postproject Analysis for a Customer Onboarding Team

Several years ago, the new-client onboarding team approached me just before their busiest time of year. They were in a state of panic. Their forecasts told them they weren't staffed adequately to handle the volume of work coming their way, and the team wouldn't be able to hold the one-on-one calls needed to walk clients through the system setup process. They had come up with a solution that would allow them to educate clients at scale through a series of live webinars—they just needed L&D's help to create and facilitate them. Their thinking was that webinars educate multiple clients at once, reducing the need for one-on-one calls and scaling the workload. And, because the webinars would be live, clients could still ask questions and wouldn't be left to figure out the system alone.

By the time the request reached me, stakeholders in senior leadership and sales had already signed off. I was skeptical that webinars would solve the problem, but my questions were immediately squelched. My team had no time to delay; we had to take and deliver on this order.

We took it to heart. My team gathered information, wrote scripts, created visual aids, and worked overtime to complete the project. We carefully designed each webinar so clients could follow along on their screens, completing the onboarding steps in real time. I was proud of my team's efforts.

Unfortunately, soon after we launched the webinars, my early skepticism was validated. Very few clients attended the webinars, and those who did frequently encountered tech issues. The facilitator spent half the time troubleshooting or calling in IT while everyone without a tech problem waited for the webinar to get rolling. Even worse, the number of one-on-one calls for the client onboarding team *didn't decrease at all*. The webinars did not solve the problem.

When the volume of new clients subsided and we had time to breathe, we looked at our abysmal numbers. We had spent more time and resources than ever before and hadn't helped the onboarding team at all. We initially thought the project was a complete failure.

But was it? When we started, I had seen an opportunity to do our analysis after the fact instead of before. Thinking like an SBP, I made an intentional ask at the beginning of the project that would set us up to partner with the onboarding team more proactively in the future. I agreed to provide L&D's best team resources for the webinar project with the caveat that, at the conclusion of their busy season, they would let me conduct a full level 3 analysis of the new-client education process. This would allow us to better help them prepare for the next busy season—without the time crunch. They agreed, and I followed through.

After completing the analysis by interviewing team members, observing the work (gemba), and reading process documents, I found that the process surrounding one-on-one onboarding calls—not the calls themselves—was extremely inefficient and clunky. The onboarding team members had to run multiple reports each day to determine if they had any new clients assigned to them and which clients weren't keeping up with their onboarding tasks (indicating the need for a call). Each report had to be sorted and combed through manually, which took a minimum of an hour per report. Every. Single. Day.

To make matters worse, passwords for the system were provided to clients once in an initial email, and they couldn't reset or change them without an onboarding team member's help. Finally, the majority of client communication was done via email, and each template had to be updated manually before sending.

We discovered that each onboarding team member spent multiple hours a day completing these routine manual processes—all time that could have been spent helping clients with specific questions. The symptom that led to the creation of the webinars was the onboarding team's inability to complete needed phone calls for client education. Through our postproject analysis, we diagnosed the root cause as inefficient processes, not a lack of knowledge or skills. The webinars would never have fixed those inefficiencies.

Once we were able to show stakeholders the real problem, they immediately connected with IT to begin automating and streamlining the administrative processes before the next busy season. We earned some serious street cred for our ability to help find the root cause and corresponding solution.

As a bonus, after my postproject analysis, the new-client onboarding team never came to me with a prebaked L&D request again, and they became one of my team's strongest partners, involving us at the beginning whenever they discussed new challenges.

It may seem backward to do an analysis after creating a training program instead of beforehand. But, in this instance, the benefits far outweighed the costs, especially because it led to my L&D team jumping across the continuum from order taker to SBP.

3. Add Measurement

Most training orders won't come to you with a corresponding request to measure impact. If the orders are compliance related, you might receive a request to measure compliance, but that isn't the same as measuring a change in performance—and it certainly doesn't help you make future business decisions.

As an SBP, you will continuously search for measures to help everyone make informed business decisions. Even when taking an order without a measurement request, try to add value by adding measurements.

Guerilla Effectiveness

Do you remember the term *guerilla effectiveness*—meaning small, unconventional tactics—mentioned in chapter 3? Joe, the L&D director who introduced me to the term, adds measurement without prior authorization (knowing that it will prove valuable later) as one of his tactics.

In my previous example about new-client onboarding webinars, I also added measurements to the project when it wasn't requested. My team kept records of the number of webinars offered and how many clients attended each one. We also estimated the average cost per client by dividing staff hourly salaries by the number of clients attending. I worked with new-client onboarding leaders to obtain data about the number of clients and one-on-one calls, despite the webinar strategy. I told them I was gathering the numbers so we could gauge the impact of webinars on workloads and determine whether to continue them in the future.

I also added one more piece of data collection based on a strategic ask I had made at the beginning of the project. As a backup to the webinars, I suggested we break down and screen record the content in one-to-five-minute segments, turning them into a series of short, on-demand videos that each new client could access through their landing page. It was a fairly light lift but had the potential to inform business decisions in the future.

So, in addition to tracking the number of people attending the webinars, the cost, and the impact on workload, we also tracked the number of people who viewed those on-demand videos. The results didn't surprise me and won't surprise you: More people watched the inexpensive videos than attended the costly webinars.

The data from all these measures showed the webinar strategy's failure even more starkly, but it also supported my request to complete a full analysis of the customer education process. It provided additional depth and insight. As the onboarding team worked to automate processes, they also partnered with us to create more short on-demand videos because our data showed clients engaged with that medium.

If I hadn't pushed for any of those measures, my L&D team's frustration would have remained high. We would have felt our training solution was a failure without having any real data or solutions to share. Our measures were a value-add that informed business decisions and increased the credibility of L&D as an SBP.

4. Share a New Vision

Even within the confines of an order that you must take, you may have an opportunity to share a new vision of what L&D can do when working as a strategic partner. Depending on the project, you may be able to directly articulate a new vision in small or big ways.

A Push Back In (Not On) the Ask

A new C-level leader joined the small healthcare technology company where Denise was the training and development manager. The new leader decided that the company needed to focus on performance management—specifically, the proper way to write a performance improvement plan (PIP) for people who weren't meeting expectations. He asked Denise's team for a condensed training program on performance management and coaching, focused on PIPs and he wanted them to deliver it in a shortened timeline.

Denise knew that, for political reasons, she couldn't push back on the order. Instead, she used one of her favorite strategies: *Push back in the ask, not on it.*

Instead of telling the new stakeholder that her team would not cover PIPs per his request, she pushed back on *how* they would cover them. She asked to break the program into two phases—the first phase would feature coaching, which would allow employees to make behavior modifications and improve skills. If the employee was still struggling after the coaching, phase two would involve implementing a PIP. She also pushed back on how condensed the training would be to ensure it would be more effective through hands-on practice.

Neither pushback was extensive, and Denise's response established her team as the company's learning experts.

A New Definition for Learning

Travis—the senior VP of talent at a midsize insurance, financial services, and HR consulting company—seized a much more dramatic opportunity to share his new vision for L&D as a strategic partner shortly after entering his role. At the time, the marketing team was running a series of annual internal events for other teams throughout the company. The events included a national sales team kickoff and a summer gathering for all client services teams. When he was hired, the marketing team told Travis that these were their largest internal training events, and L&D needed to take them over.

Travis was immediately skeptical. As a leader with expertise in L&D, he knew that effective learning didn't happen within a one-time event. Before agreeing to take them over, he attended one of the events and then debriefed with the chief operating officer (COO), who asked him how the event could be better. In this one-on-one, Travis explained that training isn't an *event* and that the necessary learning couldn't happen in just a few days each year.

The COO was curious and asked Travis to speak at the next event—not to train the group, but to help the entire company get ready to learn with a brief, 10-minute talk.

The result? Travis introduced the entire company to Hermann Ebbinghaus's Forgetting Curve. He told everyone that much of what they would hear in the next two days would be forgotten unless they thought more intentionally about how learning works.

"The way it really works," Travis said, "is by training the mind the same way we train the body." He explained that people don't get in shape with one 30-minute workout but by consistently participating in multiple 30-minute workouts over time. Travis then suggested that participants in the event revisit or apply what they were learning for 20 to 30 minutes two to three times a week, just like a workout.

Travis took the opportunity to share a different way of thinking about learning and used that to kick off a full campaign in which his L&D team helped leaders across the organization understand how learning does and doesn't work. Most importantly, the campaign emphasized that future learning events would be a waste of company time unless they did things differently. The path Travis took led his team from being seen as order takers to working as SBPs.

This simple opportunity *within* the order allowed the team to shift their position on the SBP continuum.

The work needed to become a strategic business partner isn't easy and can't happen overnight. As an L&D leader, you will always live on a shifting continuum between taking an order and working as an SBP. In the middle is a wide ocean of opportunities to make small changes that eventually lead to the big ones you desire.

YOUR TURN

When You Must Take the Order, Find the Opportunity
The next time you are faced with a request for training or a learning solution that you cannot deny, look for the opportunity. Could you do any of the following?
- Add unexpected value that shows your ability to work creatively and strategically.
- Work backward by adding analysis elements after the fact that will lead to more strategic work in the future.
- Measure results without being asked to do so.
- Share a new vision for L&D through your work.

Summary

The work of L&D as an SBP exists on a continuously shifting continuum with order taker at one end and SBP at the other. Even those working as SBPs sometimes need to take an order. But orders provide opportunities to make small changes that lead to bigger ones. Remember, some of the most common situations in which L&D leaders have to take orders include:

- A compliance or regulatory request
- An unforeseen critical business need
- An opportunity to build a needed relationship with a key stakeholder
- An opportunity to build trust
- An opportunity for increased visibility
- A political necessity

SBPs take the order in these instances, but then they work differently to begin shifting perceptions within the ask. You can do this by:

- Adding unexpected value
- Working backward
- Adding measurement
- Sharing a new vision

Sometimes, the best way to begin working as a SBP is to make small changes within the order that open the door to larger ones later.

Conclusion
Become a Strategic Business Partner

Here we are at the end of this guide to becoming a strategic business partner in your organization. If you've ever felt like an order taker at a drive-thru window, I hope that feeling is diminishing—or maybe gone for good.

I've shared how so many of us ended up in a difficult and powerless position, why we remain in that position for much longer than we want to, and how we can change our circumstances. We've considered three keys to transformation: shifting our individual mindsets, putting new foundations in place to support becoming true business partners, and adopting new practices in our everyday work. I've provided lists, tools, stories, and examples of what works and what doesn't. After all, we usually learn the most from our mistakes.

Now, it's your turn. Take the ideas and stories that have resonated most and use them to transform your mindset and build the foundation and practices that will make you an effective SBP in your organization. It's time to roll up your sleeves and do the work. Be prepared—it won't be easy. It's a continuously shifting dance along the continuum between taking orders and working as a partner with stakeholders. Some days, you'll see yourself making progress, but then others will put you right back behind the counter taking orders. Remember, this is normal. I've yet to meet a colleague who says they are *always* working as an SBP. The goal isn't perfection; instead, it's to eventually spend more time as an SBP than not and to keep moving forward every day.

This work is about constant change and the ebb and flow of your efforts to make a real difference. Envision yourself on a beach, down by the water where the sand is wet and packed down. You want to make a footprint. You lift your leg and, with the full force of your body weight, slam your foot into the sand. Unfortunately, you've barely made an impression.

So, you take a different approach. Instead of a forceful slam, you stand still. You gently apply pressure to the sand underneath one of your feet, wiggling it back and forth ever so slowly from side to side. After some time has passed, you've made a deep impression.

The change in the sand didn't come from a one-time action, but from patience, small movements, and consistent gentle pressure—just like the work of becoming an SBP. One action, by itself, won't make much difference. And if that action is too forceful, it will be rejected quickly and dismissed. But, if you continuously apply a gentle pressure, a little at a time, using the techniques outlined in this book, you will eventually make a significant impression. And unlike a footprint in the sand, your impression will last. You just need to keep at it.

Look at where you are right now, today. Start doing the little things that will lead to the big things. If you slowly watch your mindset and approach to L&D work change, you'll become a better leader for your team and help your organization's leaders know how best to work with you. You will gain credibility by demonstrating your business knowledge and become a better partner to your stakeholders. And you'll start to develop and work within a carefully aligned L&D strategy. Your *yes* will become strategic. You will build a consistent plan to measure learning outcomes that will inform business decisions. Most importantly, you will develop a team of people who think like partners.

Finally, something you may not have anticipated will happen. Your actions will help change the way the L&D profession as a whole works, escaping legacy patterns and expectations in favor of partnering to solve talent challenges creatively and collaboratively.

Let's stop worrying about our position as L&D order takers and start doing the hard work to change that.

You've got this.

Acknowledgments

I'm forever grateful to the McDonald's regional manager who made me start thinking at a young age about the best way to make an impact through the work I love. He planted a seed that took root and many years later blossomed into new ways of looking at our L&D challenges. I'm also grateful to all the people who helped me nurture and grow the ideas that led to this book. Thank you to Kara, Jodi, Lindsay, Brent, and my entire team at Discovery Benefits. I wouldn't have figured out this secret sauce without your trust, questions, challenges, collaboration, and brainstorming.

Thank you also to the many L&D leaders who shared their experiences with me, allowing this book to become a collective story of common struggles and practical tools for change within our profession. Thank you to my L&D mentors, including Chelle and Elaine, who taught me about true collaboration and measuring for impact, respectively. To my team of ATD National Advisors for Chapters whose ability to believe in and empower each other is unparalleled. And there are so many ATD authors and speakers who sparked ideas that led me to think differently that I can't name them all.

Finally, thank you to those who have sat by my side throughout the writing process. My husband is simultaneously my rock, my teddy bear, and the voice of logic. My best friend, Katherine; daughter, Greta; sister, Eva; and parents, Mary and Keith, are the best cheerleaders and always ready with the biggest hugs. And my son, David, is the most patient listener I've ever met.

Jess Almlie
Phoenix, Arizona

References

AllenComm. 2016. "The History of Training and Development." AllenComm, April. allencomm.com/2016/04/history-training-development-infographic.

Defelice, R.A. 2021. "How Long Does It Take to Develop Training? New Question, New Answers." ATD Blog, January 13. td.org/insights/how-long-does-it-take-to-develop-training-new-question-new-answers.

Friedman, J. 2010. "The Most Important Marketing Acronym: WIIFM." Writer's Digest, June 9. writersdigest.com/general/the-most-important-marketing-acronym-wiifm.

Garner, R., and O. Ferguson. 2023. "The 20-Year Evolution of L&D." *The Mind Tools L&D Podcast*, May 16.

Gilbert, T.F. 2007. *Human Competence: Engineering Worthy Performance.* Pfeiffer.

Grossman, D. 2024. "Face-to-Face Communication: 6 Benefits of Leading in Person." The Grossman Group, July 8. yourthoughtpartner.com/blog/bid/44390/leading-in-person-6-reasons-to-communicate-face-to-face.

Institute for Experiential Learning. n.d. "What Is Experiential Learning?" experientiallearninginstitute.org/what-is-experiential-learning.

Kirkpatrick Partners. n.d. "What Is the Kirkpatrick Model?" kirkpatrickpartners.com/the-kirkpatrick-model.

Lencioni, P. 2012. *The Advantage: Why Organizational Health Trumps Everything Else in Business.* Jossey-Bass.

Mostrom, S. 2024. "How to Avoid the Dreaded 'Learning Cliff.'" *Develop Daily*, January 14.

Pepperdine Graziadio Business School. 2023. *Backstabbing, Credit Snatching, and Blame Gaming: Disrupting the Toxic Office.* Pepperdine Graziadio Business School. bschool.pepperdine.edu/academics/research/millennial-research-report.

Phillips, P.P., ed. 2025. *ATD's Handbook for Measuring and Evaluating Training*, 2nd edition. ATD Press.

Robinson, A. 2022. "History of Team Building." Teambuilding.com, September 27. teambuilding.com/blog/team-building-history.

Rogers, E.M. 2003. *Diffusion of Innovations*, 5th edition. Free Press.

The Henry Ford. n.d. "Ford Motor Company Sociological Department and English School." thehenryford.org/collections-and-research/digital-resources/popular-topics/sociological-department.

Tréguer, P. 2018. "Meanings and Origin of 'Flavour of the Month/Week.'" World Histories Blog, September 22. wordhistories.net/2018/09/22/flavour-month-week.

University of Minnesota. 2010. *Organizational Behavior.* University of Minnesota. open.lib.umn.edu/organizationalbehavior.

Vance, D., and P. Parskey. 2021. *Measurement Demystified: Creating Your L&D Measurement, Analytics, and Reporting Strategy.* ATD Press.

Varghese, T. 2015. "Here's Everything You Need to Know About Hamburger University." *BrainGain*, November 11. braingainmag.com/here-s-everything-you-need-to-know-about-hamburger-university.htm.

Wiggenhorn, W. 1990. "Motorola U: When Training Becomes an Education." *Harvard Business Review*, July–August. hbr.org/1990/07/motorola-u-when-training-becomes-an-education.

Wiseman, L. 2021. *Impact Players: How to Take the Lead, Play Bigger, and Multiply Your Impact.* HarperCollins Publishers.

Index

In this index, *f* denotes figure and *t* denotes table.

A

accountability, 29, 95, 105, 106, 107, 284–286
   See also roles and responsibilities, clarification of
acronyms, 80
   See also terminology and language
adoption/innovation curve, 182–183
The Advantage (Lencioni), 92
annual employee engagement surveys, 193–194
asks and requests. *See* requests and asks
audience, defining, 92
autonomy, lack of, 16–17

B

behavioral expectations, in L&D, 103–106
Behavior Engineering Model, modification of, 227*f*
big-picture, small-step thinking, 40–42
big-picture view, 161
   See also mission statements; vision sharing
bonuses, 228–229
   See also recognition and rewards
book clubs, 280–281
bosses, 132–134, 269
   See also managers
brand guidelines, adherence to, 99
business basics funnel, 67*f*
business cases, making, 137
business operations
   adding value to, 48–52
   basic knowledge about, 66–81
   big-picture, small-step thinking in, 40–42
   importance of understanding, 27–29, 141–142, 152–154
   inserting oneself into, 44–47
   lack of goals and objectives in, 17–18
   making unsolicited recommendations about, 47–48
   organizational culture and processes and intersection with, 78–81
   ways to improve knowledge about, 82–85
   See also goals and objectives
buy-ins. *See* adoption/innovation curve

C

cadences, 74–75
capacity tracking. *See* workload and capacity tracking
CBT (computer-based training), 6–7
challenges, business, 75–76
champions and influencers, 162–163, 184–185, 222–223
   See also key performers
coaching and mentoring, 274, 283–284
   See also mentors, business
collaboration, 36, 52–54
commonalities and criticalities, 195–196

311

communication, 164–175, 208–209, 210–211, 268–271
See also consultation and analysis, decision trees for
compliance training, 24–25, 26, 222, 293
computer-based training (CBT), 6–7
consultation and analysis, decision trees for, 219–244
consultation conversations, 224–225
contacts, key business, 111–112
content discussions, 280–281
content review cycles, 100
corporate universities, 5–6
critical needs, training requests for, 222, 293
culture. *See* organizational culture and processes
curriculum. *See* L&D strategies; *learning entries*
customers, understanding, 68
See also audience, defining

D

data and documents, 238–239
See also metrics
data gathering, 265–267
data review and analysis, 267–268, 298–299, 300–301
day-to-day operations, 71–77
See also business operations
decision trees, for consultation and analysis, 219–244
definitions, key, 119
designer standards of work, 102
difficulty versus impact, 200–203
dive deeper decision tree, 221f

E

educational experiences, traditional versus common workplace, 8–10
See also formal learning
effectiveness. *See* "guerilla effectiveness"
effectiveness measures, 253–254
efficiency measures, 253
ego control, 26–27
e-learning. *See* computer-based training (CBT)
employee training, evolution of, 5

executives and senior leaders, 136–137, 270
expectations. *See* behavioral expectations, in L&D
expenses and revenue, 73–74
expertise, engaging others', 52–53, 205–206, 288–289
See also subject matter experts (SMEs)
external L&D playbook, 114–126, 171–172

F

face-to-face meetings, 167–168
See also touch-base meetings
facilitative leadership, 177–179
facilitators, 275
facilitator standards of work, 102
feedback, 172, 180, 228, 286–287
See also annual employee engagement surveys; data review and analysis; metrics; stakeholder feedback
flavor-of-the-month approach, 22–23
follow through, 174–175
Ford English School, 5
formal learning, 4–7
four-question decision tree, 219–244
Friedman, J., 175
frontline and middle managers, 137–139, 270–271

G

gemba, going to the, 84–85, 236–238
Gilbert, T., 227
goals and objectives
    idea generation, for L&D strategy, and, 191–192
    idea scrutiny, for L&D strategy, and, 198
    intake process and, 116
    L&D team as leaders in setting and monitoring, 39–40
    for L&D team development, 284–286
    lack of specificity in, 17–18
    level of business maturity and, 81
    understanding priorities in, 70–71
"guerilla effectiveness," 50, 300–301
    See also proactivity

H

helpfulness, as self-sabotage, 20–21
Hermann Ebbinghaus's Forgetting Curve, 302
hiring profile, for L&D team, 275–278
history of L&D, 3–13
HR business partners (HRBPs), 134–135, 270

I

idea generation and scrutiny, for L&D strategy, 190–207
impact versus difficulty, 200–203, 223
influencers and champions. *See* champions and influencers
initiatives, early involvement in key, 37–38
innovation. *See* adoption/innovation curve
intake process, 115–119
internal L&D playbook, 90–114
involvement in key initiatives, early, 37–38
I-RECCOM, 71–77

J

job descriptions, 94

K

key business contacts, 111–112
key definitions, 119
　See also acronyms
key performers, 233–236, 246–247
Kirkpatrick Levels of Evaluation, 253
Kolb, D., 281

L

L&D library, 220
L&D measurement plans, 252–271
L&D playbooks, 90–126
L&D strategies, 23–24, 190–212, 215–216, 217–219, 250, 251–252
　See also decision trees, for consultation and analysis
L&D team, 39–40, 130–132, 269, 273–290, 294
　See also internal L&D playbook; strategic business partners (SBPs)
language and terminology, 71–73, 170–171
Lao Tzu, 220
leadership support, lack of, 17
leading up and down, 132–134
learning, new definition of, 302–303
learning, reinforcing wrong purpose for, 24–26
learning cliff, 11
learning content creation. *See* L&D strategies
learning experiences, traditional versus common workplace, 8–10
　See also formal learning
learning experience team and facilitators, 275
　See also L&D team
learning modalities, history of, 7–8
learning purpose meetings, 149–150, 152
learning responsibility, sharing, 53
legacy mindsets, 10–11, 22
Lencioni, P., 92, 172
listening, strategic, 83

M

managers, 236, 248
　See also frontline and middle managers
mandatory training, 24–25, 26
　See also compliance training
Mann, H., 4
marketplace trends, 23–24
maturity, business, 80–81
McDonald's Hamburger University, 6
measurement. *See* metrics
measurement audits, 254–256
measurement before design, 257–259, 262–263
measurement consistency cycles, 265–271
Measurement Demystified (Vance and Parskey), 253
meetings, 43, 44–47, 83
　See also face-to-face meetings; learning purpose meetings; touch-base meetings
mentors, business, 83–84, 162
　See also coaching and mentoring
metrics

lack of showing results through, 29–30
order taker/deliverer identity and adding, 300–301
qualitative versus quantitative, 249–250
reasons for using, 251–252
understanding business, 77
See also data and documents; L&D measurement plans; performance measures; projects, timelines, and results, typical; workload and capacity tracking
middle managers. *See* frontline and middle managers
mindsets, xii–xiv, 11–12, 17, 217–219
See also big-picture, small-step thinking; legacy mindsets; order taker/deliverer identity; partnership mindset
mission statements, 66–68
See also purpose statements
Mostrom, S., 11
motivation. *See* recognition and rewards
Motorola University, 6
Myers-Briggs Type Indicator, 6

N

negotiables lists, 206–208, 210
networking, 280
See also partnering
no, mastering the strategic, 223–225, 243–244

O

observations. *See* gemba, going to the
OJT (on-the-job training), 5
onboarding
adoption/innovation curve and, 183–184
business operations knowledge about, 153
measurable results about, 124
partnering on performances measures around, 261–262, 266–267
postproject analysis of, 298–300
scaling of trainings for, 199
stakeholder feedback and, 194

using stakeholder language about, 170–171
one-thing-at-a-time approach, 173
on-the-job training (OJT), 5
order taker/deliverer identity
as best option, 292–294
blockers promoting, 16–30
history of L&D as, 3–13
inherent flaws in L&D promoting, xi–xii, 10, 186, 216
as a leveraging point, 295–302
and mindset shifts to SBPs, 226, 305–306
as a point on a continuum, 291
self-assessments, 32–33
organization, of business, 76–77
organizational blockers, promoting order taking/delivering identity, 16–18
organizational culture and processes, 16–17, 42–44, 78–81, 118–119
organizational politics, 42–43, 160–164, 294
organization charts, internal, 95–97
outcome measures, 254
See also metrics

P

Parskey, P., 253, 254
partnering, 39, 207, 224, 241–243, 259–263, 287–289
See also strategic business partners (SBPs); subject matter experts (SMEs)
partnership mindset, 185–186
performance improvement, learning as solution for, 25–26
performance influencers, 227–228
See also champions and influencers
performance issues, symptoms of versus solutions for, 226–240
performance measures, 107–108, 253–254, 256, 261–264
personal blockers, promoting order taking/delivering identity, 18–30
personality assessments and team building, 6, 23
personal response rules, 218
Phillips POI Methodology, 253
"playing pharmacist," 54

policies and procedures manuals. *See* external L&D playbook; internal L&D playbook
prioritizing business improvement, 42, 47–48
proactivity, 44–48, 82–85
products and services, understanding, 69–70
professional association memberships, 279–280
project processes, 100
project reviews, 99
project roles and responsibilities, 124–126
See also roles and responsibilities, clarification of
projects, timelines, and results, typical, 119–124
project templates, 99
project tracking software, 109, 111, 117–118
purpose statements, 91–93, 198
See also mission statements
pushback, 301–302

R

rapport, reputation, and relationships, 36–37
recognition and rewards, 286–287
recommendations, making unsolicited, 47–48
reflections, on projects, 85
reflective practice, 281–283
regulatory request for training. *See* compliance training
remote work, 25, 85, 97
requests and asks
    decision-making strategies for, 219–248
    effects of saying yes to all, 215–217, 234–235
    mindset shifts to deal with, 217–219
    simplifying, 172–174
    See also order taker/deliverer identity
resources, finite, 18, 136–137
response rules, personal, 218
results. *See* projects, timelines, and results, typical
revenue and expenses, 73–74
rewards. *See* recognition and rewards

Rogers, E., 182
roles and responsibilities, clarification of, 94–97
    See also project roles and responsibilities

S

scaling of trainings, 51, 198–200, 223
scrap lists, 197, 198, 200, 203, 205, 207
Sealtest Dairy, 22
self-assessments and tools
    business basics, 87
    key and standard performers, 246–247
    L&D strategy creation checklist, 213
    managers, 248
    SBPs, 56–57, 58–61
    strategic yes and no, 245
    why do you stay stuck, 32–33
self-sabotage, unintentional, 19–30
senior leaders. *See* executives and senior leaders
services and products, understanding, 69–70
silo wall busting, 53–54
skill gaps, identification of, 192–193
SMEs. *See* subject matter experts (SMEs)
social learning, 4
Socratic dialogue, 4
stakeholder feedback, 172, 193–194
stakeholders
    assumptions about need for training solution by, 21
    best practices for partnering with, 159–187
    as business mentors, 84
    communicating metrics to, 268–271
    communication preferences and expectations of, 164–175
    decision-making strategies and building trust with, 222–223
    determining key, 129–139
    external L&D playbook and, 114–126
    and increasing L&D business knowledge, 147, 152–154
    as part of hiring process, 276
    perceptions of L&D made by, 10–11, 140–148

relationship improvement with, 146, 148–152, 294
trust in expertise of, 175–177
See also L&D team; partnering
standard performers, 233–234, 246–247
standards of work, in L&D, 101–103, 107–108
strategic business partner continuum, 291–292, 305–306
strategic business partner formula, 140–142
strategic business partner grid, 142–148
strategic business partners (SBPs)
    defined, 35
    developing a team of, 273–290
    external indicators of being, 36–38
    internal indicators of being, 38–54
    L&D strategies and, 215–216
    metric use by, 250, 252
    mindset shifts from order takers to, xii–xiv, 226, 305–306
    self-assessments and tools, 56–61
    within the order taker/deliverer identity, 295–302
    See also external L&D playbook; partnering; stakeholders
strategies, L&D. *See* L&D strategies
strategy lists, 200, 204, 206, 210
subject matter experts (SMEs), 119, 209, 278, 284–285
    See also expertise, engaging others'
success sharing, 181–185

T

team building and personality assessments, 6, 23
templates, project, 99
Teresa, Mother, 175
terminology and language, 71–73
    See also key definitions
TILT journals, 282–283
timelines. *See* projects, timelines, and results, typical
time management, for strategic thinking, 218–219
time tracking, 99
    See also workload and capacity tracking
tools. *See* self-assessments and tools

touch-base meetings, 150–151, 152, 168–169
    See also face-to-face meetings
town hall meetings, 46
trainers, 275, 277–278
trainings. *See* L&D strategies; *learning entries*; onboarding; scaling of trainings
trust
    decision-making strategies and building stakeholder, 222–223, 243–244
    face-to-face meetings and, 167–169
    follow through and, 151, 174–175
    HRBPs and, 134, 135
    order taker/deliverer identity and building, 294, 300
    stakeholder expertise and, 175–177

U

unintentional self-sabotage, 19–30
unwritten rules, 43, 78–79, 163
    See also organizational politics

V

value-adding strategies, 48–51, 296–300
    See also scaling of trainings
values, business, 79, 198
    See also mission statements
Vance, D., 253, 254
vision sharing, 273–274, 301–302
    See also mission statements

W

WIIFM ("What's in It for Me?"), 175
Wiseman, L., 136
workload and capacity tracking, 108–111, 204–206, 240–241
    See also roles and responsibilities, clarification of
work processes, in L&D, 98–101
work standards, 101–103, 107–108

Y

yes and no, mastering the strategic. *See* requests and asks

Z

zone of proximal development, 80–81

About the Author

Jess Almlie is a seasoned leader and advocate for transforming the L&D profession. Throughout her 30 years of experience in the field, she has continuously focused on improving the impact of L&D in the organizations where she's worked. During her time as a vice president of learning, Jess led teams through complex initiatives, blending her expertise in learning strategy, performance consulting, and leadership development to deliver effective, business-aligned outcomes.

In March 2023, Jess founded Almlie Consulting, a firm dedicated to upleveling the work of L&D to be more strategic, intentional, and measurable. As a learning and performance consultant, she works with small and large organizations to create strategic learning blueprints. She also equips L&D leaders and teams with the tools and confidence to shift from reactive order takers to strategic business partners.

Jess is a sought-after speaker and consultant, known for her practical insights, engaging storytelling, and ability to inspire action through small steps that add up to big changes. She believes that by aligning L&D strategies to business goals, organizations can foster growth and innovation while empowering their people to succeed.

Jess holds a master's degree in educational leadership from North Dakota State University where her thesis research focused on whether leadership skills can be learned in a classroom. She also holds a bachelor's degree in organizational communication from Concordia College Moorhead.

When she's not working, Jess is usually spending time with her family and friends, hiking, cycling, or binge-watching baking competitions.

Check out Jess's podcast, *L&D Must Change*, or connect with her on LinkedIn at linkedin.com/in/jessalmlie. Learn more about her writing, consulting, and speaking at jessalmlie.com.

About ATD

atd The Association for Talent Development (ATD) is the world's largest association dedicated to those who develop talent in organizations. Serving a global community of members, customers, and international business partners in more than 100 countries, ATD champions the importance of learning and training by setting standards for the talent development profession.

Our customers and members work in public and private organizations in every industry sector. Since ATD was founded in 1943, the talent development field has expanded significantly to meet the needs of global businesses and emerging industries. Through the Talent Development Capability Model, education courses, certifications and credentials, memberships, industry-leading events, research, and publications, we help talent development professionals build their personal, professional, and organizational capabilities to meet new business demands with maximum impact and effectiveness.

One of the cornerstones of ATD's intellectual foundation, ATD Press offers insightful and practical information on talent development, training, and professional growth. ATD Press publications are written by industry thought leaders and offer anyone who works with adult learners the best practices, academic theory, and guidance necessary to move the profession forward.

We invite you to join our community. Learn more at **TD.org**.

www.ingramcontent.com/pod-product-compliance
Ingram Content Group UK Ltd.
Pitfield, Milton Keynes, MK11 3LW, UK
UKHW021832140426
5217IPUK00021B/1414